# THE No-Nonsense NINE

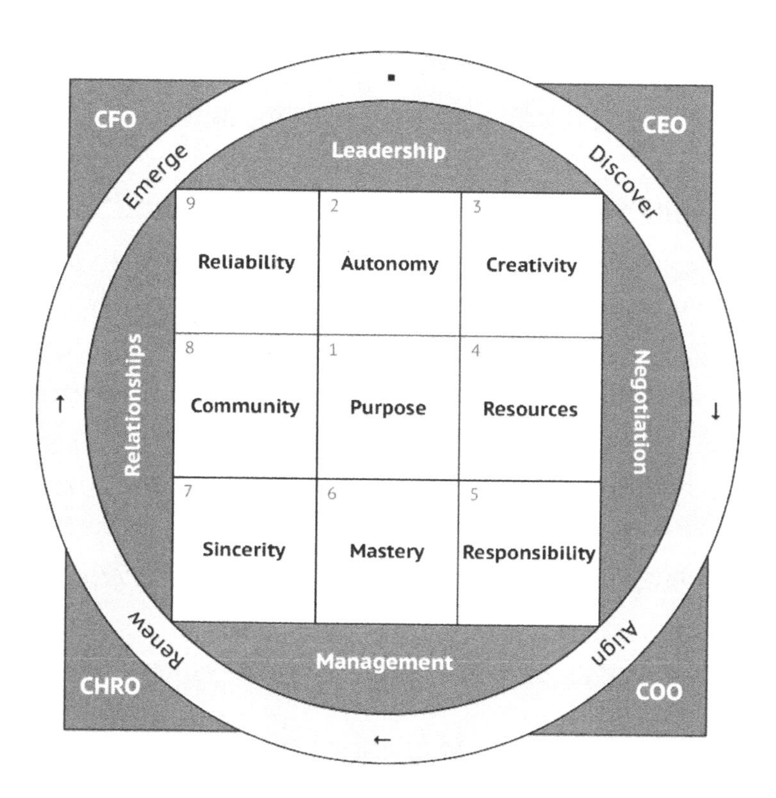


## NINE PRINCIPLES OF TOP-QUALITY VALUES-BASED LEADERSHIP SPIRIT

(To Help People Work Better Together)

By

CLARK ANDERSON RILEY

# CONTENTS

# OPENING STATEMENT: YOU ARE INVITED

Welcome. This is an invitation. By working your way through the No-nonsense Nine book, what you will come to realize is that what is urgently needed in the workplace today is for us to be (a) engaged, (b) connected and (c) supportive as a work community. By doing that, true business success will be achieved by being able to Work Better Together (WBT)… And the numbers, the operations such as manufacturing, and the delivery, and ultimately the customer service, will collectively end up being very, very good.

But you must do the work… the learning work: By being (1) engaged, (2) connected and (3) supportive.

The author wishes to thank Management Professor Extraordinaire, Henry Mintzberg of McGill University in Montreal, for the three key words of this opening statement: "Engage, Connect and Supportive." This he believes is what managers, as learners, must do now if they are to succeed in helping curtail what Mintzberg calls, the "mindless, reckless behavior that has brought the global economy to its knees."

Thank you, Henry: We have much work to do.

*Henry Mintzberg OC OQ FRSC is a Canadian academic and author on business and management. He is currently the Cleghorn Professor of Management Studies at the Desautels Faculty of Management of McGill University in Montreal, Quebec, Canada, where he has been teaching since 1968.*

# PREFACE: THE FIVE FOREMOST LEADERSHIP SKILLS

The Five Foremost Skills of Leadership Spirit

1. Be positive
2. Be honest
3. Be strategic
4. Be action-oriented
5. Be balanced

Early on in my career, I came to pursue close to a dozen interesting jobs that included a ton of sales-like activity and conversation, business negotiating debates, and many other similar happenings that a shy person would ordinarily not relish. Along the way I somehow luckily found out that plain old "common sense" made it all so much easier: Finding common sense balance takes its place as the central, fifth skill I label as a chief part of "strategic" above, which pulls the full five together – and something I now see that ties the ancient leadership skills and philosophies such as Yoga and Zen together with the latest thinking in our most modern theory of all - the new science of Complexity.

Over the years I must have studied more than a thousand books on leadership, personal development and self-help – more than enough to show they all point to these same five basic qualities of leadership. After 30 years teaching, coaching and training multiple hundreds of managers and executives, I could see even more clearly how these five operate in all sorts of practical situations. I trust you agree that seeing them so clearly makes them easy to explain – frankly something I haven't found in any other books. I believe this can be helpful to so many people in leadership and management positions.

The OSHAM acronym below represents Life's 5 Illusions of the Workplace: Objectivity, Scarcity, Hostility, Activity and Measurability. OSHAM's illusions are as follows:

**OSHAM** (The Acronym)

1. **O**BJECTIVITY (has to do with a person's IDENTITY)

   Love is based on what you do. (The Workplace illusion: Objectivity)

   My self worth comes from my functioning:

   Success is based on "what I have." (Versus "who I am")

   (Evidence: low self-esteem)

   (The Positive Polarity: trust)

2. **S**CARCITY

   Provisions are scarce. (The Workplace illusion: Scarcity)

   The law of human nature is "scarcity." (Versus "abundance")

   (Evidence: jealousy)

   (The Polarity: letting go)

3. **H**OSTILITY

   The world is hostile. (The Workplace illusion: `Hostility)

   Life is "conflict and control" versus "community and collaboration."

   (Evidence: competition)

   (The Positive Polarity: curiosity / intuitiveness / innovation)

4. **A**CTIVITY

   Gifts are hard-earned vs. natural and free. (The Workplace illusion: Activity)

   Our lives should be organized around what we have been trained and rewarded to do (are paid to do). You do what you "ought to do." (Versus "ought to love")

   (Evidence: stress and mid-life crisis)

   (The Positive Polarity: ability, achievement / strengths focus)

5. **M**EASURABILITY

   Measurable effectiveness of work is the standard. (The Workplace illusion: Measurability)

   Do you want to know why society today is so rarely addressing the great needs of humankind? A "logic of results" that makes our work more and more trivial.

   (Evidence: Trivializing and hopelessness)

   (The Positive Polarity: compassion / hope / "generativity")

| The 5 Foremost Qualities of Leadership Spirit | Life's 5 Illusions |
|---|---|
| * "Effectuation" Terminology | ("OSHAM") |
| 1. Positive attitude (Subjectivity) | Objectivity |
| * "Bird in Hand" | |
| 2. Honesty (Abundance Thinking) | Scarcity |
| * "Affordable Loss" | |
| 3. Sustaining Balance (Community) | Hostility |
| * "Lemonade" | |
| 4. Building Improved Habits (Ability) | Activity |
| * "Patchwork Quilt" | |
| 5. Creative Thinking (Purpose/Resolve) | Measure-ability |

* "Pilot-in-the-Plane"

*The above Effectuation labels are per the research and writing of Professor

Saras Sarasfathy of The Darden Business School at the University of Virginia.

Effectuation: in contrast to causal logic, according to the effectuation logic you can maintain control by taking small steps in one direction instead of working towards long-term goals with unpredictable outcomes. By approaching decision making this way, you avoid investing time or money that you are not actually willing to lose.

Entrepreneurial people constantly make decisions and take action. The big question is, "Are there any universal methods or principles that they use?" To answer this question, Dr. Saras

Sarasvathy, a cognitive scientist with the Darden Business School, conducted a study of expert entrepreneurs.

The result? Effectuation. To make this easier to understand, she broke the effectuation process into 5 self-descriptive steps as displayed in the left-hand column shown below:

| Effectuation Model | Top Leadership Spirit Skills |
|---|---|
| 1. Bird in hand | 1. Be Positive |
| 2. Affordable Loss | 2. Be Honest |
| 3. Lemonade | 3. Be Strategic |
| 4. Patchwork Quilt | 4. Be Action-Oriented |
| 5. Pilot-in-the-Plane | 5. Be Balanced |

These five effectuation steps are described in detail in Addendum #2. These match up well with the foremost leadership spirit skills, as displayed in the right-hand column above. These also align well with the thinking behind OSHAM, as described earlier.

Whatever you call these (and you'll see below there are many words to describe each), the five Leadership Spirit qualities remain essentially simple actions we already know how to do. Each builds on the others if we carry them out together:

1. **Positive attitude** (a quality of our SUBJECTIVITY) – also called agent, hope, faith, belief, confidence, courage, commitment, extroversion, energy, etc. – all feelings of motivation – the stuff motivational speakers prize and promote. Though we don't always admit it or work consistently at it, we know very well how to act positively and that if we do so, we'll end up feeling more positively ourselves and add to our success. This is entrepreneurial thinking

2. **Honesty** (a quality of our RES0URCES) – especially honesty about feedback – also called truth, integrity, being in touch with reality, down-to-earth, connected, listening, accepting feedback, agreeableness, etc. These are all things that some people class as too "negative" to be thought about too much – roadblocks or challenges to be overcome – stuff we're often told not to dwell on, but which will rise up to bite us if we don't. We are perfectly capable of being honest, facing feedback and putting it into perspective – all stuff that's not really negative at all, but tremendously valuable and rather difficult to actually get. This is at the heart of calculating affordable loss.

Feedback helps us move forward and improve. Honesty helps us build and maintain relationships not destroy them, but only if it's handled positively. The five skills must work together. Again we know how to be honest, but we often aren't. We're dishonest mostly in small ways – because it's easier to say nothing or make stuff up… or because we don't think it's important. If we fail to take the trouble to look for ways to get closer to truth all-round, to be in touch with reality and concrete facts, yet also positive at the same time, admittedly a tough challenge, we fail to practice useful skills that could help in many situations.

3. **Sustaining Balance** (a quality of being "in" COMMUNITY) – The middle skill is to maintain all 5 in balance while heading as quickly as conveniently possible toward our goals: being strategic. The core, central skill is unique, because it includes making sure the others are all functioning. When they are, we say we are "in the zone," in balance. Things seem to happen as if by magic. They feel great, easy and fast. This is also called coordinating, focusing, driving toward goals, building momentum, using common sense, keeping things in perspective, not sweating the small stuff, keeping one's balance while moving forward.

4. **Building Improved Habits** (a quality of our ACTion) – also called developing skills, changing behavior, persistence, conscientiousness, consistency, hard work etc. This process produces the only actual action elements among the five – the stuff we know we should be doing, but think we're too lazy to work on. We're NOT at all – not when we see why action is needed and choose to do it for ourselves. We know from hundreds of books that simply struggling through 20 to 30 repetitions of any behavior makes habit start to flow smoothly and automatically: We overthrow the willingness to fail. We can also note the practical fact that when behavior becomes habit through repetition, it soon feels comfortable, so qualms about avoiding uncomfortable change disappear if we simply convince ourselves to persist. I can tell you that after 20 or 30 speeches to corporations, and leading small learning groups and performing well at quasi-public meetings that I was no longer shy about that challenge. In fact, I've chosen teaching others to teach as my next career. We enjoy overcoming past limitations and we get good at it.

5. **Creative Thinking** (the quality of our PURPOSE) – also called contrarian or paradoxical thinking, creativity, vision, openness, asking hard questions, etc. This is stuff many people think they're not good at, but every human being can develop effectively with a particular type of simple practice, to maintain balance. Everyone automatically thinks creatively when they confront both honest facts and at the same time have positive wishes or goals (a "purpose"). The contradictions, apparent puzzles or "paradoxes" that emerge between these opposites, cause our human brains to dream up varied answers. Some will work, some won't. The way to find out is to test them – mentally or in actual practice. This leads from thinking up solutions to the next skill - better action. All the skills only function effectively

when working together in balance to create a total result. Just as working to be positive balances against the challenging honest facts we face, great ideas balance against our practical abilities to try them. Practice makes us good at these and other new skills that are required.

Regarding #5 above, I generally refer to this skill as "dynamic, active or flexible balance," not being "off balance," and it includes a sense of something greater, a deep spiritual sense, what I in my training and writing I call "Leadership Spirit." This "spirit" isn't about finding God, this simply means being in tune with the universe, seeing the unity or how things fit together. This feels mystical, magical, but is very well known. It only takes coming together of all five skills in one workable stream that propels us to success. This results simply from doing the other four simultaneously, and practicing often enough to be good at them. Practice and persistence over time makes this occur and when it feels right, it truly is magical.

In many presentations I use the simple skill of juggling three objects to illustrate these five skills and how they come together in balance. It even makes the third skill "visible" to some extent. People can imagine that you don't "know" how you make the leap from simply practicing with the three objects to suddenly finding that you can keep them all three in the air simultaneously. It just happens… after considerable steady practice. It's no wonder we sometimes imagine this is magic, but we "make luck happen…" when steady preparation using the five skills meets the opportunities that always exist to create new results.

In my presentations I encourage people to test this simple approach to analyze their own examples as well as those I offer. I try for examples that will illustrate how easily they work for individuals, teams and major organizations. Modern complexity and chaos theory explain how it is that the same principles generally work at every level. Anyone can now read about those, but why it works is not nearly as important as learning to make it happen for you.

With practice, using the five to coordinate effective balance becomes easy and it also becomes easy to see these skills at work in everything we do. Examples from books and motivational speeches start to connect with examples in one's own life where focusing on these simple basics makes more things effective. Examples help, but actually using the skills in one's own life is even better. I can attest to the success this can bring. This is in fact what all those motivational books lining store shelves have to say – different stories, same principles.

So why do people want to hear about this? Because we all need motivation and examples of success to measure our own challenges against from time to time. I'm able to fit examples into nearly every type of work and many life situations since I've worked through so many over the years myself, from volunteer organizations and boards, to big companies and corporate environments plus a good many life experiences that all can be seen to contain the same basics and improve with the use of these skills.

As David Crisp previously head of HR of Canada's Hudson Bay Company shared with me before he retired: "The great thing is these ideas are ultimately free and can be amazingly helpful in explaining all that we see. One can use them to figure out what to do next. The best part is it's so simple. There's no hocus-pocus. You see it work and understand why." My goal, as it was for David, is "to SIMPLIFY, to make it easier for people to succeed, to cut out the complexity so they can see results and learn that things are easier than they appear." Thank you, David, for your lessons on Leadership: I agree as David once wrote to me, "If everyone could excel at legitimate means to get what they want, using just a bit of practice with these fundamental skills, there'd be no need for crime or war." A grand thought, but perhaps not as out-of-reach as it first might seem. Let us all encourage each other, and everyone else, to try and spread these ideas for maximum impact on many more groups.

- **Be positive**: If you say or even think that someone is stupid or lazy, you'll get what you expect along with powerful passive resistance. Praise them for forward thinking and they'll strive even harder to supply it. Jump to take your share of the blame if things go wrong. Shield them; you're the leader!

- **Be honest**: If "we're" not there yet, say so. We can all get better, but encourage them with support, brainstorming that includes their ideas, and then get them motivated to try again. Don't sigh and do it for them – see #1! Express faith!

- **Be strategic**: This requires combining 1 and 2 with their ideas to find a new way to forge ahead. That's a challenge, but one worthy of the thinking time it takes. Successful companies like Toyota, Google, Apple and Wal-Mart constantly implement many small ideas suggested by staff at every level – true learning organizations.

- **Be balanced**, continually: Balance is the key in every aspect of these and much more. Avoiding 'dismal practices' means finding and balancing many factors including what's good for the individual and the organization every time, not just when it's convenient, a balance between "urgent today" and "creating a base for a better future" and many, many more.

- **Be action-oriented**: That means trial and error, not waiting for grand scale perfection. Better habits grow with practice.

A culture is no more or less than everyone's habits so make it a learning one in which errors in good faith are not just OK, but valued.

The five questions for Leadership Spirit are:

1. How's it going? (Overall, what progress do I feel I'm making or not making?) (Positive spirit)
2. What do you really want? (Honest Motivation)
3. What needs to happen? (Strategic goals)
4. What needs to be different? (What action do I need to take, how can I change my own approach to balance and impact the situation?)
5. What habits or skills do I need to start working and acting upon consistently to develop and to achieve this?

   Really a repeat of number 1 – we should determine how often to ask, "How's it going" – for follow up, for reminders of our plans, to check progress, etc. (This is both the start and the finish of the 'loop' of leadership coaching or Manager/Leader-as-coach "Leadership Spirit.")

The recipe? Dozens of books, articles and long experience boil down to just five skills:

- **1. Be positive**: If you say or even think that someone is stupid or lazy, you'll get what you expect along with powerful passive resistance. Praise them for forward thinking and they'll strive even harder to supply it. Jump to take your share of the blame if things go wrong. Shield them; you're the leader!
- **2. Be honest**: If "we're" not there yet, say so. We can all get better, but encourage them with support, brainstorming that

includes their ideas and get them motivated to try again. Don't sigh and do it for them – see #1! Express faith!

- **3. Be strategic**: This requires combining 1 and 2 with their ideas to find a new way to forge ahead. That's a challenge, but one worthy of the thinking time it takes. Successful companies like Toyota, Google and Wal-Mart constantly implement many small ideas suggested by staff at every level – true learning organizations.
- **4. Be action-oriented**: That means trial and error, not waiting for grand scale perfection. Better habits grow with practice. A culture is no more or less than everyone's habits so make it a learning one in which errors in good faith are not just OK, but valued.
- **5. Be balanced** continually: Balance is the key in every aspect of these and much more. Avoiding 'dismal practices' means finding and balancing many factors including what's good for the individual and the organization every time, not just when it's convenient, a balance between "urgent today" and "creating a base for a better future" and many, many more. The mark of Leadership Spirit is the ability to balance and make steady progress among competing demands by testing better and better solutions with at least the objective that everyone wins. Recognize that change takes time and consistent effort. But the rewards are huge and build momentum both in individual careers and organization success.

## LEADERSHIP SPIRIT

LEADERSHIP

RELATIONSHIPS

| 9 Reliability | 2 Autonomy | 3 Creativity |
|---|---|---|
| 8 Community | 1 Purpose | 4 Resources |
| 7 Sincerity | 6 Mastery | 5 Responsibility |

NEGOTIATION

MANAGEMENT

**The No-Nonsense Nine Principles.**

The No-Nonsense Nine isn't a theoretical model. It's an important practical tool that creates awareness and leads to better action, and builds what is called “Values-based Leadership Spirit.” This is not the same as “Spiritual Leadership.” They are not the same thing… Dr. Richard Blackaby is a Canadian Minister and author, and is prolific on the topic of what he calls “Spiritual Leadership:” Thirty-five books about experiencing God. This book is not that. This book is about having what is called “Leadership Spirit. ” This comes from understanding of what is called the No-nonsense Nine Principles and by practicing what is called the No-nonsense Nine Disciplines. In brief, the No-nonsense Nine are progressing touch points, much like the hours on the face of an old fashioned clock, circular in motion. Creatively imagine the No-nonsense Principles as if these principles were literally assembled upon the face of circular clock, as a guiding compass. The No-nonsense Mandala image shown on herein however, means much more than just being a handy reference. Systematized together as a framework, they become a strategy to serve you as instant cues for enabling your conversations, evaluating your business situations and providing you with useful insights about problems that must be solved and opportunities that must be considered. Together, the No-nonsense Nine provide a framework of understanding for you. More importantly, you will find through teaching them that they will also help others: managers and executives… to build strong, resilient businesses. You will find that it is a workplace tool to help you build a better sense of Leadership Spirit into workers, managers, and executives. This book is not about finding God in your life, it's about finding your way on the job, and with these insights, helping others do the same: Helping people Work Better Together (WBT).

To help you get a sense of how these universal principles apply in practice, ask yourself the following questions about your own workplace. When you have competed that task, you will be asked to do a mini- exercise to think further about the ways that a fuller expression of these universal principles could help you, help your people and help your company to Work Better Together (WBT).

### The No-nonsense Nine Questions

1. **Purpose**: "Is a sense of PURPOSE present in my work and in my environment? Do the people around me work with a clear sense of purpose? Does our work feel meaningful?" Do I begin at the epicenter of my being, with my life story, within my heart, and with purpose?

2. **Autonomy**: "Am I granted the AUTONOMY to feel ownership of my work and to do my work in a style that suits me? Am I granting the dignity and empowerment of autonomy to others?"
3. **Creativity**: "Does my environment foster CREATIVITY? Does it encourage the development of new approaches and new solutions? Do I welcome change?
4. **Resources**: "Are RESOURCES being used to their fullest potential, or are they being hoarded and squandered?" From who and where do my energy come?
5. **Responsibility**: "Do people take RESPONSIBILITY for their actions? Do they assume responsibility for the wellbeing of the organization and for the wellbeing of each other? Do I know that they'll take care of things, even when no one is watching? Does a healthy business attitude exist? Is it encouraged?
6. **Mastery**: "Am I building and demonstrating MASTERY in my work? Do my colleagues and co-workers value mastery? Does this environment support and encourage the development of mastery?"
7. **Sincerity**: "Do the people around me speak and act with SINCERITY? Do they really mean what they say and care about the way they affect other people?" Is a true sense of humility present?
8. **Community**: "Does this feel like a good COMMUNITY? Do I respect and trust these people? Do we support one another and give each other the benefit of the doubt? Do we share knowledge and resources? Do we inspire each other and coach each other?"
9. **Reliability**: "Do people around me practice RELIABILITY? Do they follow through and make good on their word? Do I know that they'll get the job done and come through for each other?"

## Working Better Together (WBT) Exercise A.

Now, stop a moment and spend some time to think about the ways that a fuller expression of these No-nonsense principles could benefit you, your people and your company. Take a moment, look back and re-visit the questions.

In time you will find that the No-Nonsense Nine Principles, Disciplines and Questions are strategic and progressive. Like a clock, they begin in the middle at the very heart of the No-nonsense Mandala, with the first and central principle of "Purpose," and then they spiral straight upward to "Autonomy," and then to the right and around, clockwise, through the remaining No-nonsense Principles. Picture the increments of this progression in your brain.

This clock-like spiral symbolizes opportunity, growth and change: As Angeles Arrien, Basque-American cultural anthropologist, educator, author, lecturer and consultant, best known for her book "The Four-Fold Way," writes about spirals in her spirit-filled and captivating 1992 book, "Signs of Life:" "*This is a process of coming to the same point again and again, but at a different level, so that everything is seen in a new light.*" (P47).

There is a simplicity and yet elegance in her expression of faith. In learning and using the No-nonsense Nine, you will find "new light" over and over, again and again. These No-nonsense Principles for Values-based Leadership Spirit in the Workplace can help and guide you. In today's workplace, sadly work can be hurtful, even painful… so dull and dark if you let it be, so bring new light. In today's remote, rushing, isolated and struggling workplace, you truly do earn and deserve it everyday: New light.

So now, again, before you read the remainder of the "Leadership Spirit" Introduction that follows: "think about the ways that a fuller expression of the principles could help you, help your people and help your company." Stop, right now, and think: "what are the ways that a fuller expression of the principles could help and benefit you, your people and your company:" Write a short 30 to 50 word refection directly below:

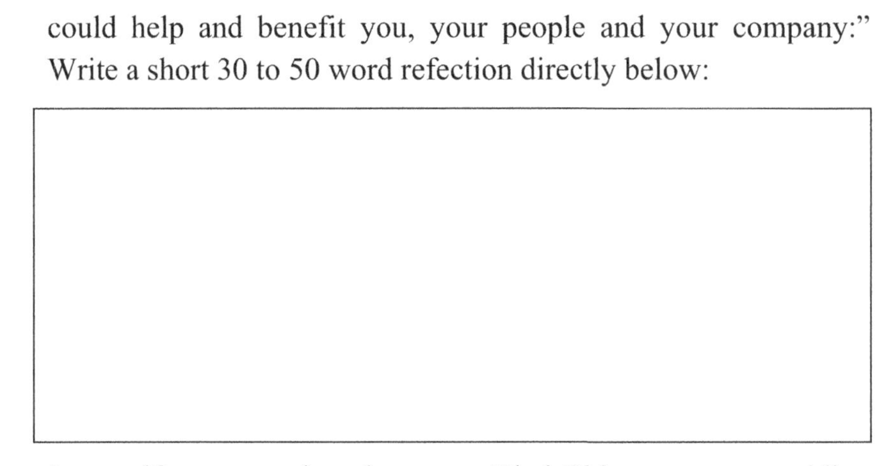

Just as if you were learning yoga, Thai Chi or any new guiding discipline, this is how you will begin to learn the No-nonsense Nine and its benefits: First through contemplation, and then through conversation. Beyond contemplation, which can be powerful alone, an even more formative way you will learn is through the No-nonsense disciplines of conversation, with either (a) your coach, or (b) within your small group of cohorts.

**The No-Nonsense Nine Club**

Look at this as though you are a new member of "The No-nonsense Nine Club." A small team of 5 to 7 learners.

Do not learn the No-nonsense Nine all alone, without companionship. So, first contemplate, and then second and more importantly, have a conversation. Contemplation first and then conversation, and being part of a small group: these practices are much of what this "work" book is about... so that you will eventually get Working Better Together ("WBT"). And the best way is to just begin by either working through the No-nonsense Nine in small doses with either a companion coach or, more ideally, as part of a small group of cohorts... Your very own "No-nonsense Nine Club:" on a recurring schedule, you assemble 5 to 7 participants to learn within a small group. Receiving this sort of "other help" is part of the ultimate goal: Learning and utilizing the No-nonsense framework together... Learn together what in time will be called your workplace "No-nonsense Nine Mandala," as well as the principles and disciplines **by heart (memorized)**, so that you work better with all others and improve your overall work productivity. Improvements such as (a) how you lead, (b) how you manage, (c) how you negotiate, and, most importantly, (d) how you build and maintain relationships. These four are like four No-nonsense Mandala gateways: Leadership, Management, Negotiation and Relationships. These four, as you can plainly see, surround what will become **your** No-nonsense Nine Workplace Mandala.

The No-nonsense Nine is a Discipline or a Practice, much like Yoga or Thai Chi, especially if you are burned out on business and still need to learn to find a way to positively focus.

Worried about investing the time and energy? When you are maintaining a pretty tough regimen, as most people are, what can you do? A good way is to begin with the Principle of Autonomy: You must begin with the Discipline of "Still Point." But for right now, look at and become comfortable with The Mandala diagram.

On the first Introduction page, the No-nonsense Nine Principles are displayed as a part of a Mandala. Mandala is a Sanskrit word meaning "circle." Simply put, the No-nonsense Nine is a workplace improvement Mandala. It's designed for easy recall, in order to save time and energy: So, start at the top... The No-nonsense discipline of Still Point is at 12 o'clock high on the face of the No-nonsense Mandala

In the business world, "Still Point" is code for "meditation." In the Buddhist and Hindu religious traditions their sacred art often takes a mandala form. The basic form of most Hindu and Buddhist mandalas is a square with four gates containing a circle with a center point. Each gate is in the shape of a "T." Mandalas often exhibit what is called "radial balance." In brief, a Mandala's purpose is to help transform ordinary minds into enlightened ones. In your work life, this begins with you being able to achieve "Still Point."

Much like the traditional Hindu or Buddhist Mandala, the No-nonsense Nine Mandala has 4 "gates:" Leadership, Negotiation, Management and Relationship. You can enter these gates and find the No-nonsense Principles and accompanying No-nonsense Disciplines.

These Mandalas, concentric diagrams, have spiritual and ritual significance in both Buddhism and Hinduism.

Within business, the No-nonsense Nine Principles are the components of what is called "Leadership Spirit." In business today, you are asked to work very, very hard; as a result, you can get tired and lost and even "spiritually wounded." The need for "Soul repair" from Workplace abuse is not uncommon, and can be damaging to the very people trying hardest to do a good job. Often called "Burnout," PTSD (Post Traumatic Stress Disorder) is not uncommon amongst workmates. Burnout is prevalent in "first responders," such as within fire and police departments and hospitals, and is not uncommon with Military working in businesses. Burnout happens, and it happens within the body, brain and soul. You and your cohorts are not immune. Working remotely and in relative isolation alone can take its toll. "Burnout" is often accompanied by addictions such as drugs and alcohol abuse.

These simple No-nonsense Principles and Disciplines are components that can help you find your way to more peace and kindness and productivity at work. This is a big part of what's needed today: A Mandala: The term is of Hindu origin and appears in the Rig Veda as the name of the sections of the work, but is also used in other Indian religions, particularly Buddhism. In the Tibetan branch of Vajrayana Buddhism, Mandalas have even been developed into sand painting. They also are a key part of certain yoga meditation practices. In the United States, there has been a successful Contemplative Prayer movement (called "Centering Prayer"), made famous by an author and world-famous Trappist Monk named Thomas Keating, a close friend in his life to the 14th Dalai Lama. That practice to this day is what is called "Still Point" as a Discipline, which is one of the No-nonsense Nine's Disciplines to be learned. "Still Point" accompanies the Principle of Autonomy and is a close cousin discipline to Steadfastness. A Still Point practice (aka, "meditation") can be like a regular yoga practice, to help you find your way, as well as a motivation for you to interact with care and generosity with others, in community.

These "No nonsense Nine" workplace principles and their accompanying disciplines have been "uncovered" over the span of a quarter century within business coaching assignments and within hundreds of small cohort-group communications skills training programs for global corporations and international professional services firms located in a variety of countries. The inklings of "Principle and Disciplines" came first from hosting "Clearness Committee" meetings in the 1990's within Hewitt Associates, the giant HR Benefits Consulting firm. The meetings were patterned upon a discussion-prompting paper based upon a sermon and a handout of the same name written by a Quaker and Social Activist author, Parker Palmer. This created an avenue of discovery to more of what Parker Palmer provided as guidance to his niche of universities and colleges. The critical awakening catalyst was an address he delivered to several hundred professionals and business people invited within a gothic church setting near Chicago in 1990. The sponsored address he gave was entitled, "Leading From Within." The audience was captivated.

It has an essential, powerful message for every leader today, whether that is within education, government, not-for-profit, business or healthcare. The most recent version of this essay can be found today in Parker Palmer's book, "Let Your Life Speak: Listening for the Voice of Vocation" (San Francisco: Jossey-Bass Publishers, 2000). It is also available via searching the Internet.

The No-nonsense Nine Principles respond to the root of that first address. Within the address, Parker speaks of "Life's Five Shadows," which have been reworked and transcribed as what are called "the Five Workplace Illusions." They are as follows: as an acronym called "OSHAM," a made up word based upon an acronym standing for the five (5) main workplace Illusions as follows:

**OSHAM**

| | |
|---|---|
| 1. Objectivity = | "People are objects" |
| 2. Scarcity = | "Resources are Limited" |
| 3. Hostility = | "The World is Hostile" |
| 4. Activity = | "I am what I do" |
| 5. Measure-ability | "I have control" |

These are the five (5) workplace illusions that the No-nonsense Nine Principles are designed to react and respond to within businesses. They are as follows:

1. **Objectivity**. The workplace illusion: *People are objects.* The "**O**" in OSHAM represents the workplace illusion

that people are **O**bjects. – Truth is, People are subjects – they have hearts and feelings and can be frail and in need. Point is, too often in business, people can be treated as if they are objects.

2. **Scarcity**. The workplace illusion: *Resources are Scarce.* The "S" in OSHAM represents the workplace illusion that resources are limited, are Scarce- The truth is, Resources are only as scarce or as limited as someone perceives them to be – when you enter into a conversation or a relationship with a "scarcity attitude," that scarcity perception or "mindset" alone will influence what and how you discuss things, and what and how you decide to share within the relationship. Scarcity thinking is a workplace nemesis, and every manager's worst enemy when it comes to managing other people, assets, energy and all other resources. It breeds jealousy and petty competitiveness. Scarcity thinking is what empties the glass to half full.
3. **Hostility**. The workplace illusion: *The World is hostile.* The "H" in OSHAM represents the workplace illusion that the world is hostile – The truth is, the world is not a hostile world. Sure enough, people can be hostile, but don't be blaming the world or some generalized or universal idea for hostility beyond that. School shootings, workplace abuse and downsizing layoffs are specific. They are awful. But they are human generated. People can be greedy, selfish and possessive and insecure and many other nearly intolerable negative ways as well. Never meet those ways with force. Diplomacy, acceptance, kindness, patience and conversation are what you must deliver, and if that and all else fails, greet hostility finally with a "kindly goodbye," and simply get out of harms way to be safe. A big part of possessing

Leadership Spirit is to help others get out of harm's way. Be sure to be safe. That is ultimately how hostility fails.

4. **Activity**. The workplace illusion: *I am what I do.* The "A" in OSHAM represents the workplace illusion that "you are what you do." – In addition to succumbing to scarcity thinking or to becoming hostile, people can also become activity junkies, usually out of fear, thinking that if they just keep busy doing and doing, that all else that is good will follow. The counter balance here is to work from self worth and to develop your ability. Think "ability" instead of "activity." Combating OSHAM requires the help of others, which is simply not always the case, especially in the workplace. Managers and workers need to focus on replacing activity, pure blind activity especially, with ability. They also need to add a practice called "other help" to do that. As with addressing hostility, addressing hyper activity in the workplace, and rebuilding activity into true ability takes diplomacy, patience and reaching out, like a good coach. People in the workplace, especially, need to know that they are valued for being who they are, and not for just what they can do. In the working world, we are more remote and more time deprived than ever before. As a result, people want some sense of control, which their high paced activity seems to be grasping for. Perverse advice as it may seem to give them, yet what they really need to do is to calm down and to slow down. But this to them is often unwanted, often frightening. Shortening lists, eliminating lists and delegating or off-loading burden is frequently a good start. But activity junkies will need a helping hand - and just as in sports as a metaphor, they need a disciplined and caring manager-coach to get them operating with ability. As John Wooden, UCLA's "most

winning ever" basketball coach was famous for saying: "Don't mistake activity with achievement." Ability is the difference maker. Wooden built ability: Coach Wooden's most insightful model to discuss his idea is the methodology he used to prepare, execute and improve his practices. He was not satisfied with simply having achievement in each activity, but rather he sought to maximize achievement without stifling initiative.

The 4 components Coach Wooden utilized:

(1) Proper planning and execution of the plan
(2) Relentless attention to detail
(3) Maximizing the use of time
(4) Post-practice analysis for improvement

He describes the importance of each in his refreshing 1988 classic coaching book, "Practical Modern Basketball."

5. **Measure-ability**. The workplace illusion: *I have control.* The "M" in OSHAM represents the workplace illusion that people have control, which is untrue from the get go"– There is an old saying, "If you can measure it, you can manage it." Many managers and workers live their work life this way, as a measurement. This reveals a win-lose mentality; one that often times places you in opposition and keeps you out of cooperation, removes you from being in true community with your co-workers. Have you ever been in a brainstorming session with the goal, for example, of coming up with a cleverer, new, different or more creative way to do something? These sessions are a "slippery slope" – mostly in the search for finding a way to measure. Brainstorming sessions can become a battlefield of "one-upmanship" especially if not

managed properly. Hundreds of brainstorming sessions have gone cockeyed because most people do a marginal job of running them. Even if they think they are good at it, running them is always risky. So, why breed hostility when you can choose another way that instead breeds a more solid community? Don't "brainstorm," instead do "NGT."

### NGT – Nominal Group Technique

Nominal Group Technique (NGT) is defined as a structured method for group brainstorming that encourages contributions from everyone and facilitates quick agreement on the relative importance of issues, problems, or solutions. NGT is a discipline and a practice to be learned and used regularly with intentionality. NGT helps build a sense of Community. Here's how: Team members begin by writing down their ideas, then selecting which idea they feel is best. Once team members are ready, everyone presents their favorite idea, and the suggestions are then discussed and prioritized by the entire group using a point system. NGT combines the importance ratings of individual group members into the final weighted priorities of the group.

Use NGT especially when:

- Some group members are much more vocal than others
- Some group members think better in silence
- There is concern some members will not participate
- The group does not easily generate quantities of ideas
- Some or all group members are new to the team
- The issue is controversial or there is heated conflict

When working with your small learning group, you'll succeed when using the NGT philosophy and approach.

As with NGT, all of the "No-Nonsense Nine" Principles and Disciplines have a subtle difference, yet are very accurate behavior indicators that serve as helpful communication improvement aids for (a) improving everyday conversations, (b) for refining your self-reflection, and (c) for improving results of on-the-fly executive and manager coaching that takes place in the workplace. A growing concern also, much of today's communications and conversations are being done remotely. "It's a sign of the times" as the old saying goes. Isolation can be a spirit killer.

**Values-based Leadership Spirit.**

When you look down upon the No-nonsense Nine Mandala shown at the opening of the Leadership Spirit Introduction, you would intellectually think that Leadership Spirit itself radiates directly down from the Leadership medallion inscription shown at the very top center of the No-nonsense Nine Mandala. Not so. Values-based Leadership Spirit radiates and reflects sideways and sort of backwards from that (left to right, precisely). Instead of coming by edict from above, true Values-based Leadership Spirit emanates most powerfully from the left side, from the Relationship Medallion, which is the inscription shown at the left center of the No-nonsense Nine Mandala (at 9 o'clock).

Values-based Leadership Spirit comes mostly from the Relationship Medallion and from its three component squares of Sincerity, Community and Reliability. These are the three (3) "relating" principles and skills. They are more supportive. They are not assertive. Across from this on the face of the Mandala, the requiring principles and skills of Responsibility, Resources and Creativity are the three component squares of the Negotiation Medallion. These are the "requiring" principles and skills.

Twenty-seven years ago, the methodology of being principle-based was simply called "the 9-Square" by me. They were used daily by me as an executive coaching aid mainly, and through my repeated "delivery" (use) for my coaching clients. It became a logical process tool for me, especially when I'd coach my clients in one-on-one coaching sessions, either in-person or on the phone. I use this now more often virtually online. I felt guided to do so by these four original "foundational" expert resources: David Maister, Aaron Antonovsky, Richard Rohr, and Peter Friedes.

1. **David Maister**: His many "Trusted Advisor" books, but most relevant with the No-nonsense Nine, is his best selling book, "Practice What You Preach."
2. **Aaron Antonovsky**: His 2 main books explaining his groundbreaking Salutogenisis Theory, including his "Sense of Coherence" (SOC) scaling research and survey.
3. **Richard Rohr**: His descriptions of an ancient personality system and mandala design called "The Enneagram," as portrayed especially by him as a Franciscan Monk and his co-author Andreas Ebert in their book entitled, "The Enneagram." This was a Christian Perspective first published in Germany in 1989. Amusingly, some small co-hort learning group members actually describe the No-nonsense Nine as a dumbed-down version of the Enneagram, except meant for today's high-stressed, time-deprived business boss. I consider this a compliment.
4. **Peter Friedes**: Hewitt Associates' CEO Peter Friedes ' early research and writing from Hewitt's in-house first draft "workbook," which back then was simply called

"2Rs" (for "Relating" and "Requiring,"). Those were Friedes' terms (versus an earlier HR Department version that I simply called, "SAMI," which was an abbreviation by Hewitt that stood for "Supportive-Assertive Management Initiative."(See Chapter 4 for more). Note: Peter Friedes is the retired CEO of the human resources and benefits consultancy giant Hewitt Associates, is the architect of the "Managing People Better" questionnaire, which (as of this writing today) is published (with free access) on the Internet. Under Friedes' leadership, Hewitt grew 23 percent each year for 23 years and earned a continuous spot in the book The 100 Best Companies to Work For in America. While at Hewitt, Peter worked continuously to create more effective ways to develop managers. He asked, "What fundamental skills do our best managers have? How do we assess our existing managers and then help each one of them do better?" His current organization from which he is also retiring from, which he established in 2007, is "Managing People Better." This non-profit organization synthesizes over two decades of experimenting into a powerful, simple tool to help almost all managers, even if they are already good at managing.

Maister, Antonovsky, Rohr and Friedes. Each of these four thinkers/authors has played a meaningful part in the simplified design of the No-Nonsense Nine Principles; They along with Parker Palmer's vision and certain key professors, including Harry Kraemer, and my faculty and colleagues while I was in postgraduate school studying at Garrett Seminary located at Northwestern University from 1996 to 2006. Being in small learning groups goes way back to the foundation of the Methodist Church.

That's when I first began coaching executives and teaching small work groups of managers and workers. Coaching was an unheard of thing in most businesses and the workplace in general back then. I entered a new field early that would develop rapidly and mature quickly. Lots of people hung up the coaching shingle in the late 90s. Today, the market size, measured by revenue, of the Business Coaching industry is $14.2bn in 2022, with an expected growth rate of 2 to 3 percent per year.

In Chapter Four, you will be introduced to the title of Leader/Manager-Coach, especially as a manager-coach learns Supportive and Assertive Management Initiative (SAMI) and how to have people Working Better Together (WBT). With each chapter you will find the focus to be mostly upon a single No-nonsense Principle. Each principle aligns for the most part with the above listed four thinker-authors.

As an Addendum to all chapters of the book, there are also included nine companion Values-Based Leadership exercises, one per chapter, each one co-located with the ending of each No-nonsense Nine principle and its book chapter.

At the closing of each chapter, I include short writings that are called "One Sheets." These "One Sheets" are typically written as short singular one-on-one or small group "thought-provokers" to be shared as "readings" by you with your one-on-one executive coach or within your small cohort-learning group. The permissioned resource for these nine "one sheets" is from the book, "From Values to Action," written by award-winning teacher and Kellogg Graduate School Leadership Professor, Harry M. Jansen Kraemer, Jr., the former Chairman and CEO of Baxter International. These Nine One Sheets were originally published as a Values Based Leadership Series for small group learning in 2013.

Not only do I look upon the No-nonsense Nine Principle's Mandala as a clock-wise circular improvement process, I also consider it a Leadership Spirit guide and companion, a friend. I also look upon these No-Nonsense Nine principles as the key framework components for a harmonious way of strategic business thinking. A philosopher or a theologian may refer to this approach as being what is generally called "a systematic." For me, I look upon it a lot more practically, basically as a way for people to learn to communicate better, and to have easily adaptable conversations, and to Work Better Together (WBT), one understandable and usable chunk at a time.

The all-important question is this: Would you like to lead and manage your workers in small group meetings more effectively? The general problem is that too many small group meetings are wasteful and boring. The No-nonsense Nine can really help change this, but this is not automatic: the learning time, with a positive and sincere mindset, must be invested. Approach it as though you are part of a club of devoted learners, willing to help each other, because you and they are the real experts. Create your own "No-nonsense Nine Club" and in the words of Henry Mintzberg, "(a) Engage, (b) Connect, and (c) Be Supportive."

This is the direct, singular, and ultra-sincere goal of this book: To help people Work Better Together (WBT). With it you will discover what Google discovered and what over 300 companies owned by Sir Martin Sorrell discovered on their own through their own in-depth in-house research: How to Work Better Together (WBT). You will learn to Work Better Together as you learn your way through The Nine No-nonsense Principles book… one principle, one discipline, and one chapter at a time. It's methodical. It requires commitment and your gifts, but it works. Again, this has been over a quarter century journey in Leadership Spirit to get here with you. The No-nonsense Nine

Mandala has been a working workplace touchstone.... A true and loving Leadership Spirit. I am grateful to be able to share it with you.

In Chapter One, you will be given an exercise to help you determine your purpose. That will be a first step of your No-Nonsense nine-step Leadership Spirit journey, completely through the No-nonsense Nine Mandala. Plus, you will, preferably, be doing this with the help either of an executive coach or as part of a small group of your workplace cohorts, as a community of learner-experts. That method relates to another of the No-Nonsense Nine principles, namely the Principle of Community. So, you're getting a taste of the idea already: The No-Nonsense Nine Principles are interconnected and, when combined, is a systemized set of principles and accompanying disciplines. It's an organism designed to help you Work Better Together (WBT), and to help you be more successful at what you do. So, learn, enjoy and prosper! The goal is simply about being more productive by communicating in conversations better: Working Better Together (WBT).

**Who this is meant for...**

This is primarily aimed at helping people working currently within the areas of Science, Technology, Engineering and Professional Services, or what I call "STEP." STEP people rarely if ever have training in conversational skills and communicating better. Yet having good communications skills is often critical to helping members of the STEP vertical do much, much better on the job. Google's in-house Oxygen Project success and research bears witness to this. This also has gained much more importance with today's staggering growth in people working remotely and becoming more isolated at work.

## A little bit more intro

The No-Nonsense Nine is mainly one thing only: an aid for making workplace communications and conversations better: Between managers and their workers and between co-workers. Our objective is to help with performance overall.

## The No-Nonsense Nine Main Goal

The main direct goal of the No-Nonsense Nine is to improve communications so that people get Working Better Together (WBT) and, as a proven result, they can then have significant lift in the quality of their productivity and overall performance.

## What The No-Nonsense Nine is NOT!

The No-Nonsense Nine is not about following rules... the No-Nonsense Nine is about having principles as a set of values with "pre-learned" disciplines already built in... disciplines that preclude the need of any immediate manager from having to become a "ruler," an enforcer: This is of great value within today's more isolated, distributed and remote workforce...

When workers are remote, the critical question is "how do you manage them?

With the No-Nonsense Nine, the infallible answer is, "you don't... they do: the workers manage themselves - mainly because they know how to and want to."

This is about getting out front and ready: Managers and their workers each want to know what to do, how to do it, when and where to do it, and why. That is the No-nonsense Nine Discipline of what is called "Story Works" in action... so you have understanding.

Story Works is central to the meaningfulness of your work life, as is someone's purpose and answering the very basic question, "why?"

Purpose, with its companion Discipline of "Story Works," is proven to be the single most important guideline of business coaching. Key to know is that coaching is a two-part story, in which the first huge part is about accepting the invitation to believe. The second part is the believing. Workplace coaching requires "Story Works" to help assure mutual retention and initial openness of both participants, the coach and the one being coached A good Coach asks and then awaits response. Never talking inside their head. Keeping open to receive. It's interdependent.

Just like telling a story to your child, the success is less about learning the details, although they are important, and more about having the necessary relationship, and with that the necessary relationship-building skills to be able to succeed. When you know the story, the work results will follow.

The No-nonsense Nine's middle row contains three (3) principles: Community, Purpose and Resources. Story Works is the central discipline of Purpose. S H A P E is the discipline and practice for the principle of Resources (or "resourcefulness"). It's a "book end" partner discipline to S H A R E, which is the discipline and practice for the principle of Community.

These disciplines are like interdependent bookends that surround the principle of Purpose, which has the discipline of Story Works, as the center or "central" Discipline of more than just that row, but of the entire No-nonsense Nine Mandala.

As you can see, all of the 8 other surrounding squares touch the discipline of Story Works. This Story Works discipline relates directly to the structure of Kenneth Burke's Dramatistic Pentad:

1) agent (who), 2) agency (what), 3) scene (when and where), 4) act (how) and 5) purpose (why). The Pentad is from the world of rhetoric: And in real business life, it allows us to make sense of motivation, the heart and pulse of work.

**No-Nonsense Nine Productivity**

Productive work comes from healthy relationships, which each in turn come directly as a result of healthy conversational communications that build trust. This makes sense: No nonsense.

**No-mystery No-nonsense Nine**

The No-Nonsense nine curriculum, workbook and exercises are not a mystery but they are sort of magical as to how they improve the bottom line. The No-Nonsense Nine is a Business Conversation Communications enabling Toolset.

That description, however, will generally not get a sponsoring boss excited enough to approve the budget. But that's it. The No-nonsense Nine Principles as a system that has proven to work within law, HR Management, high technology, engineering, financial services, manufacturing and real estate. They Can Work For any small group, if the members want to Work Better Together (WBT).

**No-nonsense Nine is a Tool.**

The No-Nonsense Nine is a very narrowcast tool: Primarily it is meant to help you communicate better through conversation in business situations, especially if you are "working remote" or a "remote manager" trying to manage others, especially within the highly competitive world of "STEP: Science, Technology, Engineering and Professional Services."

Experts who work remotely today need to be managed by their values and principles: with trust and understanding.
This makes sense: No nonsense.

## IAC

"IAC" is the narrow-focus Umbrella terminology I crafted for describing the No-nonsense Nine Principles.

The No-Nonsense Nine is very narrowly focused. It's really mind-numbingly simple, and pretty boring until you start to use it. You learn to have it "at the ready" in the back of your head. It is not at all glamorous. But it does works.

Also, even the umbrella terminology used for the No-Nonsense Nine Principles is uninteresting sounding, too: IAC.

"Instantly

Adaptive

Conversations"

Or more simply - "IAC."

These three simple words describe exactly what IAC is meant to enable, and what the No-Nonsense Nine toolset is intended to help you with, but you will need to practice and fundamentally learn to put the No-nonsense Nine to memory as though it were second nature to you.

Don't do this alone. It requires forming your own club of cohorts. Your own "No Nonsense Club." This makes sense: No nonsense.

Instantly – you can use the No-Nonsense Nine instantly. It's easy to learn, practice and apply. It's already set up for "instant recall and use."

The No-Nonsense Nine is an instantly adaptive tool:

**What the No-nonsense Nine is NOT.**

The No-nonsense Nine is **not** a Leadership Program, but it will help you become a better leader.

The No-nonsense Nine is **not** a Manager Development Program, but it will help you manage others better.

The No-nonsense Nine is **not** a Negotiation Program, but it will help you negotiate better with others.

The No-nonsense Nine is **not** a Six Sigma Tool, but it will help Six Sigma users.

The No-nonsense Nine is **not** an Agile Tool, but it will help you as an Agile Manager in your job to do a better job of managing, and to become even more agile.

The No-nonsense Nine is about helping working Relationships. This really makes sense.

If your goal is to become an outstanding manager and/or leader as a result of studying, learning and practicing to apply the No-nonsense Nine Principles is a positive step, but there is much more to do. Strongly consider augmenting your gain in No-nonsense Nine knowledge by also becoming students of experts such as Peter Drucker, Harry Kraemer, Jim Collins and many of the top business authors and experts available.

IAC or "Healthy Business Conversational Communications" is a very narrow field, and it's also pretty intense stuff. When it comes to leading and managing, I am sub-orbital in comparison to my many heroes. I love and admire the three experts above, and many others, but as able as I am to stand in my narrow field, I am only able to stand in their shadows in their much broader arenas of teaching about managing and leading. Keep on learning and growing.... That's what is most important! The No-nonsense Nine Mandala is like a mental cue card. Use it as a tool to learn to quickly adapt your conversations on the fly... It's a great tool for that. Practice it, memorize it, use it without fear or hesitation, and then get really, really good at it.

It makes the workplace a better place to work.

**Communicating and Getting Unstuck.**

As a coach and teacher, I stick with helping people to improve their communicating. That's a niche. It is the "quick fix.". It's the key to rapidly getting people to work better together (WBT). That's also why these three creations are my main text proof resources:

1. The 2001 book, "Practice What You Preach: What Manager Must Do to Create a High Achievement Culture" by David H. Maister, published by Free Press, a Division of Simon and Schuster, Inc.
2. The December 2013 Harvard Business Review article, "How Google Sold Its Engineers on Management: Hint: It's all about the data." by David A. Garvin.
3. The 2011 book, "From Values to Action, The Four Principles of Values-Based Leadership," by Harry M. Jansen Kraemer, Jr., published by Jossey-Bass, a Wiley Imprint.

   These are three excellent and friendly resources. Easy to read, readily available, compelling and right on the money. I love these three creations. They support the No-nonsense Nine Mandala and its logic of getting unstuck via improved communication and conversations. This leads to guaranteed improvement in productivity.

Maister focuses on improved productivity and lists the top attributes that proved valid within his exhaustive research and reporting on Martin Sorrell's 300+ independently run WPP companies. In addition, The Oxygen Project is all about improving productivity: that's what Garvin's Top Ten Oxygen Project list of Manager Behaviors within Google proved.
Maister's and Garvin's creation are well researched and documented. To my way of thinking, they each are strong testimony as to what the No-nonsense Nine Principles are intended to be used for: the improvement of workplace conversations and communications on-the-job.
I have chosen these three works as my testimony, not the other way around. This No-nonsense Nine book is intended to provide a learning experience that gets people Working Better Together. (WBT)
That sure makes sense.

**David Maester**: David's book is a one-of-a-kind creation. I found the No-nonsense Nine Principles present within his research findings: the attributes of WPP's companies' productivity boost. When and if you read this book, you will find much more. The top ten attributes that are presented in this book on WPP are evidence. They align with the No-nonsense Nine Mandala's construct.

**David Garvin**: David for years was the most prolific professor at Harvard Business Review and a person whose work quality is admired universally. As within Maester's book, I find the No-nonsense Principles also align within the research and recommendations garnered by Garvin and his team from Google's Oxygen Project, which is the main subject of David Garvin's well-researched article. The top ten manager behavior qualities found within the Googleplex-based research are evidence on the value of the No-nonsense Nine; they, as with Maester's attributes, align well with the No-nonsense Nine Mandala's content, context and construct.

**Harry Kraemer**: I have selected Harry Kraemer's book, "From Values to Action," as an ideal resource to show the importance of what I call values-based leadership spirit. I add the word "spirit." His four main cornerstone values-based leadership principles are as follows:

1. Self Reflection
2. Balance and Perspective
3. True Self-confidence
4. Genuine Humility

These four values align directly with the four corner principles of the No-nonsense Nine, respectively, 1) Responsibility, 2) Creativity, 3) Reliability, and 4) Sincerity. With Harry's permission, I rewrote and condensed nine portions of his much more substantive original book published by Jossey-Bass to use as what I call class "handouts" or "One Sheets," which are like Reader's Digest versions of his book's chapters. These are short-readings, as abbreviated extracts used as "food for thought" about what I call "Principle-led leadership." I did this with the intention of supporting both executive coaching sessions and/or teacher-led small group learning discussions, led by a teacher-coach, usually me. The "From Values to Action" book content has been "re-choreographed" in this way by me to help promote conversations that are based upon the No-nonsense Nine Principles. Until 2019, these Nine (9) One Sheets were most predominantly used for improving productivity by middle manager small groups that I "coached" within Jones, Lang,

LaSalle Incorporated's Life Sciences Division, which was then being managed out of Chicago, between 2009 until 2019, before the Covid-19 outbreak changed and interrupted everything. Each participant also had Harry's book, personally autographed by him. Interestingly, this learning book you are now reading was inspired by the experience of my witnessing training and development budgets drying up, and being constrained at most companies whose workforces very appropriately and logically were being migrated rapidly to a remote-location business management model. This training and development followed this philosophy and inspiration as championed by Harry:

> *Harry J. Kraemer: "If you wish to improve your productivity, make a grid with six rows for each of the major aspects of your life." This Kraemer defines for everyone as career, family, health, spirituality, fun, and volunteering. He then suggests that you decide how much of your time you would ideally like to be devoting to each of these activities. Next, figure out how much you actually are devoting. Finally, calculate the difference.*

Like Harry, I believe in using lists and grids and imagery of them to improve productivity, and I highly respect his Leadership Spirit.

## WBT EXERCISE #1:

First-time Learning The No-Nonsense Nine Principles Model Structure

Wouldn't it be great to help people Work Better Together: to help you communicate better, strategize better, and make better decisions, Real time… On-the-job?

The answer starts with this very brief exercise, which begins with the basics.

The No-Nonsense Nine Principle's structure may look complicated, but is actually quite simple. Think, "Tic-tac-toe." To help you to understand and make use of the No-Nonsense Nine box-like Model, you first must put it to memory. Therefore, I ask you to first quickly sketch it yourself on to a letter-sized sheet of paper. Don't just look at it and skip on. Do it! Use a grade school type of pencil with an eraser, and think like a basic early-learner. Go back to the "feel of it:" Learning something by heart.

It may also help you to think of this part of the learning process more like it's doodling, or as a super-brief experiment in self-reflection.

This learning experience exercise will require you to read the descriptions and then deliberately describe a choice at the end that you will be making about yourself.

First, draw a tic-tac-toe design inside of a box-shaped square and then with your pencil, number the upper right corner of each of the squares #1 through #9: Begin your numbering with the center square of the tic-tac-toe design as the #1 square and the top middle square, above it, as the #2 Square. After that, continue this numbering process clockwise from the #3 square (the box's upper right square) to the #9 square (the box's upper left square), with the #9 square becoming the last and upper left most square of the tic-tac-toe shaped No-Nonsense Nine structure (what I sometimes still call the "9 Square").

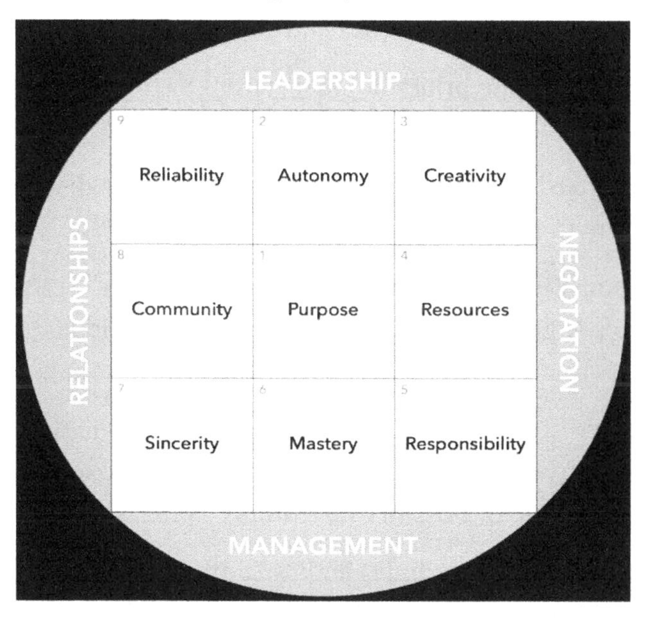


Look at the No-nonsense Nine Mandala above… you are essentially creating the same image in pencil by hand. This with intention is very basic tactile learning for you - building recall. You must do this, mainly because the end goal is to make using the No-nonsense Nine a fun and HIGHLY AUTOMATIC way for you to lift performance: "second nature" for you.

Each square has a No-nonsense principle and a corresponding No-nonsense discipline.  FYI, "Disciplines" are also called either "practices" or "skills."

With your pencil, write the principle (in the top center of the square) and the discipline (right underneath the principle in the bottom center of the square). Do this for each principle and discipline into its appropriate square, as follows:

**(Think about these as you do the labor of learning).**

#1. "Purpose" (the principle) and "Story Works" (the discipline).

#2. "Autonomy" (the principle) and "Still Point" (the discipline).

#3. "Creativity" (the principle) and "strengths focus" (the discipline).

#4. "Resources" (the principle) and "shaping" (the discipline). A good synonym for "resources" would be "agency."

#5. "Responsibility" (the principle) and "surrender" (the discipline). A good synonym for "surrender" would be "letting go."

#6. "Mastery" (the principle) and "Step Stones" (the discipline). A good synonym for "mastery" would be either "execution" or "implementation" or possibly just simply "process."

#7. "Sincerity" (the principle) and "steadfastness" (the discipline). A good synonym for "steadfastness" would be "dependability."

#8. "Community" (the principle) and "sharing" (the discipline). A good synonym for "sharing" would be "togetherness" or possibly "family."

#9. "Reliability" (the principle) and "self differentiation" (the discipline). A good synonym for "reliability" would be "consistency." A synonym for "differentiation" would be "awareness."

The Questions: In the space below, write which No-nonsense Principle and No-nonsense Discipline would be an ideal analog to represent you in the working universe of the modern day workplace? How do you "identify" and why?

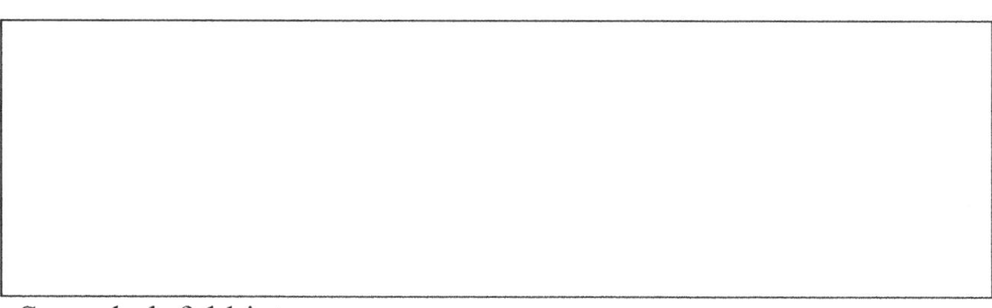

Some helpful hints:

The center column contains Daniel Pink's 3 implicit motivations.

The 3 rows top-to-bottom represent "head, heart and gut."

The left column represents "*supportive*" ("*relationships*").

The right column represents "*assertive*" (partly "*character*" *and* partly "*execution*").

All of the Disciplines begin with the letter "S," to aid recall.

Still Point is much like Thomas Keating's "Centering Prayer."

Story Works is much like Kenneth Burke's "Dramatistic Pentad."

Step Stones is patterned after Lakota Medicine Wheels as a symbol of hope and/or a stone laid before a threshold as a symbol of expected positive change

The 5 interior squares represent story ("doing")

The 4 corner squares represent 4 Cardinal Virtues ("being")

All 9 represent doing and being ("harmony" and "kindness")

The OSHAM squares are the 5 interior squares.

The "Effectuation" squares are also the 5 interior squares: See Addendum #2.

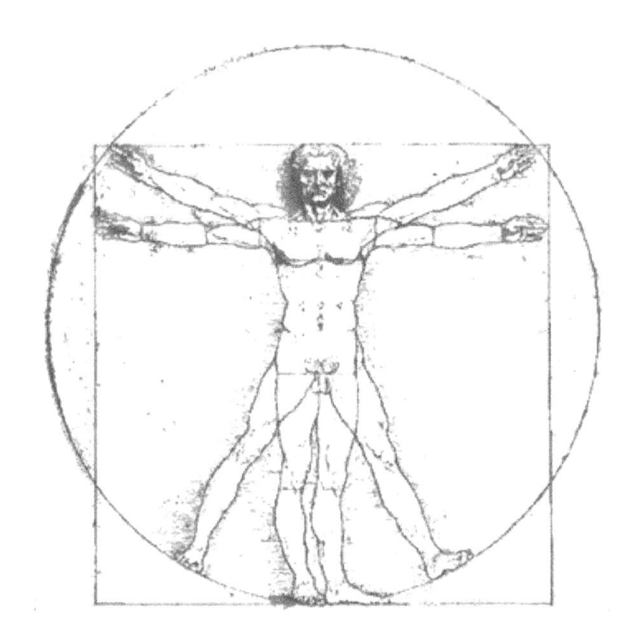

**The Vitruvian Man**

Considered today by some people as politically incorrect, this shape and symbol is Leonardo DaVinci's rendition of The Vitruvian Man from 1490, a "product" of its time. (Shown Above)

Note: This image provides the perfect example of Leonardo's keen interest in proportion. In addition, this picture represents a cornerstone of Leonardo's attempts to relate man to nature. Encyclopedia Britannica online states, "Leonardo envisaged the great picture chart of the human body he had produced through his anatomical drawings and Vitruvian Man as a*cosmografia del minor mondo* (cosmography of the microcosm). He believed the workings of the human body to be an analogy for the workings of the universe."

The No-nonsense Nine, amusing as this may seem, is <u>my</u> attempt at the Vitruvian Man for the workplace; as a different sort of, but not too different sort of, universe than DaVinci dealt with. Quite simply: DaVinci wanted to learn, and his learning steps are essentially the same as your learning steps are today: 1) Explain 2) Demonstrate 3) Practice and 4) Personalize. After that, you should have it, be able to work with it. Beyond the everyday practical skills, the No-nonsense Mandala approximates a strategy, sort of like a modern day Medicine Wheel to help explain and then connect you as a digital-age person to the workplace in a way that is highly principled and loaded with helpful skills, practices and disciplines, as a uniting system that allows you to converse and work better with others and improve your workplace productivity. The 18th century's plains people's medicine wheel, or Sacred Hoop, was a true symbol for life among Native American tribes and had many interpretations. It was comprised of four quadrants, which represented several concepts, such as seasons of the year, stages of life, cardinal directions, and the four sides of a person – physical, emotional, spiritual, mental.

The No-nonsense Nine "Medicine Wheel" doesn't describe strategy per se, it simply describes and unites workplace principles and disciplines. That's it. They are to be discussed and shared in small learning groups. Eventually this takes you to understanding "process" and helps you to begin a more expanded, meaningful relationship with the No-nonsense Nine. In time, you must eventually personalize (as within step 4, numbered just above), and then you must "own the process," which comes eventually (with step 3 "practice," also numbered just above). This is straightforward and not at all mystical or blurry, which strategy can be. But first things first, here below are the Principles, listed one at a time:

1. **Purpose**: Everything begins with someone knowing his or her own story. It's the foundation that defines a person's meaningfulness, what's in the heart. There are 5 parts to a story: Agent, Agency, Purpose, Scene, and Act. This harkens back to Aristotle's teachings, as researched and recorded within the book, "A Grammar of Motives"

(1933) by Professor Kenneth Burke, University of Chicago, wherein Burke examines how the five Aristotelian principles interrelate. As an expert on rhetoric, Burke's "A Grammar of Motives" delves into consideration of language as a vehicle of eliciting human action.

Work groups and learning groups can bond and build trust by sharing purpose through story sharing, or what I call "Story Works, " which is the centermost No-nonsense Nine Discipline. Story Works or story sharing, if you like, is the single most basic must in the executive coaching process. Story Working is especially powerful when combined with what is called "Solution Focused Coaching," which is a derivative of Solution Focused Brief Therapy Counseling ("BTC"), which frankly is mostly about becoming "Not Problem Focused." This approach is a huge opportunity to improve your work life. How much time in your career, or just today, have you wasted chasing problems up a flagpole when all you really needed was a solution. For more, see the book, "Solutions Focus," (2002, 2007) by authors P. Jackson & M. McKergow.

In a nutshell, Albert Einstein said, "Everything should be made as simple as possible, but no simpler." The answer is the "SIMPLE" process:

SIMPLE is an acronym (by Mike McKergow).

The acronym speaks for itself:

S = Solutions not problems

I = In between – the action is in the interaction.

M = Make use of what's there.

P = Possibilities – past, present and future

L = Language – simply said

E = Every case is different

Just think how much time in the workplace is wasted because a group or team is mindfully searching for the problem and trying to define it. Instead, they should think about starting working first on the solution. A true story:
Insoo Kim Berg and her husband Steve DeShazer were the co-creators of Brief Therapy Counseling ("BTC") in a counseling firm of that same name (eventually) in Wisconsin. They came from their offices in Milwaukee to present BTC at Loyola Chicago in 1996 one Autumn evening, and my Seminary Pastoral Counseling Class and I all drove north from the NU Evanston campus together to Rogers Park to attend. Insoo related this story: A businessman client of hers was troubled, and like a dog gnawing on a bone, the businessman couldn't figure out what to do about the problem. Insoo intentionally asked him what solution he could suggest instead: "What might be a better solution?" The next day he was elated. He awakened with the solution, with the "problem" no longer a concern. That day was the birth of "Brief Therapy Counseling," which in time would grow into Solution-focused Coaching, now in "full swing," 27 years later.
Remember: S I M P L E.
Dr. DeShazer that evening reported that versus traditional and personal counseling processes most popular at the time, "BTC" proved to work three times faster, often in one sitting.

2. **Autonomy**: Autonomy is about self-worth, what you "stand for." The purpose of your existence is tied in to your sense of autonomy. What you think of yourself. When you look upon the No-nonsense Nine Mandala, the Autonomy principle is placed where the head and brain

would be if the Mandala were a person's body. Capture this image in your head.

3. **Creativity**: Creativity is your thoughts filled with new and powerful energy. Creativity is the ability to make or otherwise bring into existence something new, whether a new solution to a problem, a new method or device, or a new artistic object or form. Creativity and the second Cardinal Virtue of "Justice" are connected. The No-nonsense principle of Creativity ties with the No-nonsense Principle of Mastery in importance, also. Creativity is about change as are Justice and Mastery. I have found that creative beings (including artists and writers) most often want things to be "just" right (aka "justice") and excellent (aka "Masterful"). Versus by "Causation," Entrepreneurial Creativity is born through the "Effectuation" process. (Study Addendum #2 for its 5 steps).
4. **Resources**. To be resourceful requires you to have some power, energy or capability, to have a source of supply or support, an available means (usually used in plural). Within the No-nonsense Nine, Resources means having access to labor, or to possess assets or worthwhile entities, as a natural feature or phenomenon that enhances the quality of life on-the-job, to possess "Agency."
5. **Responsibility**. Fortitude, the first of the four Cardinal Virtues, is defined as "Courage." Courage is the choice and willingness to confront agony, pain, danger, uncertainty, or intimidation. Valor is courage or bravery, especially in battle. Having responsibility requires fortitude and courage.
6. **Mastery**. Mastery is defined as control or superiority over someone or something. In his book "Drive," Dan Pink focuses upon Mastery as an implicit motivation.

This definition aligns with what is the No-nonsense Nine's Mastery Principle. The motivation and decision-making within the Mastery Principle is more about wanting to achieve excellence, about seeking perfection, about wanting to dominate something such as a skill, and not about dominating someone, such as another person or persons in your workplace. Mastery is more about the craft, such as within software coding, scientific research, or technical design.

7. **Sincerity**. A person who is sincere has the quality of being free from pretense, deceit, or hypocrisy: "the sincerity of his beliefs is unquestionable." Even more so, sincerity is the virtue of one who communicates and acts in accordance with the entirety of their feelings, beliefs, thoughts, and desires, in a manner that is honest and genuine. Sincere people embody humility and have a stick-to-it nature that let's you know that they will be there for you when you need them. They employ the No-nonsense Nine discipline of steadfastness, which comes from the heart and is unmistakably the quality of a person being the same person on the outside that he or she is on the inside.
8. **Community**. The social glue that binds us together, there are many types of community. As a No-nonsense Nine group member, you are within a small learning community. In your job as well you are part of a work community. A community is a unified body of individuals. Being in community is also often a feeling, a feeling of fellowship with others, as a result of sharing common attitudes, interests, and goals: such as, "the sense of community that organized religion has historically provided and can provide." USA Football teams are a small community, usually part of a larger

community of teams, such as a conference like the Big Ten, the SEC, or the NFL. I have a community of friends. I feel "in community" with them. Community is one of those soft, fuzzy words that many people do not fully understand and even find alienating. It is a word that gets used loosely, with the meaning confused and distorted. Community and culture are often confused. They are not the same. Organizational culture is the attitudes, customs, rituals, values, and beliefs shared by the members of an organization that govern their behavior. In business, we talk about communities of practice and communities of interest. We also talk about virtual communities, often consisting of forums. Per Henry Mintzberg, renowned management author, puts it best in his HBR article entitled, "Rebuilding Companies of Communities" (2009), he writes: " Decades of short-term management have inflated the importance of CEOs and reduced employees to fungible commodities. Middle managers, who see the connections between operations and strategy, can be instrumental in rebuilding a sense of community in businesses."

Mintzberg writes further: "Individualism is a fine idea. It provides incentive, promotes leadership, and encourages development—but not on its own. We are social animals who cannot function effectively without a social system that is larger than ourselves. This is what is meant by "community:" the social glue that binds us together for the greater good." To me, within the No-nonsense Nine Principles, the Community Principle means caring about our work, our colleagues, and our place in the world, geographic and otherwise, and in turn sharing in and being inspired by this caring. "Sharing" is the No-nonsense Nine Discipline in partnership with

Community. I think of Sharing as caring in togetherness. Many people today need more caring at work.

9. **Reliability**. The easy definition is simply, "**the quality or state of being reliable**." Reliability is the backbone of scientific proof, in medicine, pharmaceuticals, software, computer engineering, all of engineering, financial management, investing, manufacturing, business planning.

   Reliability is the cornerstone of proof. Why? Because then there is trust and candidly people's lives are at stake in this world. This is the most serious of all the No-nonsense Nine Principles. This is the corner belonging to the Chief Financial Officer, the accountants, Chief Information Officer and the Chief Technology officer. This corner principle is even superior in importance to the kitty corner No-nonsense principle of Responsibility. You can also think of it as the ability for a test or research findings to be repeatable. For example, a medical thermometer is a "reliable tool" that would measure the correct temperature each time it is used. Often times, Reliability is the responsibility of the Chief Operating Officer and his or hers cadre of experts, especially in the production arena and/or manufacturing.

   As a quick reference, below are the No-nonsense Nine principles, shown directly adjacent to each principle's companion or partner discipline:

| NO-NONSENSE PRINCIPLE | DISCIPLINE |
|---|---|
| PURPOSE | STORY WORKS |
| AUTONOMY | STILL POINT |
| CREATIVITY | STRENGTHS FOCUS |
| RESOURCES | SHAPING |
| RESPONSIBILITY | SURRENDER |
| MASTERY | STEP STONES |

| SINCERITY | STEADFASTNESS |
|---|---|
| COMMUNITY | SHARING |
| RELIABILITY | SELF DIFFERENTIATION |

The No-nonsense Disciplines: These are not taught in a classroom. They are too intimate for that. Also, since these disciplines must be yours, by default they cannot be mine. They all start with the letter "s" simply to help with recall. They each have multiple synonyms.

I can tell you what they mean to me. Then you must do the work to make them yours. Otherwise, they are not disciplines, they are rules... and I do not rule. The No-nonsense Principles are each individually less like rules and more like moral values. I'm okay with that but I seldom like specific rules. And specific rules just don't seem to work very well because people care more about themselves than they do about a rule. We are a society of jaywalkers especially if we are in a hurry. Point is, disciplines must evolve from within. You must want the discipline. I can only shine a light.

Here is the light:

1. **Story Works**: Per Rudyard Kipling, I quote the following: "I keep six honest serving men (they taught me all I knew); their names are What and Why and When And How And Where and Who." Story Works takes these basic elements and allows you to use them to explain your own self – "What is my story, dear friend?" – and to question others – "What is your story, my dear friend?" The actionable word here is "friend." Unfriendliness is nonsense... makes no sense. So build your own story as if you were your own best friend, and elicit other people's stories, as a best friend would do. People feel vulnerable when talking of themselves. So be kind and gentle, and be a friend when "working a story."

Mechanically, there are 5 parts to a story. Kenneth Burke's Pentad is a popular heuristic that allows us to analyze motivation in any dramatic situation. At a basic level, the Pentad functions like Kipling's journalistic questions. The Dramatistic Pentad comprises the five rhetorical elements: act, scene, agent, agency, and purpose, as shown below:

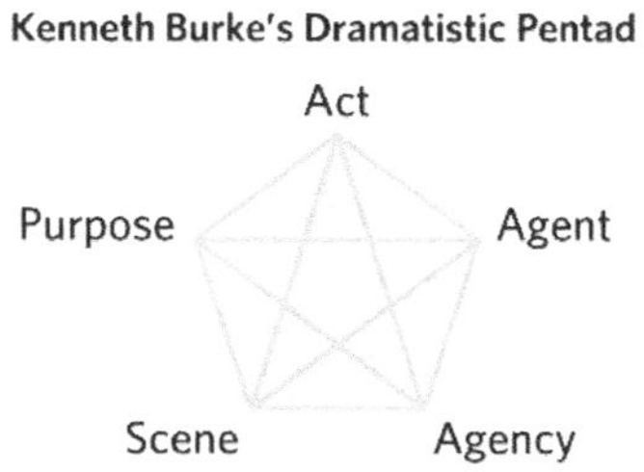

**Kenneth Burke's Dramatistic Pentad**

Act
Purpose
Agent
Scene
Agency

These work together. These words from the precious, parent-essential book "How to Tell Stories to Children" by Silke Rose West and Joseph Sarosy: "Storytelling is one of the oldest and most essential skills known to humankind: a timeless parenting tool that helps families celebrate life's joys, navigate its challenges, and raise healthy, well-adjusted kids." (Houghton Mifflin Harcourt, 2021)

Story Works is within us from childhood on, and therefore a powerful and formidable communications tool… "Storytelling is, without a doubt, the best way to imprint information or ideas on the mind of the listener. " (Jane Goodall)
The No-nonsense Discipline of Story Works is the job of crafting your own work story built around your Purpose. This "story workings" you must have "at the ready." In battle, Soldiers came charging through the forest, guns "at the ready." Synonyms for "at the ready" are: poised, waiting, prepared. So practice your Story Works that you wish to

share and be prepared, actually be proactive "at the ready." This tells people that you care. Then in truly humble fashion, ask the other person to share their story with you. And then be a good listener, first, by not talking, and then, second, by using active listening. Active listening is a way of listening and responding to another person that improves mutual understanding. It's about being present, listening to understand (not to respond), and showing active interest and engagement in the dialogue. Be positive and kind, but be active, proactive. This can help build rapport, relationships and can promote empathy.

2. **Still Point**: This is my way of meditating, but for business. Many high tech people and business executives who have tried meditating don't stick with it. A lot of that is due to time pressure on the job. The No-nonsense Discipline of Still Point is the job of crafting your own sense of peace built around your Autonomy. The Still Point discipline I teach is an Eastern version of Centering Prayer, which was taught to me by a Monk in Snow Mass at St. Benedict's Monastery. If you're time deprived, it's natural to be wary. At first it took time, but now it's really quick… 15 to 30 minutes. I set my alarm for it. And it's very beneficial. In working within law, medicine, high tech and pharma and such for many, many years, I have found there is little resistance to meditating. Meditators "on-the-job" I have observed, however, in fact seem to process anxiety a little differently. I believe that is what "Still Point" is, it's a bit different that way. The time deprivation concerns they had seem to go away. They figured it out. That's key. One of the biggest differences is that they often know how to turn their anxiety into a source of energy rather than seeing it as purely an obstacle. That's classic "Still Point." One meditator I know calls her meditating "enervating," in that it lifts her energy and helps her

prioritize objectives and goals more accurately. She was initially skeptical, but now she says that her meditating (aka, "Still Point") practice actually "kicks the time clock's backside." (her words). I have found the same reaction personally for me with "Still Point" for over 20 years now.

3. **Strengths Focus**: This is about sticking with what you are good at and letting the other stuff fall back behind where it belongs. And knowing to not try and turn a weakness into "a strength: " Just stick with the strength!" I learned this first from the previous president of Gallup, Don Clifton, by reading his book, "Soar With Your Strengths" (1992), before he bought Gallup.
4. **Shaping**: Shaping is about being proactive in your mental conversation, just before and as you are speaking. Be sure not to be blind and watch for physical signs of reaction by your partner in conversation. Shaping is also about softly breaking the intimacy barrier that people have. Never cut off your partner's words. Take a breath. Lean in to get closer and respond with a quiet voice. Pause and be quiet until you know they are listening. Not a whisper, just quieter, so that the partner must almost have to lean in also to hear you. Shaping is about softly breaking the intimacy barrier that people have. Loud partners will naturally soften their voice and quiet down their voice volume if you persist in Shaping the conversation in this manner. When on a phone call, you can imagine what they look like as they speak and almost mentally see them in your mind: their reaction, and physical look. Overly shy and conversation-resistant partners must never be bullied with a louder voice. Do not ask them to speak louder. Instead say you are having trouble hearing them: "I'm sorry, I couldn't quite hear you, would you repeat what you just said." Or, "Can you repeat that? I didn't catch everything you said, and it's important to me."

5. **Surrender**: This is the discipline of knowing to let go, not necessarily just **when** to let go, but much more: Surely Disney had no idea how viral the song, "Let it go," would become. In fact, before the canonical version sung by Idina Menzel was released, Disney had released another version by Demi Lovato. It has different words, and a less challenging musical structure. It was designed for radio play, with all the conventional features you expect in that genre. It must have come as a shock to the Disney people that the soaring and hyper-dramatic version by Menzel became the radio hit. I believe that our work culture is open to the idea of people letting their egos get out of the way. So, on-the-job, learn to let go and let someone else do the work. This is a solid sign of a healthier workplace.
6. **Step Stones**: Step Stones is being incremental. Stuart Diamond, the internationally recognized expert and award-winning professor of the famed negotiation course at Wharton Business School concludes his entire book, "Getting More: How to Negotiate to Achieve Your Goals in the Real World," with a single graphical image, and concludes his 383 page book by coming back to the summary of his course. His model (see Addendum #A, B and C) in a nutshell shows a parabola arch with multiple short arrows, front-to-end, stepping across the bottom of the arch as a straight yet segmented line, captioned by the words: "pictures in their heads." This is what you must learn to do with the No-nonsense Nine Principles and Disciplines: picture them in your head incrementally, just like they are, as Step Stones. Bring this image to your mind, and practice its use.
7. **Steadfastness**: Is about being true. Steadfastness is Biblical, and harkens back to 30 parables in the New Testament, alone illustrating the importance of Steadfastness.

8. **Sharing**: Is about trusting within community. Sharing is equally about having a process for communication. In the workplace, trust and process are yoked together. I recommend knowing the No-nonsense Mandala by heart. And when sharing, also have a conversation process that can allow you to touch into it easily. I use the acronym "D.A.R.E." as a memory aid: "Discover, Align, Renew, and Emerge." I use one "memory cue" for each corner starting with and proceeding clockwise with the CEO corner, as follows:

   CEO: Discover (This is a top priority for CEOs)
   COO: Align (This is a top priority for COOs)
   CHRO: Renew (This is a top priority for CHROs)
   CFO): Emerge (This is a top priority for CFOs)

It's like a driving circle or a steering wheel graphically, surrounding the No-nonsense Nine principles. I highly recommend and teach participants to use a "memory cue" devise like DARE: superior to "DARE" is another memory cue construct called, "The Six Conversations That Matter." I prefer this and/or "DARE" as ways to maximize the value of the No-nonsense Nine Mandala. "DARE" is rather simplistic. Very basic. The Six Conversations is more complete... a unifying system (a series) of conversations described by notable business author and world-renowned training development designer/developer, Peter Block. He is the recipient of the Organization Development Network's 2008 Lifetime Achievement Award

Preferable to the DARE acronym, the Six Conversations, as described in Peter's book, "Community," helps participants move through the process of building a community based upon accountability and commitment. Descriptions of the Six Conversations process are listed within the next few pages.

The process is fantastic as a method for sharing in community. I recommend aligning the six key words as "memory cues," as displayed within the circle on the No-nonsense Nine's book cover: Commit this to memory.
To build a new community or open one to an alternative future, start with the Invitation conversation.
The Six Conversations progress as a circle from one to the next. Some of the conversations may overlap, and any given conversation may be revisited after it has begun.
Some of the conversations are more challenging than others, especially when individual members of a community are being called to interact with each other in new ways. The more challenging conversations present greater risk to the participants and require the development of deeper trust.
For best results in sharing, begin with less demanding issues and objectives before addressing more difficult ones.
In addition to describing the process of sharing to build community, the Six Conversations model also applies to the process of developing trusted partnerships between individuals and successfully initiating change.
As mentioned above, Peter Block is the author of the book "Community: The Structure of Belonging," (© 2018, Berrett-Koehler Publishers), and other great books, and is a partner in Designed Learning, a training company that offers workshops on building skills. They offer a training program in The Six Conversations, as do other independent trainers and educational organizations. Another helpful acronym is ("T.I.G.E.R.S."): Trust, Interdedendence, Genuineness, Empathy, Risk Resolution, and Success. See CoreValues.com and/or Dianne Crampton, from her book on Leadership entitled,"Becoming Tigers: Leading Your Team to Success," ©2019 Three Creeks Publishing.

9. **Self-Differentiation**: Is about not being sucked in and then becoming stronger because of this through self-awareness, and a lot about not over-identifying and becoming swallowed up. Self-differentiation was first defined by psychiatrist Murray Bowen as; "A setting apart of oneself as distinct from others." More broadly, self-differentiation is the ability for a person to recognize their own thoughts and feelings, and to respect that they are sometimes different from others.

   The two charts that follow display the No-Nonsense Nine principles and each principle's companion or "partner" discipline. Each single square represents one of nine basic principles.

**The No-Nonsense Nine Principles in Mandala Order (Together)**

| | | |
|---|---|---|
| 9. RELIABILITY | 2. AUTONOMY | 3. CREATIVITY |
| 8. COMMUNITY | 1. PURPOSE | 4. RESOURCES |
| 7. SINCERITY | 6. MASTERY | 5. RESPONSIBILITY |

**The No-Nonsense Nine Disciplines in Mandala Order (Together)**

| | | |
|---|---|---|
| 9. SELF AWARE | 2. STILL POINT | 3. STRENGTHS |
| 8. SHARING | 1. STORY WORKS | 4. SHAPING |
| 7. STEADFAST | 6. STEP STONES | 5. SURRENDER |

These principles and disciplines represent motivations and decision-making. They, respectively, first **motivate** people at work and secondly influence their **decision-making** processes. To communicate conversationally with success, you must keep 1) **motivation** and then 2) **decision-making** alive in your thought processes. Stay with your process, such as The Six Conversations and always be mindful of The No-nonsense Nine. This over time is what will become your very own No-nonsense Nine systematized method.

A No-nonsense Nine Mandala is on the following page. Added to it are four corner executive typologies, along with the circling

Six Conversations process surrounding the No-nonsense Nine Principles. The No-nonsense Nine Disciplines are not displayed. These you must develop for your own self.

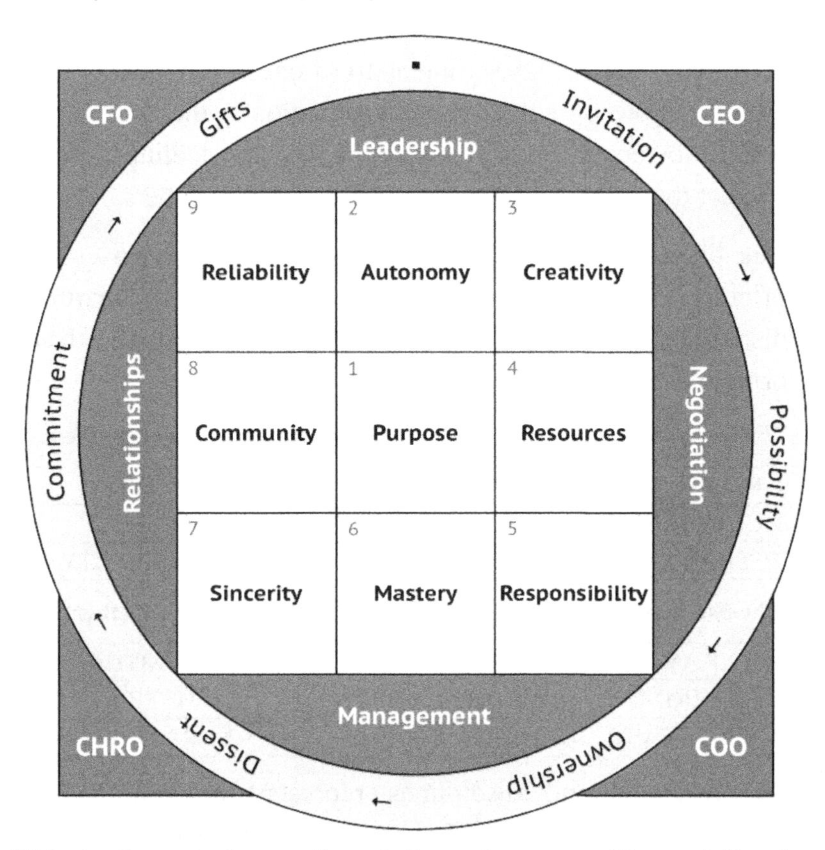


This is the art, the craft and the science, as Henry Mintzberg would say, which you need to have to be better at conversations. Above is a picture of what this looks like: Peter Block's Six-Conversations process surrounds The No-nonsense Nine Principles. Each corner labels the executive type most commonly affiliated with the No-nonsense Principles from that closest quadrant:

- Chief Executive Officer Type (upper right quadrant)
- Chief Operating Officer (lower right quadrant)

- Chief Human Resource Officer (lower left quadrant)
- Chief Financial Officer (upper left quadrant)

As stated before, it is recommended that you put the Non-nonsense Nine Disciplines to memory and "make them yours."

The logic of these attributes and behavior qualities have been uncovered over the past quarter century within hundreds of business coaching assignments and small-group teaching and training programs within client global corporations and international professional services firms. The results are that participants "see the light" and then in this way gain "Leadership Spirit" and find "new light" within their workplaces.

**LEADERSHIP SPIRIT**

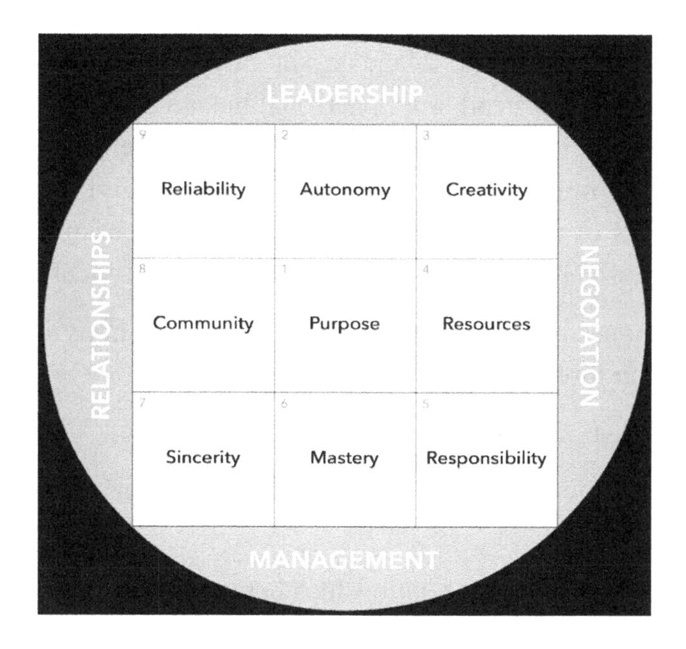


We have found that managers and workers alike easily identify with the construct and these straightforward descriptions. This makes the No-nonsense Nine readily transparent and easy to recall, especially while in the midst of a conversation.

Participants learn to capture the image, almost like a picture, in the back of their minds.

With this picture in mind, we have found that these No-nonsense principles and disciplines act as subtle yet accurate behavior indicators: They serve as helpful aids for strategy conversations, self-reflection, and on-the-fly workplace coaching. We do not think of these as personality and/or psychological typologies. The No-Nonsense Nine is different, and is useful mostly as gauging motivations and decision-making styles. It does not judge the person. In this way, we find the No-Nonsense Nine Mandala to be a helpful tool for (a) fostering conversations and discussion, (b) aiding self-reflection and making decisions and (c) assisting in the purposes associated with business coaching and small group learning programs. Easy to recall and then use, the No-Nonsense Nine Mandala, in brief, is not a validated typology, but is instead only a personal business coaching and/or small-group teaching tool to help enable constructive relationship-building conversations between individual people and groups of people working together in the workplace. The No-nonsense Nine is not judgmental. It is solution focused.

The No-nonsense Nine solution-focused conversations are highly effective in three primary area;

(1) conversations about people's character,

(2) conversations about how people execute their work on-the-job, and

(3) conversations about relationships between people on-the-job:

Character Squares, Execution Squares, and Relationship Squares, as described below.

**The Character Squares:**

The three squares in the center and the upper right (#s 1, 2 and 3.) - These are called the "character squares." These three principles, respectively, are meant (a) to invite, (b) to discuss possibility, and (c) to reflect upon ownership. (More in-depth explanation on this follows immediately when you will learn Peter Block's "Six Conversations That Matter"). Again, the No-nonsense Nine is not used for judging others.

**The Execution Squares:**

The three squares on the bottom right of the No-Nonsense Nine (#s 4, 5 and 6). - These are called the "execution squares." These three principles, respectively, are meant (a) to challenge ownership (b) defend and justify ownership (Again, more in-depth explanation on this follows immediately when you will learn Peter Block's "Six Conversations"). Again, the No-nonsense Nine is not used for judging others.

**The Relationship Squares:**

The three squares in the left vertical column make up the remaining balance of the No-Nonsense Nine (#s 7, 8 and 9). These are called the "relationship squares." They are either supportive as in SAMI or "relating" as in Friedes' "2Rs."These three principles, respectively, are meant (a) to frame the story, (b) promote dissent, (c) secure commitment, and (c) take the story from imagination into action and to "gifts conversations:" More in-depth explanation on this follows immediately as you will learn Peter Block's "Six Conversations." Again, the No-nonsense Nine is not used for judging others.

**"The Six Conversations" That Matter**

As written earlier, The Six Conversations That Matter is a series of conversations described by Peter Block in which participants move through the process of building a community based on accountability and commitment. Learn to use these in conjunction with the No-nonsense Nine Mandala framework

**Below are descriptions for each conversation:**

### The Invitation Conversation

Transformation occurs through choice, not mandate. Invitation is the call to create an alternative future. What invitation can you make to enable people to participate willingly and own the relationships, tasks, and processes that will unearth gifts and lead to success? The Invitation Conversation enables **trust**, which is a major leadership component, to emerge and grow.

### The Possibility Conversation

This conversation focuses on what you want the future to be as opposed to problem-solving the past. Focusing on "what's possible" frees people to interrelate, innovate, challenge the status quo, break new ground and create new futures that make a difference. (Note: This aligns with Solution-focused Coaching). The Possibility Conversation enables **interdependence**, which is a major leadership component, to emerge and grow.

### The Ownership Conversation

This conversation focuses on creating understanding about who effectively owns the group, processes and tasks. It challenges individuals to assume responsibility for their own contributions to both the present and the future. Confusion, blame and waiting for someone else to change are a defense against ownership and personal power. The Ownership Conversation enables **genuineness**, which is a major leadership component, to emerge and grow.

## The Dissent Conversation

This conversation gives people the space to say no. If you can't say no, your yes has no meaning. Give people a chance to express their doubts and reservations as a way of clarifying their personal roles, needs and wants within the larger vision and endeavor. Genuine commitment begins with doubt, and no is an expression of people finding their space and role in the overall mission. The Dissent Conversation enables **empathy**, which is a major leadership component, to emerge and grow.

## The Commitment Conversation

This conversation is about making promises to peers about your contribution to the success. It asks: What promise am I willing to make to this enterprise? What price am I willing to pay for success? The promise is focused on the larger purpose rather than on personal return. The Commitment Conversation enables **risk resolution,** which is a major leadership component, to emerge and grow.

## The Gifts Conversation

Instead of focusing on deficiencies and weaknesses, focus on the gifts and assets that each person can bring in order to make their best and highest contribution. Confront people with their core gifts that can make a difference and bring about lasting, meaningful change. The Gifts Conversation enables **success**, which is a major leadership component, to emerge and grow.

The Six Leadership Components underlined above as being enabled by The Six Conversations are the six leadership components taken directly from author Dianne Crampton's insightful leadership book entitled, "Becoming TIGERS,

Leading Your Team to Success." This highly effective book approaches the issue of successful teams with a balance of humor and seriousness that is rare, captivating and unique.

**In the No-nonsense Mandala, The Six Conversations are shown residing within a circle**, much like a moat surrounding the No-nonsense Nine Principles. The circle also touches and therefore connects all four corners that represent the four classic executive leadership "typologies" of CEO, CFO, CHRO and COO. This is a handy tool and, to my mind, is much like Stuart Diamond's Arch (P383) from within his book, "Getting More:" Much like Diamond's arch the Mandala is a handy picture to store in your head. The moat elements help identify and "incrementalize" the conversations and reminds the speaker what needs to come next, and will help make sure the conversation stays on track and is fruitful. Knowing "the moat" by heart keeps the conversation itself from straying or getting lost. Visually it looks like an automobile's steering wheel, which I find is a helpful reminder or "memory cue." As a metaphor, this image makes me think of the No-nonsense Nine as the automobile's engine.

**Imagine the "No-nonsense Nine engine" this way now: The Upright Heart of the No-nonsense Conversation**

The vertical central column of the No-Nonsense Nine runs perpendicularly through the diagram. This column represents the three main implicit motivations of 1) Autonomy, 2) Purpose and 3) Mastery, as identified by the author Daniel Pink within his research reported in his popular New York Time's bestselling book, "Drive: The Surprising Truth About What Motivates Us." (Canongate House, 2010)

These are the three implicit motivations that clearly influence our business conversations.

Directly below, concentrate and make mental pictures within your imagination with regard to the No-Nonsense Nine Principles:

Make this a picture in your brain. Imagine 1) the top row of the No-nonsense Mandala as being "the thinking row," 2) imagine the middle row as being the "feeling row,' and, similarly, 3) imagine the bottom row as being the "doing row." More casually now, imagine and picture these three rows, top to bottom, as 1) the head row, 2) the heart row and 3) the gut row. Commit this image to memory.

This whole No-nonsense Nine conversational structure is new, home-grown and quite a bit different than more traditionally-accepted, validated typologies: The No-nonsense Nine structure and elements deal with how you **imagine** it applies to what you find motivating, and to how you personally go about making decisions. The No-nonsense Nine Mandala is stimulating, creates interest, and can be quite helpful to aiding The Six Conversations, self-reflection, and on-the-job, live action coaching, especially in the "STEP" workplace where on-the-job, or what I sometimes characterize as "on-the-fly coaching." That is what today's high speed STEP workplace is most often all about: speed. After gaining familiarity with the use of the No-nonsense Nine Model, people have been known to think of the No-nonsense Nine as either a communication tool, a people-strategy tool, or as a "leader/manager-as-coach" coaching tool, or all three: for communicating, strategizing and for coaching with workers and groups on-the-job.

Once you get the image, it's simple to recall and easy to use. Going through the book in Group is tops. The images provided should help you picture the practice and disciplines more easily. I ask that you just give the No-Nonsense Nine Model a try. In the "STEP" world there is a lot to know about data and process when it comes to the "hard skills" of the profession, whether you are a lawyer, engineer, business executive, technician or scientist. But most "STEP" professionals rarely get the chance to discuss and develop the "soft skills" of active listening and formative conversation, personal communications processes, and building relationships. This requires imagining, and some time. That is what the No-Nonsense Nine Principles and Disciplines are here to help you do: provide you with a "soft skills" process, and the disciplines and tools you need to know and use to become more successful.

A conversation communications improvement process like this does not exist elsewhere as far as we know. If you are a STEP manager, technician or executive, we know that you're smart, but there is no other coursework in how to "Work Better Together" (WBT). This is it. This is not a leadership program or curriculum: It's a "Working Better Together" Program.

So take on the first exercise. Better yet, establish a No-nonsense Nine Club and start learning.

We begin slowly and deliberately:

**WBT Exercise #1: Head, heart, gut / supportive, assertive?**

This exercise is intended to help with your imaging the No-nonsense Nine: to assist your imagination. When it comes to your own personal motivation and decision-making style, which of these three **rows** do you most identify with? Are you more of a thinker "Head Person" (top row), a feeler "heart person" (middle row), or a doer "gut person" (bottom row)?

Furthermore, which of the three **columns** do you most identify with? We suggest that the left hand side column of the No-

Nonsense Nine as being the supportive side in that the left-side column deals more with relationships. Conversely, we see the right side column of the No-Nonsense Nine as the more assertive side. Think about this. Do you personally and professionally identify more with the supportive "relationship" column on the left, or with the more assertive "column on the right side? Or do you most identify with the center column, which is made up of Daniel Pink's three main implicit motivations of Autonomy, Purpose and Mastery? We suggest that the No-Nonsense Nine motivations are what "drive" your principles and values (what "motivates" you), as well as what influences your decision-making.

Instinctively select one of the three rows and then one of the three columns that seem to be a good fit for you... and then simply look at where <u>your</u> selected column and <u>your</u> selected row intersect: at which of the No-Nonsense Nine Principles do the row and the column intersect? Do you land smack dab in the middle on the No-Nonsense Principle of "Purpose?" Are you purpose driven? Or similalrly, did you land in the middle of the top row, are you more "Autonomy driven?" Or did you land in the middle of the bottom row and are therefore more "Mastery Driven?"

Do the principle as well as the discipline shown in the square you have highlighted best match with your most preferred motivation principle and decision-making discipline style?

In brief...

1. Row one - are you more of a thinker?yes no
2. Row two - are you more of a feeler? yes no
3. Row three - or is more of a doer? yes no
4. left column - are you supportive? yes no
5. Right column - are you assertive? yes no

6. Middle column – are you more neutral? yes no
7. Which is your main principle and discipline
8. See below - (Which of the No-Nonsense Nines is a good match?)
9. Please write and describe your reaction and rationale in one short paragraph of 25 to 50 words):

| |
|---|
| |

No-Nonsense Nine principles

| | | |
|---|---|---|
| 9. Reliability | 2. Autonomy | 3. Creativity |
| 8. Community | 1. Purpose | 4. Resources |
| 7. Sincerity | 6. Mastery | 5. Responsibility |

No-Nonsense Nine disciplines (a.k.a. "practices)"*

| | | |
|---|---|---|
| 9. Self aware | 2. Still point | 3. Strengths |
| 8. Sharing | 1. Story works | 4. Shaping |
| 7. Steadfast | 6. Step stones | 5. Surrender |

* The disciplines (These practices are to be **your** practices, otherwise they are "rules" established by an outside authority. You must make them your own and internalize them for them to be of real personal value).

How do you go about making a choice? Thinker, feeler, doer? Supportive, Assertive? Or does something else altogether about any given experience light up your imagination?

FYI: Go to Addendum #1. This is a routine public domain Social-Dominance survey that takes a few minutes. Do it just for fun. It points out the four corners of how people typically connect.

Please comment on this experience in up to 50 words:

**WBT Exercise #2: A Quick INTRO EXERCISE**

Write a No-Nonsense Nine short paragraph (less than 50 words)..."what I would like the No-Nonsense Nine to do for me or mean to me in the future?" Think of this as "Inviting Yourself" to a better understanding of your own self. This is similar to Harry Kraemer's Values-Based Leadership quality component that he identifies as "self-reflection:"

Goal:

Once you have a better understanding of your motivations and decision-making processes, you will begin to communicate with others much better than ever before.

# LEADERSHIP SPIRIT
# ("The No-nonsense Mandala")

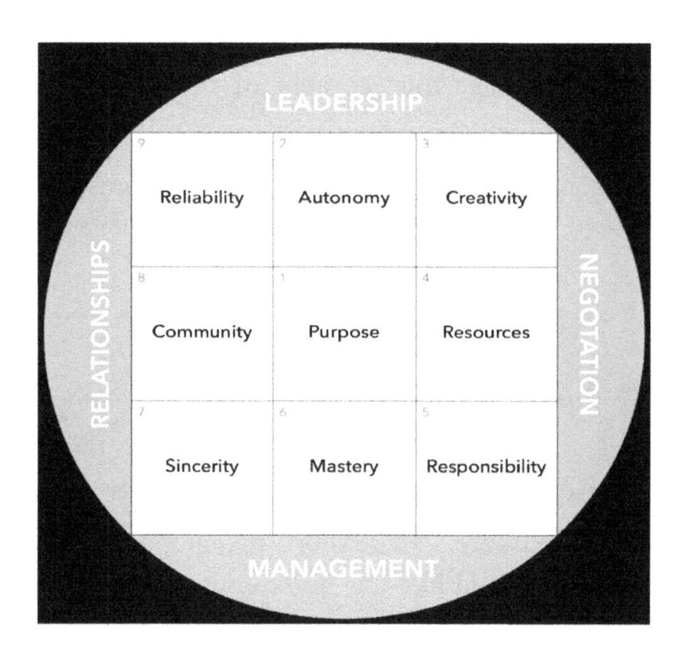


For enjoyment, the following is an experiment at aligning a type of "spirit name" with each of the No-nonsense Nine Principles:

| | | |
|---|---|---|
| Protective Spirit (Reliability Spirit) | Leadership Spirit (Autonomy Principle) | Creative Spirit (Creativity Principle) |
| Collaborative Spirit (Community Principle) | Passionate Spirit (Purpose Principle) | Survival Spirit (Resources Principle) |
| Emotional Spirit (Sincerity Principle) | Competitive Spirit (Mastery Principle) | Courageous Spirit (Responsibility Principle) |

**"Leadership Spirit" is not theological.**

In a spiritual way for me personally, the above alignment and description, as I look back, is where I began way back in Seminary after studying Rohr and Ebert's book, "The Enneagram." I thought correctly then, what I still believe, that businesses would not be accepting of the Enneagram at that time, but in my heart at the same time, I also thought that there was so much potential value in the Enneagram for people in the workspace that I was kind of torn. I felt I needed a way to deliver this value to workers. The route I took was to explore the idea of "Leadership Spirit," and to not solicit or propose any sort of Spirituality in my workplace coaching, teaching and consulting. I stayed "business like" in my demeanor. I'm delighted to say that things have changed nicely over the last 27 years, and that I see the Enneagram now being received quite well within many corporations and professional services firms.

**The No-nonsense Nine as Career Drivers (A Survey)**

The survey that follows was originally used as part of the BBC's "Confidence Lab" TV Series hosted by Dr. Ros Taylor in the years 1998 and 1999. Dr. Taylor is a leading UK psychologist, successful businesswoman, accomplished author and TV and radio presenter. A clinical psychologist and managing director, she travels the world developing the potential of employees through her "Transformation Programme." The assessment is found within her book published by Vermillion in 2000, entitled: "Confidence in Just Seven Days." Dr. Taylor acknowledges Dave Francis, author of the book, "Managing Your Own Career," published first by Fontana/Collins in 1985. Francis in turn acknowledges eight writers, ranging from Abraham Maslow to Chris Argyris and D.C. McClelland in the fields of personal development and career development as his resources. (Pg 73). In creating "The Career Drivers," the author, Dave Francis, has created a helpful survey that resembles the teamwork research of Dr. Meredith Belbin known for his leading scholarship in workteam typologies and workplace team building. In 1981, Meredith Belbin first expounded upon "Team Role" theory in his seminal book, "Management Teams: Why They Succeed or Fail." © Elsevier 1983-2010. Davis' nine "career driver" typologies have similarities, perhaps even connections, to Belbin's nine work team typologies. Both of these two author's references are "pioneer work" in the field of personal development. These are both fodder for the development of the No-nonsense Nine Principles Mandala: I wish to acknowledge and thank the above writers in the field of personal development and career management whose published work contributed to the definition of the No-nonsense Nine Principles and Disciplines.

**THE CAREER DRIVERS SURVEY (Per Dave Francis, circa 1985)**

The intructions shown directly below are Per Dr. Ros Taylor book, "Confidence in Just Seven Days," (circa 2000 by Vermillion Press, an Imprint of Edbury Press/Random House):

"Below are a listed 36 pairs of reasons often given by people when they are asked about what they want and need from their career. You must evaluate the relative importance of the statements within each pair, and allocate three (3) points – no more, no less. In other words, the possible distribution of points between the two items in the first pair, for example, would be as follows:

Choice one: A = 3 points B = 0 points
Choice two: A = 2 points B = 1 point
Choice three: A = 1 point B = 2 points

Choice 4: A = 0 points B = 3 points

"Beginning on the following page, the letters given before each item are for the purpose of scoring and need not concern you at this stage. Just make sure that when you have completed each pair, three points have been given each time."

The survey begins on the following page:

1. A ____ I will only be satisfied with an unusually high standard of living.
   B ____ I wish to have considerable influence over other people.

2. C ____ I only feel satisfied if the output from my job has real value in itself.
   D ____ I want to be an expert in the things I do.

3. E. ____ I want to use my creative abilities in my work.
   F. ____ It is especially important to me that I work with people whom I like.

4. G. ____ I would obtain particular satisfaction by being able to choose what I want freely.
   H. ____ I want to make quite sure that I will be financially secure.

5. I. ____ I enjoy feeling that people look up to me.
   A. ____ Not to put too fine a point on it, I want to be wealthy.

6. B. ____ I want a substantial leadership role.

C. ____ I do that which is meaningful to me, even though it may not gain tangible rewards.

7. D. ____ I want to feel that I have gained a hard-won expertise.

E. ____ I want to create things that people associate with me.

8. F. ____ I seek deep social relationships with other people in my work.

G. ____ I would get satisfaction from deciding how I spend my time.

9. A. ____ I will not be content unless I have ample material possessions.

D. ____ I want too demonstrate to my own satisfaction that I really know my discipline.

10. C. ____ My work is part of my search for meaning in life.

E. ____ I want the things I produce to bear my Name.

11. A. ____ I seek to be able to afford anything I want.

H. ____ A job with long-term security really appeals to me.

12. B. ____ I seek a role that gives me substantial influence over others.

D. ____ II would enjoy being a specialist in my field.

13. C. ____ It is important to me that my work makes a positive contribution to the wider community.

F. ____ Close relationships with other people at work are important to me

14. E. ____ I want my own creativity to be extensively used.
G. ____ I would prefer to be my own master.

15. F. ____ Close relationships with other people at work would give me special satisfaction.
H. ____ I want to look ahead in my life and feel confident that I will always be okay.

16. A. ____ I want to be able to spend money easily.
E. _____ I want to be genuinely innovative in my work.

17. B. ____ Frankly, I want to tell other people what to do.
F. ____ For me, being close to others is really the Important thing.

18. C. ____ I look upon my career as part of a search for greater meaning in my life.
G. ____ I have found that I want to take full responsibility for my own decisions.

19. D. ____ I would enjoy a reputation as a real specialist.
H. ____ I would only feel relaxed if I was in a secure career.

20. A. ____ I desire the trappings of wealth.
F. ____ I want to get too know new people through my work.

21. B. ____ I like to play roles which give me control over how others perform.

G. ____ It is important that I can choose for myself the tasks that I undertake.

22. C. ____ I would devote myself to work if I believed that the output would be worthwhile in itself.
    H. ____ I would take great comfort from knowing How I will stand on my retirement day.

23. F. ____ Close relationships with people at work would make it difficult for me to make a career move.
    I. ____ Being recognized as part of the Establishment is important to me.

24. B. ____ I would enjoy being in charge of people and resources.
    E. ____ I want to create things that no one else has done before.

25. C ____ At the end of the day, I do what I believe is important, not that which promoted my career.
    I. ____ I seek public recognition.

26. E. ____ I want to do something distinctively different from others.
    H. ____ I usually take the safe option.

27. B. ____ I want other people to look to me for leadership.
    I. ____ Social status is an important motivator for me.

28. A. ____ A high standard of living attracts me.
    G. ____ I wish to avoid being controlled by a boss at work.

29. E. ____ I want my products to have my own name on them.
    I. ____ I seek formal recognition by others of my achievements.

30. B. ____ I prefer to be in charge.
    H. ____ I feel concerned when I cannot see a long way ahead in my career.

31. D. ____ I would enjoy being a person who had specialist knowledge.
    G. ____ I would get satisfaction from not having to answer to other people.

32. G. ____ I dislike being a cog in a large wheel.
    I. ____ It would give me satisfaction to have a high-status job.

33. A. ____ I am prepared to do most things for material reward.
    C. ____ I see work as a means of enriching my personal development.

34. I. ____ I want to have a prestigious position in any organization for which I work.
    H. ____ A secure future attracts me every time.

35. F. ____ When I have congenial social relationships, nothing else really matters.
    D. ____ Being able to make an expert contribution would give me particular satisfaction.

36. I. ____ I would enjoy the status symbols that come with senior positions.
    D. ____ I aspire to achieve a high level of specialist competence.

Scoring The Career Drivers Survey

To score the survey, add all the points that you have given to each
of the A, B, C, D, E, F, G, H, and I items. Write the totals in the boxes
below and check that the grand total is 108.

| A | B | C | D | E | F | G | H | I | |
|---|---|---|---|---|---|---|---|---|---|
| | | | | | | | | | |
| | | | | | | | | | |
| | | | | | | | | | |
| | | | | | | | | | |
| | | | | | | | | | |
| | | | | | | | | | |
| | | | | | | | | | |
| | | | | | | | | | |
| | | | | | | | | | |

Copy these scores on to the Career Drivers Profile on the next page.

| A | B | C | D | E | F | G | H | I | | |
|---|---|---|---|---|---|---|---|---|---|---|
| + | + | + | + | + | + | + | + | + | = | 108 |

**YOUR CAREER DRIVERS PROFILE**

Mark your scores on the chart below by circling the numbers you scored for each letter. Then join the circles to give a diagrammatic profile of your personal career drivers. When you have done this, read the next section to interpret your profile.

| 24 | 24 | 24 | 24 | 24 | 24 | 24 | 24 | 24 |
|---|---|---|---|---|---|---|---|---|
| 23 | 23 | 23 | 23 | 23 | 23 | 23 | 23 | 23 22 |
| 21 | 21 | 21 | 21 | 21 | 21 | 21 | 21 | 21 |
| 20 | 20 | 20 | 20 | 20 | 20 | 20 | 20 | 20 19 |
| 18 | 18 | 18 | 18 | 18 | 18 | 18 | 18 | 18 |
| 17 | 17 | 17 | 17 | 17 | 17 | 17 | 17 | 17 |
| 16 | 16 | 16 | 16 | 16 | 16 | 16 | 16 | 16 15 |
| 14 | 14 | 14 | 14 | 14 | 14 | 14 | 14 | 14 |
| 13 | 13 | 13 | 13 | 13 | 13 | 13 | 13 | 13 |
| 12 | 12 | 12 | 12 | 12 | 12 | 12 | 12 | 12 |
| 11 | 11 | 11 | 11 | 11 | 11 | 11 | 11 | 11 |
| 10 | 10 | 10 | 10 | 10 | 10 | 10 | 10 | 10 |
| 09 | 09 | 09 | 09 | 09 | 09 | 09 | 09 | 09 |
| 08 | 08 | 08 | 08 | 08 | 08 | 08 | 08 | 08 |
| 07 | 07 | 07 | 07 | 07 | 07 | 07 | 07 | 07 |
| 06 | 06 | 06 | 06 | 06 | 06 | 06 | 06 | 06 |
| 05 | 05 | 05 | 05 | 05 | 05 | 05 | 05 | 05 |
| 04 | 04 | 04 | 04 | 04 | 04 | 04 | 04 | 04 |
| 03 | 03 | 03 | 03 | 03 | 03 | 03 | 03 | 03 |
| 02 | 02 | 02 | 02 | 02 | 02 | 02 | 02 | 02 |
| 01 | 01 | 01 | 01 | 01 | 01 | 01 | 01 | 01 |
| 00 | 00 | 00 | 00 | 00 | 00 | 00 | 00 | 00 |
| A | B | C | D | E | F | G | H | I |

| | | | |
|---|---|---|---|
| A | ___ Material Rewards | B | ___ Power/Influence |
| C | ___ Meaning | D | ___ Expertise |
| E | ___ Creativity | F | ___ Affiliation |
| G | ___ Autonomy | H | ___ Security |
| I | ___ Status | | |

## WHAT DRIVES ME?

**The Nine Career Drivers**

| | |
|---|---|
| 1) Material Rewards | Seeking possessions, wealth and a high standard of living. (9SQ: The Resources Principle) |
| 2) Power/Influence | Seeking to be in control of people and resources.(9SQ: The Responsibility Principle) |
| 3) Search for Meaning | Seeking to do things that are believed to be valuable for their own sake. (9SQ: The Purpose Principle) |
| 4) Expertise | Seeking a high level of accomplishment in a specialized field. (9SQ: The Mastery Principle) |
| 5) Creativity | Seeking to innovate and to be identified with original output. (9SQ: The Creativity Principle) |
| 6) Affiliation | Seeking nourishing relationships with others at work (9SQ: The Community Principle) |
| 7) Autonomy | Seeking to be independent and able to make key decisions for oneself. (9SQ: The Autonomy Principle) |
| 8) Security | Seeking a solid and predictable future. (9SQ: The Reliability Principle) |
| 9) Status | Seeking to be recognized and admired. (9SQ: The Sincerity Principle) |

Remember to check that your total score is 108. Now look at your profile and circle your top two or three highest scores. These are your main drivers, the sources of energy and direction that shape your life. If we are unaware of these career drivers, the danger is that we seek jobs or promoted positions because it is the next step, or we think that everyone expects it of us. If a job does not satisfy our major drivers, we become dispirited, apathetic, even depressed... certainly the opposite of motivated.

| | | |
|---|---|---|
| **Reliability** (9SQ)<br>SECURITY (CDriver) | **Autonomy** (9SQ)<br>AUTONOMY (CDriver) | **Creativity** (9SQ)<br>CREATIVITY (CDriver) |
| **Community** (9SQ)<br>AFFILIATION (CDriver) | **Purpose** (9SQ)<br>SEARCH FOR MEANING (CDriver) | **Resources** (9SQ)<br>MATERIAL REWARDS (CDriver) |
| **Sincerity** (9SQ)<br>STATUS (CDriver) | **Mastery** (9SQ)<br>EXPERTISE (CDriver) | **Responsibility** (9SQ)<br>POWER/INFLUENCE (CDriver) |

Which do you consider to be your top three? Above you can see the 3 square by 3 square box (the "9 Square") with all of the No-nonsense Nine Principles and directly below each one a cross-referenced Career Driver as revealed within the Career Drivers Survey that you just completed. In your mind, do you believe that the No-nonsense Principle as it is Cross-referenced to the Career Driver results are helpful to you? If so, two of the more important question to ask of your own self are, 1) "Does my current position satisfy my top 3 main drivers? And 2) "Does this match up well with my principles?" If not, then you must consider making some sort of change, whether that be in your current work role or whatever else you may be aspiring to become in your work life. These are tough issues: A current role change or a shift in your future aspirations is important and never as easy as it sounds. Bills must be paid, and so forth. However, there are often areas within jobs that you could volunteer for, or possibly delegate parts of your current job to someone who would be motivated by them. Two suggestions: 1) Discuss this in your cohort group. 2) Give the Career Drivers Survey to others in your department or team. You can then concentrate on the more satisfying and fulfilling elements. You will be more fulfilled and confident if you are more watchful of your undertakings. Again, the above is flexible fodder for having more meaningful conversations concerning your role and dreams within the workplace.

Compare this 9 Square Image to the previous 9 Square Image.

| **The Reliability Principle** | **The Autonomy Principle** | **The Creativity Principle** |
|---|---|---|
| 1. HJK: "Does the leader have true self-confidence?" | 5. HJK: "Is the leader capable of setting a clear direction for the team?" | 6. HJK: "Is the leader an effective communicator?" |
| **The Community Principle**<br>4. HJK: "How well does the leader manage the people process?" | **The Purpose Principle**<br>3. HJK: "Does the leader possess solid values and demonstrate them to the entire organization?" | **The Resourcefulness Principle**<br>7. HJK: "Does the leader motivate and empower the team?" |

| The Sincerity Principle | The Mastery Principle | The Responsibility Principle |
|---|---|---|
| 2. HJK: "Does the leader demonstrate genuine humility?" | 8. HJK: "Does the leader execute well?" | 9. & 10. HJK: "Does the leader have the courage to deal with constant change, controversy, crisis, and (#10.) to be a "best citizen"?" |

This above 9 Square Image is cross-referenced to the article written by Harry M Jansen Kraemer Jr. ("HJK") concerning Values-Based Leadership that published within Aon Consulting's Insights from their 2009 Client Symposium: Today. Tomorrow. Ready, which is based on an article by the author previously printed in Directors and Boards magazine. This article with my notations follows and is here with the intent to introduce and precede the exercise chapters #2 through #9. Note: The 9 Square ("9SQ") Image following is an Enneagram cross-match perspective.

<table>
<tr><td colspan="3">Autonomy - MENTAL / The Head: to have Knowledge</td></tr>
<tr><td>Stalwart (Thinker)<br>"Loyalist Skeptic"<br>Courage & Caution<br>vs.<br>Anxiety & Pessimism<br>Goal: Security<br>Fear: Abandonment<br>Practice/Discipline:<br>Self Differentiation<br>(Reliability/ Differentiation)</td><td>Thinker (Planner)<br>"Perceiver"<br>Understanding<br>vs.<br>Greed & Detachment<br>Goal: Autonomy<br>Fear: Demands<br>Practice/Discipline:<br>Still Point<br>(Knowledge/ Focus/Calm)</td><td>Enthusiast (Thinker)<br>"Charismatic"<br>Vision /Inventiveness<br>vs.<br>Gluttony<br>Goal: Status<br>Fear: Rejection<br>Practice/Discipline:<br>Strengths Focus<br>(Creativity/ Introspection)</td></tr>
<tr><td colspan="3">Purpose - EMOTIONAL / The Heart: to have Meaning</td></tr>
<tr><td>Helper (People)<br>"Nurturer"<br>Humility<br>vs.<br>Pride & Manipulation<br>Goal: Be Needed<br>Fear: Being Unloved<br>Practice/Discipline:<br>Sharing<br>(Community/ Teamwork)</td><td>Individualist (Specialist)<br>"Empathizer"<br>Individuality<br>vs.<br>Envy<br>Goal: Purpose<br>Fear: Being Ordinary<br>Practice/Discipline:<br>Story Works<br>(Purpose/Attitude)</td><td>Achiever (Planner)<br>"Wooer"<br>Passion-to-Succeed<br>vs.<br>Deceit<br>Goal: Recognition<br>Fear: Failure<br>Practice/Discipline:<br>Shaping<br>(Resources/<br>Service/Vocation)</td></tr>
<tr><td colspan="3">Mastery - PHYSICAL / The Gut: to take Action</td></tr>
<tr><td>Peace Seeker (People)<br>"Arbiter"<br>Mediation<br>vs.<br>Sloth<br>Goal: Affiliation<br>Fear: Being Alone<br>Practice/Discipline:<br>Steadfastness<br>(Sincerity/Tenacity/<br>Commitment)</td><td>Reformer (Action)<br>"Perfectionist"<br>Judgment<br>vs.<br>Anger<br>Goal: Autonomy<br>Fear: Being Wrong<br>Practice/Discipline:<br>Step Stones<br>(Mastery/Action)</td><td>Commander (Action)<br>"Emperor"<br>Productivity<br>vs.<br>Lust/Aggression<br>Goal: Power<br>Fear: Submission<br>Practice/Discipline:<br>Surrender<br>(Responsibility/ Obedience)</td></tr>
<tr><td>SUPPORTIVE<br>VS.<br>PASSIVE-AGGRESSIVE</td><td>POSITIVE<br>VS.<br>NEGATIVE</td><td>ASSERTIVE<br>VS.<br>AGGRESSIVE</td></tr>
</table>

Harry M. Jansen Kraemer, Jr. is Clinical Professor of Management and Strategy at the Kellogg School of Management at Northwestern University. He is the former Chairman and CEO of Baxter International Inc. "Values-Based Leadership and the HR Executive" (below) was published within Aon Consulting's Insights from the 2009 Client Symposium: Today. Tomorrow. Ready., which is based upon an article by the author previously printed in Directors and Boards magazine.

## "VALUES-BASED LEADERSHIP AND THE HR EXECUTIVE"

By Harry M. Jansen Kraemer JR.

"Leadership teams are being tested like never before. They must be ready to make difficult choices and lead by example. A conscious, values-based leadership style can help prepare today's leaders to meet tomorrow's challenges." (2009) Note: This brief following summary and commentary is geared towards providing information in regards to the topic and issue covered. This book is provided with the understanding that this book is commentary, educational summary, comparison, and analysis on some of the original author's main ideas and concepts.

Following are crucial characteristics to help identify and select values-based leaders. Note: I have reduced Harry's original list of ten (10) to nine (9) quotations in order to align them directly to the Nine No-nonsense Principles and Nine No-nonsense Disciplines. These also align with the "Values Based Leadership" One Sheets within this No-nonsense Nine book.

1. HJK: "Does the leader have true self-confidence?"

"True self-confidence isn't the ability to act self-confident or simply play a role. It comes from focused self-reflection and self-assessment that enables the leader to openly and honestly understand what he or she knows—or doesn't know. Self-confident leaders do not need to be right. Instead, they fanatically focus on making sure they do the right thing, clearly and openly state their values, and proudly set an example for appropriate behavior. They realize there are many people brighter, quicker, and more articulate than they are. They are okay with this because they are comfortable in their own skin." (HJK is Harry Jansen Kraemer Jr.)

Reliability:

**For me, this Harry Kraemer quotation aligns directly with the No-nonsense Mandala's Principle of Reliability and the No-nonsense Discipline of Self Differentiation.**

2. HJK: "Does the leader demonstrate genuine humility?"

"Team members constantly look to leaders to see if they are approachable, possess genuine humility, and truly care about team members as individuals. They ask: Do our leaders realize that everyone on the team is important? Do they keep their egos in check? Do they remember where they came from? Do they admit when they make a mistake? Do they give others credit when things go well and take the blame when things don't? As anyone who has ever been in a leadership position knows, balance is critical to almost every aspect of the job. In the real world, virtually every decision you make has implications for multiple constituencies. Are we managing this business for the short-term or the long-term? Are we focusing on growth or returns? The value-based leader understands this and is capable of balancing the trade-offs." (HJK is Harry Jansen Kraemer Jr.)

**For me, this Harry Kraemer quotation aligns directly with the No-nonsense Mandala's Principle of Sincerity and the No-nonsense Mandala's Discipline of Steadfastness.**

3. HJK: "Does the leader possess solid values and demonstrate them to the entire organization?"

"The leader is responsible for setting the values, culture, and expectations for the entire organization. He or she clearly articulates what is acceptable and unacceptable behavior. It must be clear to every person in the organization that the leader expects all team members to "do the right thing." The leader sets an example in every action, realizing that he or she is constantly being watched. As the industrialist Andrew Carnegie once said, "The older I get, the less I listen to what someone says, and the more I watch what they do." (HJK is Harry Jansen Kraemer Jr.)

**For me, this Kraemer quotation aligns directly with the No-nonsense Mandala's Principle of Purpose and the No-nonsense Mandala's Discipline of what I call "Story Works."**

4. HJK: "How well does the leader manage the people process?"

"To paraphrase a former U.S. president, "It's the people, stupid." Is the leader capable of attracting the best people to the organization in a highly competitive environment? Does he or she spend a significant amount of time in the people development process or simply delegate that to the human resources department and expect things to happen? Some leaders state that they would like to spend more time on talent development. Think about it. What could be more important than getting the right people into the organization in the right jobs? If the "people process" is right, you are well on your way to becoming an effective leader." (HJK is Harry Jansen Kraemer Jr.)

**For me, this Harry Kraemer quotation aligns directly with the No-nonsense Mandala's Principle of Community and the No-nonsense Mandala's Discipline of what I call "Sharing."**

5. HJK: "Is the leader capable of setting a clear direction for the team?"

"The values-based leader sets a clear direction. It amazes me how many leaders are incapable of setting a clear direction that everyone in the organization can follow. It is unreasonable to expect that multiple levels of an organization can understand and implement a direction that is complex and convoluted. A good standard is one set by Albert Einstein: "Make it simple without being simplistic." (HJK is Harry Jansen Kraemer Jr.)

**For me, this Harry Kraemer quotation aligns directly with the No-nonsense Mandala's Principle of Autonomy and the No-nonsense Mandala's Discipline of what I call "Still Point."**

6. HJK: "Is the leader an effective communicator?"

"No skill set is more important for a leader than effective communication. It is critical that all team members, regardless of their level, truly understand their role in the organization, where the business is going, and why. Team members also must be encouraged to challenge the leader's assumptions, because as noted earlier, the values-based leader is not focused on being right but rather on doing the right thing. One way to assess how well the leader is doing in this dimension is to speak to the top five executives in the organization. If you ask each about the organization's top five priorities, do you get a total of five priorities, or five times five (i.e., 25 priorities)? Values-based leaders ensure that the communication is two-way, spending significantly more time listening than talking so that team members feel that they are being heard." (HJK is Harry Jansen Kraemer Jr.)

**For me, this Harry Kraemer quotation aligns directly with the No-nonsense Mandala's Principle of Creativity and the**

**No-nonsense Mandala's Discipline of what I call "Strengths Focus."**

7. HJK: "Does the leader motivate and empower the team?"

"The true leader is well aware that without a highly motivated team, nothing positive will happen. Most team members do not want to follow someone without a pulse. Does the leader exhibit passion and excitement that is easily transferable to all team members? Does the leader empower the team and also stay close enough to the action to not detach from the business?" (HJK is Harry Jansen Kraemer Jr.)

**For me, this Harry Kraemer quotation aligns directly with the No-nonsense Mandala's Principle of Resources and the No-nonsense Mandala's Discipline of what I call "Shaping."**

***Shaping* is about being proactive in your mental conversation, just before and as you are speaking. Shaping is about softly breaking the intimacy barrier that people have. Pause and be quiet until you know they are listening.**

8. HJK: "Does the leader execute well?"

"Some individuals in leadership positions actually believe that their role is simply to think "great thoughts" and delegate the work to others so that they can continue to think. They view themselves as leaders and the implementers as the managers. This is an ineffective way to lead a team. The leader must be close enough to the action to know whether the business is on (or off) track. In a football game, there are three types of leaders. One is the quarterback, calling the plays and being involved in all aspects of the game. While there are some advantages to the quarterback's role, there are also some drawbacks: being so close to the action so as to be incapable of managing both the current set of downs and planning ahead for the remaining quarters. A second type of leader is the head coach, who walks the sidelines with a headset, takes notes, and has a strong set of advisers and assistant coaches. The head coach balances the short and long run simultaneously. This is a great position from which to exercise leadership. Unfortunately, many people in leadership roles do not want to be that close to the action, preferring instead to be the third type of leader, the one in the skybox with a case of fine wine. This leader occasionally glances down at the field to see what is happening. Unfortunately, this vantage point often ends in disaster because by the time he or she figures out what is happening, the game is over." (HJK is Harry Jansen Kraemer Jr.)

**For me, this Harry Kraemer quotation aligns directly with the No-nonsense Mandala's Principle of Mastery and the No-nonsense Mandala's Discipline of what I call "Step Stones."**

**Step Stone is about being exacting, and paying attention to the details. Step Stones, like walking a path or climbing a stairway, is a Discipline of trusting that there will be a next step, and that it will make sense. The circle has always been an important symbol to the Native American. It represents the sun, the moon, the cycles of the seasons, and the cycle of life to death to rebirth.**

9. & 10. HJK: "Does the leader have the courage to deal with constant change, controversy, and crisis, and (#10.) to be a "best citizen"?"

"As anyone in a leadership position knows, it is not a question of *"if"* there will be change, controversy and crisis, but "*when.*" The true leader is prepared due to the qualities we laid out earlier – true self-confidence, genuine humility, balance, clear direction setting, people development, effective communications, motivation, execution, and implementation."

"The values-based leader knows that the company needs to generate a superior return for its owners, but knows that focusing exclusively on "shareholder interest" is not a winning strategy. He or she knows that "doing the right thing' morally and in a socially-responsible manner as a "best citizen" will help build a great team, build rapport with customers, and lead to shareholder return. Once again, it comes back to balance." (Note: Paraphrased by Clark Riley).

**Harry Kraemer's 5 "Cs" of Change, Controversy, Crisis, Best Citizen and Courage" are a reminder to me of another "C" word, and that is "Circle," as represented in the No-nonsense Nine Mandala at the heart of this book's teachings. As symbolic of "Leadership Spirit," are you aware that everything a Native American Oglala Sioux does is also in a circle? This is because they believe the power of the world always works in circles, and everything tries to be round. This is similar to my personal experience at St. Benedict's Monastery in silent retreat as well as what I know of yoga, Thai Chi and the eastern beliefs of Hinduism and Buddhism. This is all so natural: The nature of Leadership Spirit.**

**The Oglala Sioux believed that all their power came to them from the sacred hoop of the nation; and so long as the hoop was unbroken, the people flourished. The flowering tree was the living center of the hoop, and the circle of the four quarters nourished it. The east gave peace and light, the south gave warmth, the west gave rain, and the north with its cold and mighty wind gave strength and endurance. This is mindful of the combined No-nonsense Nine Mandala principles and disciplines. This knowledge came to them from their outer world with their religion. A great Native American chief speaks of the circle:**

*"Everything the power of the world does is done in a circle. The sky is round, and I have heard that the Earth is round like a ball and so are all the stars. The wind, in its greatest power, whirls. Birds make their nests in circles, for theirs is the same religion as ours. The sun comes forth and goes down again in a circle. The moon does the same and both are round. Even the seasons form a great circle in their changing and always come back again to where they were.*

*"The life of a person is a circle from childhood-to-childhood, and so it is in everything where power moves. Our tipis are round like the nests of birds, and these are always set in a circle, the nation's hoop, a nest of many nests, where the Great Spirit meant for us to hatch our children."*

**Note: This is paraphrased from the teachings of Black Elk, Holy Man of the Oglala Sioux (Internet as resource).**

**Mandalas are a powerful symbol in Native American culture.**

*"INTUITION" IMAGE: CHURCH DOME (TURIN, ITALY)*

# #1.
# THE PRINCIPLE OF PURPOSE:
## *HAVING A PURPOSE*

"Purpose" is the reason for which something is done or created or for which something exists. For example, "the purpose of the meeting is to appoint a trustee." The dictionary tells us purpose is the reason something exists, an intended end; aim; or goal. Purpose creates meaning, offers a sense of direction and helps guide our paths, behavior and our goals when applied to our lives.

Purpose, as the center-most No-Nonsense principle, aligns with the discipline and practice of having intuitive trust. Trust is imperative to having purpose. Within the No-Nonsense Nine framework, you can plainly see that this highly important principle butts up to and deliberately touches up against all of the other eight No-Nonsense Nine Principles. They surround the principle of Purpose. You can see that it is stacked vertically in the middle within the central spinal column of the workplace's three most intrinsically motivating principles: first, Autonomy, then Purpose and then Mastery: Top, Middle and bottom within what is called the No nonsense Mandala. This arrangement of these three principles (as "motivations") is influenced by the workplace research of Daniel Pink, as described in his best selling breakthrough book about workplace motivation entitled "Drive." It's an easy read, or, you may want to study these ideas by searching out either Pink's 2009 Ted Talk or his entertaining and fact-filled 2010 YouTube video entitled: "RSA ANIMATE - Drive: The surprising truth about what motivates us."

To paraphrase Pink and cut right through to the conclusion: he says, "this is controversial, that the intrinsic motivations of Autonomy, Purpose and Mastery outperform the extrinsic motivation of cash." He concludes by highlighting the three centermost vertical No-Nonsense Principles: "If you pay people enough, there are three intrinsic motivations more powerful than money: Autonomy, Purpose and Mastery." As you see, I have employed these three centrally into the No-Nonsense Nine mandala structure as the three most important No-Nonsense Principles. Respectively, as shown within the framework mandala image, they align top, middle and bottom, with what is commonly called, "Head, Heart, and Gut" and also what the "Patriarch" of the modern day's Wellness movement, Aaron Antonovsky, in circa 1950 through 1960 identified as the three main elements of his theoretic, Salutogenic SOC ("Sense of Coherence") construct. Again, they are top, middle and bottom: 1. Head (SOC's "Comprehensibity"), 2. Heart (SOC's "Meaningfulness") and 3. Gut (SOC's "Manageability"). These are often simply called, "Thinking, Feeling and Doing".

Much akin to Daniel Pink''s research, Antonovsky's research in Salutogenesis shows that if you have all three of these "wellness" characteristics, you tend to have a healthier, more long-lasting and more productive life. This applies to you at play, at home and at work.

The five elements of narrative (storytelling or the discipline of "Story Works") align with the five principles within the interior five squares at the center of the No-Nonsense Nine.

Story is an important part of coaching, leadership and managing. If you do not know and own your story, than how can you coach, lead, or manage others? How can you offer what I call, "Other Help," the process of sharing and caring for others?

**Story**: Aristotle originated the naming of the five parts of story, which University of Chicago Professor and Author, Kenneth Burke, in the 1950s would name The Dramatistic Pentad: namely "Agent, Agency, Purpose, Scene and Act." These five, respectively, align with the five central No- nonsense Nine Principles as shown directly below:

| N0-nonsense Nine | | Burke |
|---|---|---|
| • Autonomy | aligns with | Agent (Who) |
| • Resources | aligns with | Agency (What) |
| • Purpose | aligns with | Purpose (Why) |
| • Community | aligns with | Scene (When & Where) |
| • Mastery | aligns with | Act (How) |

Just never forget that story works is more about the relationships and less about the narrative. Story is one of the greatest intermediaries of intimacy and trust. Jonas Gottschall in his influential book, "The Storytelling Animal," writes that story will make you more empathic and better able to navigate life's dilemmas and that stories are like life's dress rehearsals. No wonder Story Works as a discipline is at the center of the No-nonsense Nine Mandala. Everything rotates around your story.

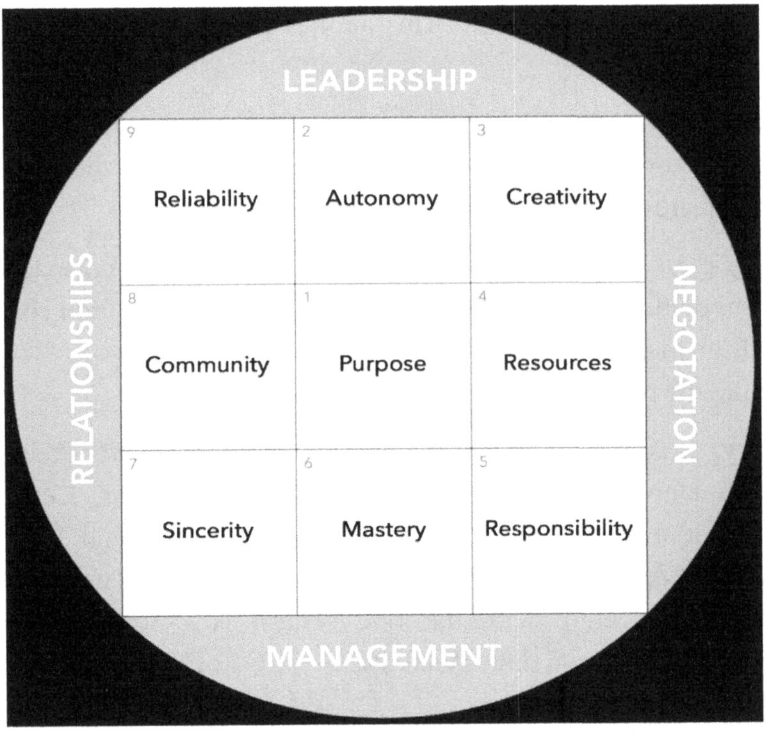

LEADERSHIP

RELATIONSHIPS

NEGOTIATION

MANAGEMENT

| 9 Reliability | 2 Autonomy | 3 Creativity |
|---|---|---|
| 8 Community | 1 Purpose | 4 Resources |
| 7 Sincerity | 6 Mastery | 5 Responsibility |

The No-Nonsense Nine Principles

| 9. Reliability | 2. Autonomy | 3. Creativity |
|---|---|---|
| 8. Community | 1. Purpose | 4. Resources |
| 7. Sincerity | 6. Mastery | 5. Responsibility |

The No-Nonsense Nine Disciplines

| | | |
|---|---|---|
| 9. Self Aware | 2. Still Point | 3. Strengths |
| 8. Sharing | 1. Story Works | 4. Shaping |
| 7. Steadfast | 6. Step Stones | 5. Surrender |

The two previous charts display the No-Nonsense principles and each principle's companion discipline. Each single square represents one of nine basic motivations and decision-making principles.

# A Harry Kraemer Inspired One Sheet: "Leading With Values"

Healthy Business Management Principles

Principle 1: Purpose

| | | |
|---|---|---|
| 9 Reliability | 2 Autonomy | 3 Creativity |
| 8 Community | 1 Purpose | 4 Resources |
| 7 Sincerity | 6 Mastery | 5 Responsibility |

Regardless of your job title or scope of responsibilities, your values will have an enormous impact—on a particular team, within a department or division, or throughout the entire organization.

Values and Leadership

Your ability to influence people depends significantly on their ability to appreciate your values. Your values as a leader should be so clearly understood that if you put three, five, twenty, or even one hundred members of your team together without you in the room, they would be able to explain what you stand for in consistent terms. The more they understand your values, the better they will relate to you and follow your lead.

Communicating your values also helps set the expectations for what behavior is acceptable and what is not acceptable. The clearer you are on this point, the better that people will understand whether their personal actions are consistent with the values you have set.

Where values do not exist or are not clearly communicated, a vacuum is created in which doubt, cynicism, and distrust can quickly take root. When people do not understand the values of the leader, the relationship is limited. People do only what they are asked to do by virtue of the fact that someone is the boss. Creativity within the organization is stifled and information in the form of feedback is withheld. Moreover, should a serious problem arise, people do not feel empowered or appreciated enough to step up and tell the boss what is happening.

The problem is that "values" is one of those words that gets overused, and not in the sincerest manner. Corporate mission statements and values statements are often either overly intellectual or totally watered down, and they tend to be so generic that they are meaningless. Values are not bullet points on a corporate website or motivational phrases on a poster in the lunchroom. Values define what you stand for and must be lived 24/7. Without values, an organization lacks cohesion and purpose.

When a boss does not have any discernible values, his team cannot relate meaningfully to him. Working for a values-based leader motivates the team members not only to do their jobs but also to take ownership of their tasks and responsibilities. Knowing that the boss wants their feedback, they speak up, and not just when asked for input. They are proud to be part of the team, knowing that no matter what the circumstance or situation, their boss is committed to doing the right thing—and so are they.

What are Your Values?

Do not wait until you are a senior leader to define your values. Even if you do not have anyone reporting to you, you should know your values. If nothing else, this exercise will enable you to discern whether you are working in the right organization. By defining and embracing your values, you will be guided in your interactions with others even if you are the most junior person on the team. In that way, you are acting as a leader.

Three things to remember:

- Clearly stated values create engagement and accountability.
- Values-based leadership provides a solid foundation for long-term profitability and growth.
- To excel as a leader, clarify your values and lead by example.

To define your values, you must engage in self-reflection. Ask yourself, "What do I truly believe? Am I willing to state my values? Am I willing to compromise my values? Are my actions consistent with my beliefs?" Once you have put your values down on paper and you are clear about what you stand for, take the time to reflect more deeply by asking, "Who am I, and how comfortable am I with myself?" For some people, realizing that it is OK to be who they are happens early in life; for others, it happens later. Sadly, for some it never happens at all. By engaging in self-reflection, you will increase your comfort level with who you are, and your values will shine through.

Values That Matter

Values are meaningful only if people understand them. If they are vague or poorly communicated, they will not be real to people and, therefore, will not guide their behaviors and decisions. A clear and specific statement of corporate values can boost the performance of the entire organization because it provides a basis for accountability. As a result, individuals no longer perform isolated jobs; they perform as part of a whole with a greater purpose.

As a manager, incorporating explicit statements of your values into informal feedback and formal performance appraisals can have a powerful impact on improving the performance and culture of your organization.

Values Help Generate Shareholder Value

Whether we are managers, functional leaders, or senior officers, it is critical that we create shareholder value by growing revenues, improving profit margins, and earning a larger profit. But what about a corporate value related to philanthropy, such as supporting the arts, science, or a particular local charity? How do those good deeds align with shareholder value? What is important to see is that good works can create shareholder value.

There are a number of factors that can directly influence the creation of shareholder value. One is the talented people in your organization. Another is having loyal customers, who are served by those talented people. When it comes to attracting the best people, extrinsic rewards such as salary and benefits are important, but for people to remain with an organization, the rewards have to be intrinsic as well: feeling good about themselves, being proud of the organization they work for, and knowing they make a difference. A company that is socially responsible and develops a positive reputation will be able to attract phenomenal people whose personal values are aligned with those of the company.

Also, customers want to do business with people they can relate to and companies they admire. If a customer has to choose between two competing products that are both of high quality and a good value, the order will most likely go to the company that has the higher values.

## What is Legal Versus What is Right

Values not only create competitive advantages when it comes to developing the workforce or customer relationships but also can guard against damage. The truth is that the boundary between legal and illegal is a fuzzy, gray, ill-defined line. When organizations allow their actions to hug that line, there is a great danger that one of these days, they'll find themselves on the wrong side, even if their practices didn't change.

Rather than focusing solely on what's legal, a company would be far better off to consider what's right. Rather than overly intellectualize, keep things simple. Ethics should always come down to doing the right thing.

Setting an Example

As the nineteenth-century American industrialist and philanthropist Andrew Carnegie once said, "The older I get, the less I listen to what people say and the more I watch what they do." For a values-based leader, this means setting a personal example in order to influence the people around you, whether it's a small team or the entire organization.

99 percent of people want to do the right thing. However, if they do not have a positive role model, they may fall short. When one person strays, others become tempted to follow, building negative peer pressure. As a values-based leader, you must continually ask yourself, "What example am I setting? Am I demonstrating a balanced life to my team? Are my actions in line with my beliefs and values?" If what you say is different from what you do, people will take notice.

As a values-based leader, you set the tone, whether within a small team or for the entire organization. Knowing who you are and what you stand for enables you to set a good example for others, so that you can create a team rooted in values. This strong foundation is critical because you will face tough decisions at times. Having a firm set of values will make your decision making clearer. This doesn't mean that your life will be easy, but you will have a compass to guide you toward the solutions that are optimal for you, your company, and all the stakeholders involved. In short, adhering to your values will keep you on track to do the right thing.

The above "One Sheet" condensation is Adapted from the book "From Values to Action" © 2011 Jossey-Bass with permission from the author, Harry M. Jansen Kraemer Jr. Note: This brief summary is geared towards providing information in regards to the topic and issue covered. This book is provided with the understanding that this book is commentary, educational summary, comparison, and analysis on some of the original books main ideas and concepts.

Questions for Discussion for Working Better Together (WBT)

1. If you were to state your values to your workers explicitly, how might doing that have a positive effect on your key performance indicators? Provide two or three specific examples.

2. If you were to state your values to your workers explicitly, how might doing that help you to save more money or grow your business? Provide two or three specific examples.

3. Have you ever worked in a "values vacuum?" What did it feel like, and how well did the people around you perform? Provide a specific example.

4. Think about your favorite leader under whom you have worked personally. What two or three values do you most clearly associate with that person?

5. In one sentence, how would you describe the relationship between values and purpose in a business environment?

*"PERCEPTION" IMAGE: CELTIC: KNOTWORK (IRELAND)*

# #2.
# THE PRINCIPLE OF AUTONOMY: *ESTABLISHING AUTONOMY*

"Autonomy" is the condition of self-governing - the freedom to be responsible for oneself. In Kantian moral philosophy, autonomy is the capacity of an agent to act in accordance with objective morality rather than under the influence of desires. In its simplest sense, autonomy is about a person's ability to act on his or her own values and interests. Taken from ancient Greek, the word means 'self-legislation' or 'self-governance.' Modern political thought and bioethics often stress that individual autonomy should be promoted and respected.

Being autonomous, along with having Purpose and Mastery, completes a powerful triad of the key No-Nonsense Nine principles. As you can see, Autonomy is located at the very pinnacle of the No-Nonsense Nine's center spinal column. It's very location makes you think about the importance of having clear thinking.

Notable researcher, Faye Tucker, from the University of Lancaster, within her thought-provoking "IFamily" website: says this: "Looked at psychologically, autonomy is made up of a set of skills and attitudes. Relevant skills include the ability to reason, to appreciate different points of view, and to debate with others. In order to do these things, the autonomous person must have a sense of self-worth and self-respect. Self-knowledge is also important, including a well-developed understanding of what matters to him or her."

Autonomy is the No-Nonsense Nine principle about the importance of thought.

This principle aligns with the discipline of perception or our ability within our careers to investigate and envision. I think of this principle as the 2nd most important No-Nonsense principle, following closely on the heels of Purposefulness. 3rd, for me, is a virtual tie between Creativity and Mastery. Is it not difficult to prefer one versus the other Having Purpose is definitely first, with Autonomy running a close second, followed by Creativity and Mastery, two important principles in what I believe is a dead heat tie for third place.

Your purpose and your autonomy are what give you the wisdom and authority to choose. Whereas Purpose is the heartfelt decision making principle, the No-Nonsense Principle of Autonomy. is the "Thinking" or "Thoughtful" Decision Making Principle. The Principle of Purpose does the heart work, whereas the Principle of Autonomy does the headwork.  Mastery does the hands-on Gut work. This triad of Thinking, Feeling and Doing right is located at the vertical center of the No-Nonsense Nine. Those people who ascribe most to the Principle of Autonomy are thought-centric. They want to know "the cause." They are planful and logical. They are more prone to causal versus effectual thinking. They are data-focused. They are open to working with others, but "conditionally" – especially as members of a highly-focused project team. This is commonplace within STEP. STEP members prefer investigating/perceiving versus doing. They are hands-off, delighting in intellectual things and knowledge for its own sake. They enjoy research, engineering and information services. As "Expert Perceivers," STEP members can talk at length about their area of proficiency, but find small talk and conversation difficult and not particularly worthwhile. Even though contemplative, dependable and respectful, a highly autonomous expert is often misinterpreted by people as being aloof or "above it all." STEP professionals have the odds against them when it comes to conversational communication that is heartfelt.

They most often avoid strong feelings, especially feelings of inadequacy, and can even become impatient or even angry when people question facts that they present. They also can be intellectually arrogant, distant, critical of others and unassertive, with the ability to become non-responsive, "putting up walls." This is not an uncommon description for people with power within the world of STEP (Science, Technology, Engineering and Professional Services), whether that be within Google, as reported on by David Garvin's HBR article about Google's Project that they named "Project Oxygen. "The December, 2013 HBR article about "Project Oxygen" is entitled, "How Google Sold Its Engineers on Management/ Hint: it's all about the data.," published in December, 2013 by Harvard Business Review) or any one of a myriad of Martin Sorrell's many smaller WPP businesses, as researched and written about by David Maister within his stellar 2001 book, "Practice What You Preach: What Managers Must Do to Create a High Achievement Culture." (Simon & Schuster, New York.).

I first became aware of David Maister in either late 1995 or early 1996 when I watched him from the back of a large meeting room address a small group of the owners at Hewitt Associates at their then headquarters in Lincolnshire, Illinois The head of HR at the time was part of their firm's 4-member top management team. They had been growing at a whopping 23% per year. How I became involved is a story about coincidence. I had been interviewed individually by 9 of their owners. Each was from a different geographic region. Although unspoken to them, the head of HR wanted each one to "soften their management style." They needed to be more "relating" and less "requiring. " (CEO Peter Friedes' words). All 9 owners had agreed to hire me as a Spiritual Mentor and Communications Skills coach. At that time along with me there was already one other main "outside" coach, a woman named Rita Cashman, a ground-breaking woman, an ex Catholic Nun, who had left her Order and was working similarly to me on healthy communications coaching for managers and executives, except that she was coaching another small group of owners. We, the owners and their coaches, had all joined together at the HR Director's request, to meet and learn about David Maister's most recent research project, which, as we were to learn, was to take root and flower into becoming his very interesting book, "Practice What You Preach," which he published in 2001. As Maister explained, he and his cohorts at the time were spending much of their time in England and Europe, interviewing executives and managers working for over 300 different WPP companies, all owned by Sir Martin Sorrell. David's top goal was to get the definitive numbers on what skills and activities cause one WPP company or office to be more profitable than another. He showed us an early causal model rendition which he would later refine and publish as his "Practice What You Preach" causal model in his 2001 book by that name. It was more than a roundtable event, with chairs set up auditorium-style. David was comfortable, laid back and as I recall.. He spoke energetically and candidly… without reservation. The work for Martin Sorrell was going quite well. David was captivating and enthusiastic. I was curious and looking forward to reading his forthcoming book. Coincidentally, I would see David again the very next week: giving a much shorter rendition of his "talk" to another one of my clients, Baker & McKenzie, at their firm's largest US office in the Prudential Building in Chicago. We spoke ever-so briefly and I expressed interest again in his forthcoming book and the Management Performance Causal Model he was building. He said it was built on actual data intake from close to 400 different WPP company offices – live interviews and a set of pre-planned quantifiable questions (and answer choices). This hit my core at the time: After all, I was coaching and teaching the lawyers who were right there, sitting in the room listening to his "talk." He seemed a bit rushed and less comfortable, but treated the occasion with respect and what I'd call courteous brevity in comparison to the more lengthy presentation he made the week before at Hewitt's Headquarters, where I simply watched from the back of the room. I would wait over two years before I was able to secure a copy of David's book. Below is a summary list (note: I like lists) of what I first called "The Top Nine Attributes of Customer Service." Essentially David's book was a progressive step in my uncovering the proof of the value of "the 9-Square," what I today call The No-Nonsense Nine Principles of Top-Quality Leadership Spirit.

Teaching each other and learning about these as part of a small group is what I have learned teaches workers to Work Better Together (WBT). When it comes to credibility, the small cohort group is the expert, not me. They teach one another, have each other's respect. That's the "magical component." A dozen years later this same thing would be confirmed to me by David Garvin's discovery as described in his December, 2013 Harvard Business Review article. The Oxygen Project list of superior manager behaviors is easily aligned with Maister's research, as was published in his 2001 book.

## David Maister's Top Management Attributes

From his book, "Practice What You Preach" (2001), here are his, top management attributes, based upon WPP's Guidelines for achievement:

1. "The quality of the professionals in our office is as high as can be expected." (Reliability**) (Practice What You Preach # 5)
2. "Around here you are required, not just encouraged, to learn and develop new skills." (Autonomy**) (Practice What You Preach # 2)
3. "We invest a significant amount of time in things that will pay off in the future." (Creativity**) (Practice What You Preach # 6)
4. "I am a member of a well-functioning team." (Community**) (Practice What You Preach # 3)
5. "Customer/client satisfaction is a top priority at our company." (Purpose**) (Practice What You Preach # 1)
6. "Those who contribute most to office success are the most highly rewarded." (Resources**) (Practice What You Preach # 8)
7. "People within our office always treat others with respect." (Sincerity**) (Practice What You Preach # 4)
8. "I get a great sense of accomplishment from my work." (Mastery**) (Practice What You Preach # 9)
9. "I have the freedom to make the necessary decisions to do my work properly." (Responsibility**) (Practice What You Preach # 7)

   Note: Below I have arranged them into the Tic-Tac-Toe Grid.

| Reliability (#5: Quality of Service**) | Autonomy (#2: Understanding /Explanation**) | Creativity (#6: Sense of Progress) |
|---|---|---|
| **Community** (#3: Access & Availability**) | **Purpose** (#1: Sense of Importance**) | **Resources** (#8: Sense of Appreciation) |
| **Sincerity** #4: (Respectful Treatment**) | **Mastery** (#9: Sense of Control**) | **Responsibility** (#7: Responsiveness**) |

## David Garvin's Google-based Top Manager Behaviors

Special note: Per December 2013 Harvard Business Review, directly below (for comparison) are David Garvin's top ten management "behaviors" from Google's Oxygen Project's findings. They are cross referenced to Maister's Top Attributes on the following page:

1. To be a good coach
2. To empower their team and to not micromanage
3. To create an inclusive team environment, showing concern for their success and wellbeing
4. To be productive and results-oriented
5. To be a good communicator – to listen and share information
6. To support career development and appropriately discuss performance
7. To have a clear vision/strategy for their team
8. To demonstrate and share key technical skills in order to help advise their team
9. To collaborate effectively across your organization
10. To be a wise and strong decision maker

In simplest terms according to Maister, the "Practice What You Preach" service "assets" or "attributes" affect a customer's perception of value, which in turn provides a basis for improved profitability:" Note: As Proven by his in-depth research in several hundred independent WPP-owned service firms: "...in essence these underpin and explain over 50% of all the variations in the profit performance of professional service firms, this in spite of country, practice size or line of business."

| | | |
|---|---|---|
| **Reliability** (#5: Quality of Service**) 2. Empower Team and Not Micromanage | **Autonomy** (#2: Understanding /Explanation**) 7. Clear Vision 10. Wise Decisions | **Creativity** (#6: Sense of Progress) 4. Create Inclusive Team |
| **Community** (#3: Access & Availability**) 5. Be a Good Communicator | **Purpose** (#1: Sense of Importance**) 1. Be a Good Coach | **Resources** (#8: Sense of Appreciation) 3. Show concern for wellbeing |
| **Sincerity** #4: (Respectful Treatment**) 6. Support Career Development and Discuss Performance | **Mastery** (#9: Sense of Control**) 8. Demo and Share Key Technical Skills | **Responsibility** (#7: Responsiveness**) 4. Be Productive and Results Oriented |

The 9-Square grid shown above compares
the No-nonsense Nine Principles to
Maister's Top Attributes and also to
Google's Oxygen Project's Top Quality Manager Behaviors
as revealed within Garvin's HBR article.
(See more about this comparison in Chapter 4)

**WBT Exercise #2**

Exercise: Achievement Analyzer

In one word or short phrase, please complete this sentence: Achievement for me is...(____________________)

For each lifetime period, briefly describe two specific things you accomplished (or will have accomplished) that you enjoyed doing and believe you did well. In your life / Note Do not look ahead within this exercise.

1. Age Early Childhood (____________________)
2. Age Late Childhood (____________________)
3. Age Teen years (____________________)
4. Age 18-24 (____________________)
5. Age 25-31 (____________________)
6. Age 32-38 (____________________)
7. Age 39-45 (____________________)
8. Age 46-52 (____________________)
9. Age 53-59 (____________________)
10. Age 60-70 (____________________)
11. Age 71+ (____________________)

After a night's rest and reflection on all this, please go to opening page #5 and circle the one No-Nonsense Nine Principle that most closely aligns with your main strength: Which Principle or principles are you most accomplished at? Circle it or them in a color such as red, green or blue.

# A Harry Kraemer Inspired One Sheet: "Setting a Clear Direction"

Setting a clear direction for your people—not just a direction, but a clear direction—is critically important to your ability to lead. In many cases, the strategy that the leaders have defined fails to be disseminated throughout an organization, and many

Healthy Business Management Principles
Principle 2: Autonomy

| | | |
|---|---|---|
| 9 Reliability | 2 Autonomy | 3 Creativity |
| 8 Community | 1 Purpose | 4 Resources |
| 7 Sincerity | 6 Mastery | 5 Responsibility |

people don't understand what they are supposed to do. Although the course of action may appear perfectly clear to the leaders who sit around a conference table and hash out the strategy, nobody communicates it to the rest of the organization in a way that everyone understands. Nobody informs the team on the front lines—those who are supposed to take the ball and run with it—what the game plan is. No wonder there are so many fumbles! You can't risk having each person moving in what she thinks is the right direction or doing what seems to make sense in the moment. If you let that happen, there are going to be many missed opportunities, much confusion, and a higher likelihood of disaster. Or, you could end up with very little action because people want to over-think every situation and decision. When setting a clear direction, you are seeking two things: simplicity and clarity.

Keeping Things Simple

As Albert Einstein said, "Make everything as simple as possible, but no simpler." How does that apply to setting direction? Admittedly, it depends on the issue. The opportunities and challenges that your organization faces may not be so simple. In fact, some of them may be quite complicated. One of the qualities of a good leader is the ability to take what is very complex and break it down into smaller components to determine what really needs to get done. Rather than becoming overwhelmed or overwhelming your team, step back, reflect, and look at the issue holistically. To use a simple analogy, it's like doing a math problem. Sometimes you're tempted to jump in and start working before you even understand the entire problem. Often a better approach is to pause, look at the problem, figure out exactly what is being asked, and then devise a way to tackle it piece by piece.

## Communicating Clearly and Broadly

Where the organization is going and why it's going there isn't something that can be communicated in one e-mail or voicemail, or that is absorbed through some invisible osmosis. People must understand the strategy or plan, and furthermore, they must be part of the process: they must be given the opportunity to provide their thoughts and feedback. Each person must understand the plan, because otherwise, they won't understand why they are being asked to perform their assigned tasks, and it will be highly probable that the directives won't be carried out as management intended. Even more important, without knowing the reason behind the plan, your people will not be able to provide feedback on how the process might be improved.

There is also a psychological reason behind communicating to every member of the team: people want to know that they are part of something much bigger than themselves. As a leader, you should strive to give every member of your team a holistic understanding, instead of just a list of tasks that must be accomplished. When your team understands how everything fits together, they will feel more empowered as individual contributors who are part of a broader overall plan. They will be much more enthusiastic and take more ownership of their work. Their projects will be meaningful to them personally and—very importantly—they will be in a position to find creative ways to achieve the shared goals more efficiently.

Setting a clear direction serves several purposes:

- It ensures a higher probability of being able to achieve the desired goal or end result.
- People will be engaged and motivated to do their best because they know that what they are being asked to do is important.

• People will understand their roles and how they fit into the whole, enabling them to provide feedback and creative input.

• Clear direction empowers people to act on their own, especially when and where there is no immediate, direct oversight.

As a leader, you will find that people at every level of the organization want to have meaning and purpose. They want to be emotionally engaged in what they do, and to know that the tasks and responsibilities they are being asked to carry out really do make a difference. For that to happen, you must give them a clear direction.

Setting Direction with Feedback

Although it is ultimately your responsibility to set a clear direction based on the organization's overall plan, it is important to gather feedback and input from all levels of the organization as circumstances change. Your first step as a leader in the process of setting a clear direction is to be a great listener. After all, it's all about people. Let your team know that you really do want their thoughts and ideas. When they are speaking, give them your full attention. Articulate team members' different viewpoints back to the team. A summarizing statement, such as "What I hear you saying is…," will let them know that you really understand their perspectives.

Three things to remember:

- When communicating direction, strive for simplicity and clarity.
- Clear direction enables engagement, action and creativity.
- Never assume that saying something once is enough;

| repeat important points as often as necessary. |
| --- |

To know what people are really thinking, you need to make the environment safe for those who are willing to speak up and give feedback. People must see that you don't just tolerate being challenged; rather, you demand that they challenge you. Some people will be hesitant to believe that it is safe to challenge you. It is your job to teach them that they can in fact share their ideas safely. In the end, your goal is not to be right but to do the right thing by drawing fully upon the expertise and knowledge of the entire team.

Effective Communication

Effective communication doesn't happen automatically. Effective communication is clear, simple, straightforward, and concise. It does not rely on acronyms and buzzwords, and it certainly isn't meant to show off how smart the speaker is. Effective communication is about being able to convey information and ideas in an open way so that the message is understood by others.

Numerous factors can undermine effective communication. First, because leaders are very busy and, therefore, usually in a hurry, some may think that a quick explanation is all that is needed. After all, they tell themselves, if the values and the right people are in place and they have taken the time to set a clear direction, how much communicating do they really need to do? Granted, it would be nice to have a staff meeting and explain what is being done and why, but there's no time for that. They've got too much to do. What these leaders fail to realize, however, is that by taking the time to communicate effectively, they would strongly increase the probability of getting things accomplished.

Effective communication is one of the most critical components of leadership because everything else hinges on it. There is no such thing as being too busy to communicate.

## Never Assume

Never assume that you have communicated enough. Remind people what issues are still at the top of the list. Let's say you've told your team that it's essential to watch expenses. There are going to be those who didn't like the directive in the first place and who are waiting for it to blow over or fade away. If an issue is still important, then keep it top-of-mind for your team.

Be precise about what you mean. Although an issue or idea may seem completely obvious to you, don't assume that it appears that way to everyone. Say exactly what you mean, exactly as you mean it, and always make sure that you aren't leaving out "obvious" details that other people might need to know or hear again. It bears repeating: simply tell people what you know, what you do not know, and when you will get back to them with an update. This may sound like commonsense advice, but leaders do not follow it often enough.

## Key Components of Communication

You must be credible and trustworthy, a good listener, aware of what makes communication effective, and able to relate to each member of your team. Being credible and trustworthy is absolutely essential if you want people not only to listen to you but to believe what you say. You can be smooth and articulate, but all the polish in the world won't help you if you are not credible and trusted.

- Make sure you are not doing all the talking.
- Demonstrate to them that you are really listening.
- Solicit feedback from others.
- Practice letting go of the need to always be right.

Finally, consider how you relate to your team members. Are you able to connect with those with whom you are communicating?

At any given moment, you may have to relate to people at levels above you and below you. When your team has an issue to deal with or an opportunity to capitalize on, you need to communicate effectively. The more you relate to them, the more you will be able to bring out the best in each person. Your heart must be in it.

When People Relate, They Will Follow

If you want to know if you are an effective leader, turn around. If nobody is following you, then you've received some bad news. If others relate to you, however, they will gladly follow you and give their all for the organization. This requires that you are both authentic and sincere. You must tap into and exercise your natural curiosity about other people. Make a point of learning about them and relating to their views and interests. Ask them questions and observe the way they think and feel about things. Seek to understand their wants and needs.

**Adapted from the book "From Values to Action"**
**© 2011 Jossey-Bass with permission from the author, Harry M. Jansen Kraemer Jr.** Note: This brief summary is geared towards providing information in regards to the topic and issue covered. This book is provided with the understanding that this book is commentary, educational summary, comparison, and analysis on some of the original books main ideas and concepts.

Questions for Discussion for Working Better Together (WBT)

1. How does clarity of direction relate to key performance indicators (KPIs) and financial performance in an organization? Answer in one or two sentences.

2. On a scale of one to ten, how well do you think the people around you understand (a) what your leaders want your organization to accomplish and (b) how their individual projects and activities relate to those goals? Rate for different groups of people if necessary.

3. On a scale of one to ten, how well do you think you understand (a) what your leaders want your organization to accomplish and (b) how your projects and activities relate to those goals?

4. What are your organization's top three strategic objectives for the next three to five years?

5. What are two or three specific things that you could do to help create more clarity about direction in your organization?

6. Have you ever worked in an organization where clear direction was sorely lacking? How would you describe the engagement level, effectiveness, creativity and general mood of the people there? Name the organization(s) and describe using concrete examples.

7. Have you ever seen a project or initiative die because people felt it was burdensome, and they were allowed to ignore it without consequence? Describe what happened.

8. Think about your favorite leader under whom you have worked personally. How would you rate that person's ability to give clear direction? Describe that person's communication style, and provide a specific example to illustrate. Also, how would you describe that person in terms of authenticity and sincerity?

9. In one sentence, how would you describe the relationship between clear direction and autonomy in a business environment?

*"ENTHUSIASM" IMAGE: CATHEDRAL WINDOW (NYC, USA)*

# #3.
# THE PRINCIPLE OF CREATIVITY: *FOSTERING CREATIVITY*

Google has proven to be a highly creative organization. Their research and discovery of what makes a great manager in my opinion aligns directly with the No-Nonsense Nine, as defined within their December, 2013 Harvard Business Review article: The Oxygen Project:

On March 12, 2011 in a New York Times article by business writer and editor Adam Bryant, he reported on "Google's Quest to Build a Better Boss." That was his headline. The article opened a trail which leads to the identification of 10 key behaviors that these creative managers undertake with consistency, which we provided in list form in Chapter #2.

These behaviors reflect and characterize the Google Manager's motivations and decision-making characteristics.

## Utilizing Creative Strengths

Decision-Making Characteristics

Your decision-making Characteristics and your motivations are kindred human elements, nearly one-in-the-same. Within the world of workplace relationships, there are several reasons why people find themselves in leadership and management positions.... First because they make decisions, and second because they make those decisions based upon their motivations. In between these two, the discipline of Still Point helps them find their way: Healthy business management begins with story (the "Story Works" Discipline), moves to self knowledge (the "Self Differentiation" and self-awareness Disciplines) and then goes to making choices. What kind of decision maker, motivator, leader/manager and story worker are you? Read on...

***Inspirational leader/managers***

Some people possess the knowledge, sway, charisma, contacts, rewards, work or what ever else it is that people seek. So long as they are seen as the source of these assets or attributes, people will follow them. Come the day a manager loses their ability or that their followers become fully satisfied with what they have gained, the management attraction soon dissipates or evaporates entirely.

***Powerful leader/managers***

Some people gain management power through sheer presence and strength of will: they have an overwhelming need to be in charge. More often than we admit, many of us accept this kind of leadership/management . . . for a while. Eventually, though, the simple need to manage is insufficient to retain willing followers.

### *Enduring leader/managers*

Those few people who achieve positions of leadership/management and retain them for long periods of time pull it off largely because of whom they are, rather than the rewards they can distribute, or their controlling need to be a leader/manager. In his research-based writing, Jim Collins describes these durable managers as "Level 5 Leaders"... those people who have been proven to take a Healthy Business Management approach.

Certain leadership/management Characteristics are tangible, measurable. Being smart, physically-fit, energetic, and socially adept are recognizable without much difficulty. Specialized expertise in a particular field is quantifiable and therefore verifiable also, as is the ability to be a "rainmaker." Yet, the No-nonsense Nine key characteristics that contribute to the success of a manager are not so easy to recognize and confirm. They're not obvious.

Below are the nine somewhat intangible qualities (not "typologies") that personify the management of choosing. These Nine (9) are based upon motivation and decision making style. Whatever motivating and decision-making characteristic is dominant within a person will more heavily influence how a person views matters of importance, makes decisions and leads and manages others. They do all this based upon their concentrations. Nobody is 100% "strong" in all nine or "100% strong (or "weak") in any one of these motivational characteristics, yet all people have all nine of them to a greater or lesser degree. And in life, we are all managers, to one degree or another. The extent to which someone has these management characteristics, and in which concentration, is an indicator of a decision-making and motivation style,

1. Judgment
2. Humility
3. Passion
4. Intuition
5. Perception
6. Integrity
7. Enthusiasm
8. Productivity
9. Mediation

Nothing is new here, is it? Nature and nurture: As to "nature" we all know that people are part born with a mix of these and that via "nurture" we continue to develop these characteristics over a lifetime. We are most likely more "nature" than "nurture" – or so some of the scientists say - and up until now it has not been likely to even clearly measure them. In practical terms, even a close friend may see these qualities differently in a person than even the person does. As you read about these No-nonsense Nine Principles and their Characteristics and "favored" strengths, ask yourself the following key questions about each one:

- On a 1 to 10 scale, how do I rate myself?
- What should I do or stop doing to improve my leadership and management ability?
- How would others rate my leadership and management strengths?

### *1. Judgment*

Judgment is the ability to make sound, just and wise decisions, particularly in complex or ambiguous situations. Nearly everyone thinks that he or she has good judgment. This is simply just not true.

Good judgment involves several related abilities. One is the ability to understand the essence of the problem, while another is to know how alternate solutions (re-forming) will possibly affect other people. Poor judgment often involves getting caught up in the peripheral details and proposing solutions long before understanding the entire problem. Another source of poor judgment is letting ego, time constraints and predispositions get in the way so that quality listening and talking evaporates, causing participants to dig in their heels or ignore other points of view. As examples, lawyers, who are trained to swiftly find the holes in other arguments and pounce upon them, and doctors, who restlessly search to eradicate the illness, are each in their professional lives warily familiar with this important yet burdensome Characteristic.

Those few judgmental individuals who can curtail their swiftness and discipline their restlessness will more consistently make sound judgments and end up in leadership/management positions, simply because others learn to trust the deliberate and well-focused decisions that they make.

Akin to the No-nonsense Nine Principle of Mastery

### *2. Humility*

Humility is the mother of all management characteristics – because it promotes stewardship. With humility, everything else that is good will work better, because it is the backbone of mentoring and teamwork achievement.

Humility stands in contrast to those who focus on power, wealth, fame, position and possessions. Prideful managers breed competition, whereas humble managers breed cooperation. Until people have the spirit of service, they might say they care for their partners, the company, or a cause, but they often despise and reject the demands these make on their lives. This double-mindedness, having two conflicting motivations or interests, is a wedge that inevitably conflicts them and their people and turns their work environment sour. Humble management in contrast endures. Empathy and compassion toward others endow the humble manager with an outgoing and natural altruism.

Humility is characteristically the most exceptional management ingredient, a Characteristic that statistically generates long-term success. Recent research shows that modest management peppered with a strong dash of personal tenacity is a proven healthy business management Characteristics mix. Benjamin Franklin was known to list character qualities that he wished to develop within his own self, mastering one virtue at a time then moving on to the next. He did well, he said, until he got to humility. Every time he thought he was making significant progress, he would be so pleased with himself that he became proud. Humility is a remarkable yet elusive virtue, and an especially influential management Characteristic, especially when strong personal will becomes its sturdy mate.

Akin to the No-nonsense Nine Principle of Sincerity

### *3. Passion to succeed*

The passion to succeed is often the added energetic ambition that leads to victory. This raw enthusiasm, however, is a two-edged sword. When combined with integrity, good judgment, and concern for others, personal passion can become both powerfully and positively contagious. On the other hand, if success-orientation is purely individual and self-centered on the leader/manager, the passion to succeed can become destructive, alienating and potentially revengeful. Still, there is no question that the self-confidence and enthusiasm that come with a genuine passion to succeed have a way of inspiring others. Others "pick up" on the confidence and enthusiasm of a passionate manager.

No one follows another who cares little about succeeding, lacks self-confidence and enthusiasm. Confidence inspires confidence when a leader/manager truly "walks the talk." Passionate leader/managers who want to succeed know that saying you care and really caring are not the same. Passionate leader/managers let their followers know that they are important. Passionate leader/managers who succeed listen passionately to what others say. To be lasting, leading with passion requires balance. This means steering clear of angry arguments, taking responsibility (having courage) rather than blaming others, being consistent and sincere, and keeping emotions under control. Otherwise, being passionate is a brand of leadership/management that repeatedly burns bright but short. In contrast, passion under control is success unto itself, and an even greater inspiration to others. The grand value in inspiring people is that they become "believers" beyond mere passion. They gain the confidence and commitment to work hard toward a mutually beneficial reward. With so many people working remote these days, passion as aligned with having purpose is surely important. My sense is that remote workers today have the independence to follow the passion and purpose. Setting rules and being an enforcer is not the answer to remote worker productivity. Remote workers must want to do the work more than have to do the work. Use passion and purpose as a leader/manager. It's the game changer. This isn't just cheerleading, there has to be substance, reward and recognition behind the passion and purpose

Akin to the No-nonsense Nine Principle of Resources.

### *4. Intuition*

Intuition is "the faculty of knowing by instinct, without conscious reasoning." There are certain professionals and business executives who just seem to have a "feel" for what needs to be done.

No one knows precisely where higher instinct comes from, but all of us have at one time or another experienced "gut feel." More often than not the intuition is accurate. The insight sees beyond the obvious, sometimes past anything a person can even explain. Highly intuitive people are important when there is a great deal of confusion, ambiguity, and high stakes: when logic or procedures are not enough to show the way. In those foggy situations, the intuitive person is likely to be "the one others choose to follow."

Healthy leader/managers are always on the lookout for the intuition of others as a key resource. This process combined with the trust in those who have a past track record of providing worthwhile, perceptive suggestions is a leadership/management art form. Watching others for their uniqueness of thought, originality and emotional sensitivity forces the best leader/managers to not only get outside the box but to even forget about the box altogether. Healthy leader/managers recognize the authority of the "best ideas" and track them down to their source, then work with these intuitive people as a primary management resource. They learn to rely on the instincts of others, reaching out for guidance beyond and in balance with their own gut instinct.

Akin to the No-nonsense Nine Principle of Purpose

### *5. Vision*

Vision is the ability to imagine a bright future, especially when others see only problems. Having leadership/management vision (or perception) is the capacity to dream powerful and tangible outcomes, and to then paint that dream in such realistic colors and terms that others are inspired by it as well. The words of Martin Luther King's "I have a dream" speech is a good example of making a dream powerfully tangible to others.

Vision requires the willingness to study the alternatives, root out the causes, look beyond the present situation, and to overlook personal needs. When a situation is fraught with problems and barriers, to consider only personal needs is automatically self-limiting. As someone consciously imagines a future and considers the firm, the business or the work group as a whole is when the vision starts to come together. The visionary person, with clear and studious insight, has a very important role in the organization, mostly because so many people are hard at work "in the trenches," battling their own daily problems and too busy to look up toward the horizon.

Yet vision is also quite simple, a combination of three business basics:

- Mission: reason for existence beyond money
- Principles: core values within the partnership
- Target: important and ultimately achievable aspiration

Of these, the most important to the enduring organizations are the core values: which is where healthy leader/managers begin. They identify and canonize these core values first, as a solid foundation upon which to build their organization's future.

Next, a healthy leader/manager looks beyond what will happen to the firm in the next few months or year. A solidly based leader/manager acquires knowledge and maintains objectivity, observing how current decisions will impact the business today and how those decisions will most likely impact it in the future. Through intellectual analysis and acquisition of vital information, healthy leader/managers investigate and then visualize things that have potential beyond their current generation, even at times when there is no direct tangible evidence or outward signs that such potential exists.

There is a big difference between being an organization with a vision statement and becoming a truly visionary organization. The difference lies in the organization creating alignment, alignment to reinforce its mission, preserve its core values, and keep its aim on-target.

Akin to the No-nonsense Nine Principle of Autonomy

### *6. Integrity*

Integrity is a discipline and a practice. Integrity measures the degree to which others can trust you, and believe in you. Integrity measures moral strength, and the extent to which others can rely on you to be fair when it is not in your best interest. People of high integrity feel a duty to be fair and honest no matter what, and they have the courage and loyalty to be that way in spite of the consequences.

Integrity breeds loyalty and a strong commitment to the traditions and institutions of the firm, company or small work group. For perhaps obvious reasons, this is a person others trust instinctively, because they know this person will never talk behind their back, never reveal a secret, and never go back on his or her word. Their word is accepted as their bond.

Integrity is a virtue often challenged. When there is a lot at stake, including perhaps your own reputation or political popularity, it is tempting to say or do something that erodes your image of integrity. The ability to withstand that temptation is both the measure of your actual integrity, and the Characteristic that most wins others lasting trust.

Akin to the No-nonsense Nine Principle of Reliability

### *7. Enthusiasm*

Enthusiastic managers are typically oriented to the real world of things and sensations. The fact is—it is more fun to be with people who embody happiness than with others who do not. It is likely that if you have the chance to select someone to be a manager of a team or a group, you may choose to pick someone who embodies "joy de vivre." These highly responsive and free-spirited managers exemplify resilience, are practical, productive and prolific – people of action and energy. The person with such an up attitude provides an interesting and often disquieting counter-balance to the normal pathology focus prevalent to the practice of law or accounting and many other professions. The ease of optimism associated with these individuals The “Rainmakers." This Characteristic tends to direct them into areas of customer contact and business development. Here these leader/managers can best display and reward their sense of spontaneous enjoyment outwardly.

Enthusiastic leader/managers tend to have mastered many important life skills, fostering the tendency to try many things, which can be viewed by other specialists, such as doctors, engineers or lawyers, as a negative. This tendency also requires tough adherence to acquiring the best possible specialized support for their selves in their leadership/management positions. For example, when other enthusiasts support enthusiasts, their combined work output usually lags behind the norm. Therefore, maintaining strict recruiting guidelines for support staff is especially important when an enthusiast is in a key management position. However, since enthusiasts tend to fully enjoy the company of other people, they are disposed to be considerate of others needs, appreciate their knowledge skills and work exceedingly well as team leader/managers. More than anything else, though, they typically love what they do, throw themselves into their career, and drive up morale. For them, work is not just a job or a way of making a living; it is a calling.

Akin to the No-nonsense Nine Principle of Creativity

### *8. Productivity*

During management programs, the number one response to the question "how do you lead?" was "I lead by example." Obviously, setting an excellent example is important: significantly for maintaining high work standards, attracting high quality work from customers, and retaining highly valued employees to do the work. Generally, powerful managers have the capacity to gain and use power to bring about positive change and to protect those who are less powerful. They stand up for what they need and want. Geared mainly on output, with action-oriented, can-do attitudes, powerfully productive managers typically love a challenge and are resourceful self-starters, taking the initiative and making things happen. They value independence and foster it in others. At their best, they are magnanimous and compassionate. At their worst, they are control freaks and tyrants. Within law, medicine and engineering, however, an interesting caveat is that the real power itself resides with the work. That is the reality of subject-matter expert's power: whoever has the work has the power. The reality of the rainmaker's power is that whoever holds the revenue has the power. In reality today, it is the customer who has the real power. Remote workers are usually close to the power.

Leadership/management in relation to productivity, therefore, means much more than just being personally powerful or working harder and longer hours than the other people around you. Leadership/management means working smarter, producing higher results, sharing the workload and serving the end user. Those who consistently produce high-value shared results are the ideal examples for others to emulate.

The fact that a professional, an executive or a group leader/manager may work very long hours does not by itself contribute to their role as a manager. As a manager, being powerful requires making the highest and best use of your time and the time and talent of your fellow workers. That includes delegating properly and making the time and effort to teach. The manager with the reputation for making it happen for others will naturally attract and retain a higher percentage of client-committed followers. This is especially important with today's drive to building remote work superiority.

Akin to the No-nonsense Nine Principle of Responsibility

### *9. Mediation*

Some people are asked to lead because they have the capacity to be "the non-anxious presence." These are individuals who, for one thing, are content with themselves and their role in life. They are more than willing to consider others points of view, and they seldom become emotionally involved, even in highly heated situations.

When things are "hitting the fan," these are the people who calm others down, maintain their self-control, and encourage others to adapt more reasonable stances. Small wonder then that others seek their mediation or arbitration services. It should also be noted that true mediators are inherently altruistic. They are primarily interested in fair solutions for everyone, not simply the best solution for him or her. They keep an eye on what's good for all.

Akin to the No-nonsense Nine Principle of Community

**WBT Exercise #3**

## Utilizing Creative Strengths Exercise

How did you rate?

*Decision Making Characteristic*

| | *My Rating* * | *Others Rating Me*** |
|---|---|---|
| Judgment | ________ | ________ |
| Humility | ________ | ________ |
| Passion to Succeed | ________ | ________ |
| Intuition | ________ | ________ |
| Vision | ________ | ________ |
| Integrity | ________ | ________ |
| Enthusiasm | ________ | ________ |
| Productivity | ________ | ________ |
| Mediation | ________ | ________ |

* The number 10 being "great" (Hint – try placing them in priority order)

** Ask 3 or 4 people who know you well to rate your Characteristics & compare

How do the Creative Strengths characteristics compare to the characteristics shown within the Career Drivers Survey?

* * * * *

# The Discipline of "Creative Strengths" in Five Dimensions

***Identity***

Our creative strengths are anchored within our relied-upon force and vigor… within our individual visceral enthusiasms - in the creative and *enthusiastic* part of our decision-making.

***Understanding***

When operating within their own particular zone of creative strength, people are always more motivated, inspired and enthused than otherwise. Their own creative strengths are what buoy them up and then in turn inspire others. We all get juiced on our own creative strengths… what we are good at. To be specific here, there are those leader/managers whose oomph and energy is their main creative strength - found right within their purebred enthusiasm in and of itself.

Beyond being inspired and inspiring, these creative and enthusiast-leader/managers regularly get high on fun, are generally charming, and are those exceptional individuals who colleagues and workers seem to always find easy to talk to. These highly evolved enthusiasts are any organization's cheerleaders, because of their natural optimism. They are the leader/managers who focus most of their energy on the long-term perspective and future possibilities. Near term challenges are longer-term opportunities

***Challenging***

Most important to these purebred creative enthusiasts is getting equal time and their fair share. As a result, they will sometimes work around regulations or "slightly bend" the rules to better fit their needs and wants. High enthusiasm can appear exaggerated or even egotistical to onlookers. The ethereal joy itself can trigger endless one-sided anecdotes that unknowingly and mistakenly (and often painfully) exclude the involvement of others. The enthusiasts own exuberance will blind them to the needs of others or to the truth or even to the importance of showing common courtesy.

The words "just kidding" and the act of easily glossing over issues are perceived as lacking substance and analytical ability: Oversimplifying and skating over the surface is a credibility killer. Their driving force of seeking pleasure can be a mask for low self-esteem or lack of self-awareness or confidence, and in some part is forced to help avoid the pain that can come with the "bad" news – resulting in creative enthusiasts (most often) only wanting to hear the "good" news.

***Believing***

"I always see the bright side of things."

"I've found that if you understand a few basic principles, you can run just about anything."

"I'm always the one at leadership retreats to figure out what we'll do for fun."

"I escaped from my family's problems with a rich fantasy life."

***Performance improvement suggestions:***

Performance development options include contingency planning for problems, eliciting and accepting feedback, using negative reframing to counter "rosy optimism" and—particularly—gaining the discipline themselves to follow through on their own development, which is hard work! Their key development need is temperance and the ability to maintain a sense of proportion—living and working in the present, expending only as much energy as is called for.

When under-resourced, having "true inspiration" is a fabulous strength, especially for those times when tenacity alone won't yield positive results. Of course, having just tenacity, with no inspiration, can frankly be just downright annoying.

Yet overall, a little well placed 'inspiration' (and sincere charm) can become extremely motivating and work wonders. The best under-resourced managers are like that. When around them and the enthusiasm level is right, the inspiration can become contagious. Truly inspirational managers are passionate about what they are doing and confident about their odds of achieving success.

Without rose-colored glasses, experienced inspirational managers have learned through experience to draw upon their own creative strengths and the strengths of others, as they are hyper-driven to "just make it happen." Like anyone else, they may have self-doubts when they are alone looking in the mirror, but a colleague or subordinate would never know it from seeing them in action in the workplace.

As a manager-coach with creative strengths, you must consciously prepare yourself if you are to be ready to inspire others. Place a mirror to yourself and be ready in advance: Here is one way to prep your own self, to keep engaged and to become inspiring to others… For example, when watching someone else present an idea that *they say* that they "believe in" – just ask yourself this: "Can this person inspire others? Then stop a moment and ask yourself what you would do in their shoes. Energy, enthusiasm, charisma, oomph and evangelism are so important because not only is "inspiration" required to hire and manage a team, but they are vital to getting people to work with you under many other circumstances. People quit almost 100 percent of the time because of their immediate boss. And they stay for the same reason too. Be inspiring!

Your own specific strengths and your own kind of inspiration are tightly connected. Pulling inspiration from nothing falls short. Inspiration that is shallow and essentially just "charismatic" is never enough on its own. True inspiration requires strength of character: idealism and activism... not just charisma. A "charismatic manager" who doesn't really know their own creative strengths and gets things done accordingly and follow through inadequately on delivery will never endure… because true and lasting inspiration requires both enthusiasm and perspiration.

Be a model as a manager-coach. Be certain to manage your weaknesses, but really be sure to maximize your strengths: That is the truest form of inspiration for others.

The Discipline of "Creative Enthusiasm" is the creative personal inspiration that is part of us all.

## A Harry Kraemer Inspired One Sheet: "Balance and Perspective"

When we account for perspectives and consequences beyond our own limited knowledge and immediate self-interest, and when we achieve balance in the ways that we use our time and energy, we become agents of creativity within our organizations and throughout our lives.

Healthy Business Management Principles
Principle 3: Creativity

| | | |
|---|---|---|
| 9 Reliability | 2 Autonomy | 3 Creativity |
| 8 Community | 1 Purpose | 4 Resources |
| 7 Sincerity | 6 Mastery | 5 Responsibility |

**The Nature of Balance**

Balance is the ability to see issues, problems, and questions from all angles, including from differing viewpoints, even those that are diametrically opposed. Through balance, you gain clearer perspective on virtually any topic or issue that you encounter. With balance, you are able to make decisions explicitly with an understanding of the broad impact, instead of focusing narrowly. In all aspects of your life, professionally and personally, pursuing balance will give you a richer, more holistic perspective. You move beyond what you see and know in order to consider what others have to say. Sometimes you will change your mind; at other times, your opinions will be affirmed. Whatever the outcome, you will become more knowledgeable and gain confidence in your decision making because you are more balanced.

**Balance and Leadership**

Balance is the ability to understand all sides of an issue. Leaders who pursue balance realize that their perspective is just that: theirs. By purposefully seeking input from others, especially those who have opposing opinions, you gain a global perspective that enables you to make choices that align with your priorities. You become stronger and more informed as you genuinely seek input, opinions, and feedback from all members of your team before making a decision. By pursuing balance, you can also communicate your views much more effectively. Instead of engaging in a tit-for-tat argument, you can usually draw parallels where the various viewpoints agree, and explore contrasts where they do not.

No matter your position, balance will help you become a well-rounded, global-thinking person with more meaningful and satisfying interactions with others. People will know that you are listening and, even more important, that they are being heard. Your ability to influence others will be even greater when you take the lead in seeking to understand first, before you are understood. Seeking input from others and taking their perspectives into account is crucial for developing genuine followership, which is the hallmark of true leadership.

Balance and Decision-making

Truth be told, most of us are very quick to express our views. We've thought about an issue, and we know what the answer is—or at least we think we do. Our focus is often to convince everyone else why we are correct. There is a flaw in this thinking: it's based on the assurance that our opinion is the "right" one.

There always are multiple perspectives, viewpoints, opinions, and even multiple “realities” to consider. When you couple the practice of self-reflection with the discipline of balance by seeking input from many people, your leadership is elevated. You not only improve your success rate when it comes to making good, well-thought-out decisions; you also demonstrate that you are committed to doing the right thing rather than being right. In order to become balanced, you must first dismiss one big myth: that the leader is the all-knowing person with all the answers.

Inherent in the decision-making process is the need for another kind of balance: you are seeking enough input to make a decision aligned with your values and those of the organization, while also avoiding "analysis paralysis." It is the job of the leader to make the final decision in a timely manner after taking in all the input. After all, leadership is not a democracy. If there are ten people on a team and you had to wait for every person to offer an opinion, not much would get done. Seeking input should not be an excuse to slow down or procrastinate. The reality is that there is a business to run, there are competitors to face, and technology is always changing.

As a leader, you will face many situations in which you will have to make decisions with less than perfect information or when not all of the variables are known. You cannot wait until things become crystal clear because it's rarely going to be that way. However, if you find out down the road that you've chosen the wrong fork, you should take the necessary steps to make a midcourse correction rather than sticking to a faulty decision just to keep going. The goal, after all, is not to be right but to do the right thing.

**Balance for Healthy Business**

Balance is not just critical to making good decisions. It is also an important aspect of how an organization operates. In many organizations, the following is a frequently asked question: "Are we running the organization for the short term or the long term?" The answer that people want to hear is "for the long term." If you answer anything else, you will appear naive. But if you say you are managing for the long term, the most likely next question will be, "Then why are we spending 95 percent of our time focusing on the short term and the current quarter?" Answer: It is important to run the organization for both the short term and the long term. You also have to manage the short term because you have the responsibility to report your progress quarter by quarter to senior management, the board of directors, and shareholders.

There are many scenarios in which you must balance two different goals—for example, managing the company for growth and also for return, or treating every person on the team with respect and managing a lean organization that may have to lay off ten percent of the workforce in order to be globally competitive. These are not "either-or" scenarios; rather, they require a balance between two objectives. Your actions will sometimes lean toward one end of the spectrum, and at other times the opposite. What is most important is to be mindful of the entire spectrum so that you can keep everything in balance.

**Life Balance**

The better a manager you are, the more opportunities you will have to make a difference in many areas. This means that you will face choices. The same strategy of seeking a balance of perspectives to help you make better decisions at work should be a part of other areas of your life as well. As a leader, you must not only balance your professional and personal life but also model this thought process for others, to set the example of leading a balanced life, pursuing meaning and satisfaction in every area that matters the most to that individual.

Three things to remember:

- Balance is the ability to take all sides of an issue into account when making decisions and taking action.
- Balance increases our understanding, our influence, and our ability to lead people beyond conflict.
- Put aside the desire to be right, and focus on doing the right things.

We must balance all aspects of our lives. When you pursue something to the exclusion of everything else, you run the risk of exhausting yourself, which is not healthy for you or your organization. A full and satisfying life must consist of more than just your job. When you identify too closely with your work, you can easily lose perspective and become unable to look at all the angles in a situation. And when that happens, you are in danger of making decisions that don't honor your values, what matters to you most. Life balance enables you to be a multifaceted person, someone who can connect with people on multiple levels because you have more interests to share with them than just work.

Managing Time and Energy for Life Balance

No matter who we are, what we do for a living, where we live, or how productive we are, we all get the same amount of time: 168 hours per week. The difference among us is in how we spend that time. Here are six buckets to consider: career, family, spirituality, health, fun, and social responsibility (or making a difference). You may have more than six; you may have fewer. If you are living a truly balanced life, you will spend at least part of your time and energy in each area over a period of a week or two or even a month. One exercise that may be helpful is to construct a grid reflecting each area in your life that you identify as important.

Keep in mind that, in reality, no two weeks will be the same. Unless you measure how you spend your time, you cannot make meaningful changes that will positively impact the quality of your life and, by extension, your leadership. You also need to be realistic and honest with yourself about the trade-offs you are willing to make in order to lead a balanced life. None of us will ever get everything done; therefore, the key is to consider the trade-offs between what needs to be accomplished immediately and what can wait another day so that you can invest time and energy in your other life buckets.

**Adapted from the book "From Values to Action" © 2011 Jossey-Bass with permission from the author, Harry M. Jansen Kraemer Jr.** Note: This brief summary is geared towards providing information in regards to the topic and issue covered. This book is provided with the understanding that this book is commentary, educational summary, comparison, and analysis on some of the original books main ideas and concepts.

Questions for Discussion for Working Better Together (WBT)

1. How does the ability to balance conflicting perspectives and competing interests relate to key performance indicators (KPIs) and financial performance in an organization? Answer in one or two paragraphs.

2. On a scale of one to ten, how well do you think the people around you demonstrate balance in their decision-making, actions and communication? Rate for different groups of people if necessary.

3. On a scale of one to ten, how well do you think you demonstrate balance in your decision-making, actions and communication?

4. How does practicing balance relate to upholding personal and organizational values?

5. Have you ever worked in an organization or team where balance was sorely lacking? What happened? Describe with concrete examples.

6. Think about your favorite leader under whom you have worked personally. How would you rate that person's ability to maintain balance? How did that person exhibit a skill for practicing balance? Describe with concrete examples.

7. What are two or three specific things that you could do to help create more balance in your organization?

8. In one sentence, how would you describe the relationship between balance and creativity in a business environment?

9. Tailor the following list to suit your life and your values: career, family, spirituality, health, fun, and social responsibility. What one to three things can you do weekly in each area to create more meaning and fulfillment in your life?

*"PASSION" IMAGE: CELTIC STONE, ANGUS, SCOTLAND*

# #4.
# THE PRINCIPLE OF RESOURCES:
# *BEING RESOURCEFUL*

## Introducing SAMI: Supportive-Assertive Management Initiative

Small Groups are the single most powerful management tool of all time. Small Groups operate everywhere: within large multi-billion dollar corporations and start-ups, within huge multi-office international professional firms, and within single-city, single-service niche operations. Small Groups are ubiquitous, from the military to not-for-profits. The methods by which we teach are built around the simple principle that "small groups make it happen" across the entire enterprise spectrum. For that reason, our working philosophy and practice is to champion the small group, the manager-coach and the individual worker. Our experience is that when those three components are operating in harmony, business just seems to be healthy all over the workplace.

*SAMI Purpose*

At the heart of healthy business management is SAMI, our approach for working productively in small groups. SAMI stands for Supportive-Assertive Management Initiative. SAMI's purpose is to help managers learn and take into practice a "manager-coach" approach to working with subordinates and peers. This approach provides measure-able, accountable improvement of interpersonal skills and the accompanying skills of healthy business management that improve communication, foster professional and personal growth, and enable excellence at the individual, group and organizational levels.

***SAMI Values***

- People
- Integrity
- Excellence
- Collaboration

*SAMI Goals and Possibilities*

- To satisfy employee work experience
- To provide highest quality service
- To be financially successful
- To be a strong, growing organization

There are Four Main Manager-Coach Positive Attitudes

1. Helpfulness

"I can help others, and enjoy helping and teaching people. I don't know nor have all the answers. Right process will allow me to get good answers most of the time. People want to achieve individually, and they want to be a part of a winning team. I'm not better than those I manage. I may be more experienced, or have more knowledge, but I am not necessarily better. Someone may have more potential, and if they have more, my role is to help them realize their potential contribution."

2. Mutual Responsibility

"I work for each person who "reports to me," and each of them works for me. Responsible professionals are mobile: Though I may influence their pay and promotions, they can influence me, other managers and their peers, and if they so choose, they can leave. We therefore must be mutually responsible for each other and have a mutual responsibility to each other. I enjoy finishing team tasks and enjoy seeing those I "manage" do good work."

3. Supportive & Assertive (Nurturing and Challenging)

"I want to develop to be a supportive (nurturing) and assertive (challenging) manager. I care about my people, and I care about delivering excellent work from my team or group. I can learn from those I manage - they can tell me things they see and feel about me and that can help me grow to be a better manager. I enjoy coaching - helping people understand how they can be more effective and how they can grow. I have respect for each individual."

4. Change Confidante

"I strive to be open to change and proactive to positive movement. I will work to recognize and agree with the problem, and to understand the impact of potential solutions and business consequences."

In order to have change occur, I must:
Want to change,

Know how to change,
Gain the confidence to change, and then
Take action to change.

*SAMI Guidelines*

Decision Making

Stay open (mentally) for new information until you must decide. Making tentative conclusions is okay, but if you lock into them, you won't hear data that suggests a different solution, and you will too easily hear confirming data. Stay open longer for better problem solving.

When someone else suggests something you know you do not like, ask the following question of them: "What problem are you trying to solve with that solution?" You will find you often agree with the problem but not with that particular solution, and you can say so, which then has you both back problem-solving again, together.

Creating Teamwork

There are several ingredients to healthy teamwork:

- Clarity of purpose, goal or “mission”
- Common commitment allows providence to join the team
- Hiring and working with cooperative people
- Sharing information—more than you have to. This is the best advice going.
- Pre-starting-date communication and then creating first-day belongingness
- Allowing team members to participate in decisions that affect them
- Eliminating barriers to teamwork, like profit centers or under-budgeting

Managing Process

Recognize that every interaction you have is on two levels of People and Process:

People: Relationship building involves questions like these: Can I trust this person? Do I want to go back again and talk to this person? Do I want to make any more suggestions?

Process: Resources and structure deals more specifically with the task-at-hand, such as completing an assignment, developing a plan, recording points of conflict, asking questions, resolving a dispute, getting direction or mapping out an agenda.

Communicating and conversation:

This is critical to future success. After completing a project with a subordinate, co-worker or a superior, make it a practice to take the time to give and receive feedback. Talk about it. Have some conversations about the tactical issues (the tasks accomplished), and then take time to review with the individual how you each handled matters on the relationship-building level. If you find you are coming up short in the latter area, you yourself need to do something about it, to help yourself make a repair. You must improve your conversation capability.

Collaborating:

As co-worker and as a leader/manager-coach in this feedback process, you become the de facto example (the mirror or the mentor) by which your co-workers and subordinates see how they come across. You are leading by example, but it is they who must choose to follow. Control and command is short-lived at best. Therefore, it becomes their job to change if how they come across in a relationship falls short. And change only takes place when someone wants to change. In brief, the leader/manager-coach's job is to (1) be supportive, (2) be assertive, (3) be a positive example, and (4) hold up the mirror and help those who try, to change.

Change:

For someone to really change, they must:

- Recognize that a problem exists
- Accept responsibility
- Want to change
- Know how to change
- Do it

Being a leader/manager-coach is taking people through the process of change. This demands clear conversation.

Look for Excellence

Who to hire is so terribly important. All the great supervision in the world is not worth one-fifth of the importance of hiring excellent people in the first place. The most satisfied people will be those with healthy attitudes about themselves and about life and realistic expectations (which the organization then must meet). People come and go for a variety of reasons, not necessarily because of dissatisfaction. And every time someone leaves an organization, that organization has the opportunity to "upgrade" and to improve the spirit of the organization by making a stronger hire.

Within any kind of organization, but especially within the corporate suite and the professional services arena, people given responsibility for hiring typically judge other potential employees by their own criteria, and usually that criterion is what the "judger" is good at. Analytical individuals judge by thoroughness and accuracy on details. Sales people judge others by whether they have neat business development ideas and the like. In contrast, the best leader/managers are well balanced and have wide criteria—they value all contributions, not just the kind of contributions they make well.

Manage to Expectations

A. Anticipate when expectations might be apart on items: Expectations both inform and then form a person's reality.

B. Satisfaction is a function of expectations and what really happens. Degree of dissatisfaction is proportional to how long someone is allowed to have expectations that won't be met.

If someone expects more than you are going to deliver, tackle it, talk to him or her, incur the tough conversation earlier, not later. Protect you and them from severe disappointment. Remember, having conversation makes all the difference very often.

Some managers do not do this well because:

A. Some are trying to please the person on each interaction , which cannot happen because healthy management works on pleasing workers over the long haul.

B. A fear that the person will leave. Typically leader/managers' fears here are exaggerated. Where will they go that is better than where they are currently employed?... Note: if the organization deals straight with everyone, everyone wins.

Reward Excellence

Recognize and reinforce healthy performance. Catch somebody doing something right. This is very powerful. Also, poor or marginal performers must certainly be confronted because their negative impact is at least double what is suspected. Again, have the conversation!

The marketplace will no longer allow the luxury of ignoring performance issues. Conflict is normal. Teach others that any organization of individuals will have multiple goals, and therefore will always have conflicts. Also, help others improve their ability to determine exactly where their particular disagreement lies. Talk about it.

Show Appreciation

Most everyone has this one management weakness that is reflected throughout every organization that needs to be greatly improved upon: that weakness is "showing appreciation." Employees do good things all the time. The SAMI guideline is simply to catch them at it and genuinely thank them. Converse with people… No false praise—just look consistently for things to appreciate and then give honest praise. Voice it! This practice is contagious: noticing and pointing out good things others do will surprisingly inspire others to be more observant of what you are doing that deserves appreciation. They will then begin to use it. There is strength within any successful organization—organizations are generally much stronger than those within it realize because they are in it every day. Their people are strong. Plus, most successful organizations have processes (systems) that are well in place and functioning well:

- How they acquire business
- How they attract new people
- How they get most people committed to a organization's mission
- How they impart the importance of quality work
- How they train people
- How they pay people
- Their policies and procedures
- How they get work done together
- Using their past experiences
- Consulting with each other
- Use of employee surveys and evaluations

- Monitoring of others' satisfaction
- Use of methodologies to monitor and quantifiably manage for improved interpersonal and communication skills

Have More Fun

- Your outlook is your own, so own it!
- Find your passion
- Lighten up with others - find your humor again.
- Disciplines & practices—one per month, to be engrained in the culture
- Most important: Harmony in being supportive (nurturing) and assertive (challenging)

Relationships and Networking

Change is constant in the world of business. Change that is meaningful in the workplace means the willingness and fortitude to change how you relate to others. The constancy of change means that you have to be vigilant about your business relationships and how they need to keep changing. Otherwise, your working relationships will grow old and die, just like an untended garden will turn to ruin.

The most powerful way to properly tend to business relationships is through networking. Networking is a supportive system of sharing information and services in relationship with individuals and groups having a common interest: an extended group of people with similar interests or concerns who interact and remain in formal or informal contact for mutual assistance or support. Properly tending to business relationships and effectively networking are metaphorically speaking two sides of the same coin.

## Leader/Manager-as-Coach Paradigm

Think of tending to relationships and networking as one-in-the-same and as diligently working to do something better and most often different with your own life. In order to change, you need to be constantly aware of the possibilities that are put in front of you. You have to know what you want and to be able to recognize it or something better when it occurs. And you can invoke the help of others around you as part of your broader network, as part of your workplace relationships, and as part of your action plan. You are then working consciously, intentionally and effectively.

## Stretching

Within the Leader/Manager-as-Coach paradigm, mentors and leader/manager-coaches and those within that sphere of learning will find that they are consistently being invited or simply moving into action in ways that encourages them to stretch, to achieve something new or to become someone beyond where they currently are operating. Within Leader/Manager-as-Coach, people are encouraged and taught what it means to be in a network of relationships at work, how to serve as an example for others, to be a Leader/Manager-as-Coach to superiors, to peers, and to subordinates.

Leader/Manager-as-Coach is an attitude of how to approach and work with others, But Leader/Manager-as-Coach is also a highly important activity – and while nurturing and challenging co-workers and teaching subordinates often do involve coaching techniques – the relationship employees have with their workplace command-and-control managers differs from the relationship that leader/manager-coaches have with their peers and subordinates: Most important is the fact that leader/manager-coaches and their subordinates are creating and then operating within a Healthy Business environment, a culture that is grounded in excellence of process, of more gentleness and kindness and tolerance of people. If workers are to stretch and grow, they need a solid healthy base.

Cooperating

The Leader/Manager-Coach is a prime example of the Healthy-Business concern for the whole person, both in and outside the workplace. The Leader/Manager-Coach and subordinate relationship is most definitely a two-way street approach. Leader/Manager-Coaches and subordinates together decide upon the goals, the content, and even the style of management that occurs, based upon their own personal needs and interests. In this sense, Leader/Manager-Coaches work "for" their subordinates… as long as everyone pulls their own weight. This self-managing approach goes only as far as having an attitude of self-responsibility. When self-management works the results are powerful. It is what helps remote workers succeed. If it struggles, then a review of what makes it powerful is important.

Action

Following are a number of reasons SAMI and the leader/manager-as-coach process work:

- A Leader/Manager-Coach pays strict attention to the subordinate.
- A Leader/Manager-Coach may be more experienced - yet is open and earnestly listens
- Paying close non-selfish attention encourages subordinates to trust and develop
- A Leader/Manager-Coach "teaches" by causing learning, as an enlightening discovery process
- Leader/Manager-Coaches typically are savvy, knowing the organization inside and out

- Subordinates have the chance to learn without experiencing the woes of trial and error
- There is indirect reward and benefit to the Leader/Manager-Coach as a byproduct

Being a Leader/Manager-Coach is inherently satisfying and engenders the same kind of satisfaction that all good teachers and parents are familiar with, or the joy and pride that a winning coach has for a team. Just as with being a new employee who is "green" with inexperience takes effort, being a Leader/Manager-Coach takes effort, too, and most definitely takes time... but the payoffs on a personal level to both parties are invaluable. This has been the experience of people throughout the ages.

**Looking Ahead**

As you conclude reading Chapter Four with the SAMI Tool, you will find that you have been unknowingly prepared to take a bigger step in pulling together a discovery about the heightened value of what is called Effectuation versus Causation within the world of STEP. As to causation, you have looked into the summary list pertaining to the writings of David Maister from his best selling book "Practice What You Preach: What Managers Must Do to Create a High Achievement Culture": which he published in the year 2001. His book is built around a specific causal model that he researched in the late 1990s within the many dozens of the communications services and marketing services companies owned by Sir Martin Sorrell the CEO of WPP (Wire and Plastic Products, PLC). In 1985, Sorrell privately invested in WPP, a British wire shopping basket manufacturer, and joined it full-time as chief executive in 1986. He began to acquire "below-the-line" advertising-related companies, purchasing 18 in three years, including in 1987 when he stunned the agency world with a $566 million hostile takeover of J. Walter Thompson, followed in 1989 with another dramatic hostile take-over of Ogilvy and Mather. Since 2000, WPP also acquired two more integrated, global agency networks, Young & Rubicam and Grey.

At the time of Maister's research that evolved into his book, "Practice What You Preach," the initial goal was to understand what made one WPP-owned services company more profitable than another WPP-owned services company. As an end result, Maister reported WPP's "TopTen," what I call "Dave Maister's Top Quality Attributes."

After that you read and learned more about the altogether different "Top Ten," as researched and reported upon in an article written by Harvard Professor, David Garvin, as published by the Harvard Business Review in 2013, I call them "Google Oxygen's Top Quality Behaviors." These are based upon what David Garvin and his team's Harvard Business Review article entitled:

"How Google Sold Its Engineers on Management. Hint: It's all about the data."

Coincidentally these two Davids of Harvard, David Maister and David Garvin, each prove and publish the same following result separately… namely, "*that people in business who Work Better Together (WBT) turn out to be more productive and more profitable.* "

But neither of the two Davids provide the tools to actually learn and apply the disciplines. Perhaps because that wasn't the assignment, but first off, they simply don't provide the tools. Because that was not their job. Their job was to describe the needs and desired outcomes, but was not to chart the road to "how to" by teaching others. That's why the No-nonsense Nine Tool Set is so helpful: the No-nonsense Nine gives people what they need to Work Better Together (WBT), and thereby with that knowledge, begin to improve performance that ultimately lifts productivity and profitability.

The big question is… "If it's proven that people who work better together perform better, and are therefore more productive and profitable, then how on earth do you get them to learn how to do just that?" After all, it's people that we are dealing with here, and they need help.

The case being made within this book for this is that you must first Learn the No-nonsense Nine Principles, and then, next, practice, practice, practice the No-nonsense Nine Disciplines.

In today's world of instant gratification, that's a hard sell.

After all isn't that what the violinist was told when he or she asked, "How do you get to Carnegie Hall?

Of course, the old, old, old answer is, "Practice, Practice, Practice."

Frankly, that's exactly how we recommend (and know) you can get to be a successful Leader/Manager-As-Coach in today's increasingly, highly competitive workplace. Note: More about Leader/Manager-as-Coach is in the following Chapter Five.

But for now below is some more about SAMI:

**SAMI (The Practical Tool)**

*Supportive-Assertive Management Initiative*

Each Manager-Coach relationship is unique and every single employee has his or her own strengths.

Remember to ask this of yourself: "What does this co-worker need from me?"

Considering your answer to the above question, and then circle those things from the following list that you are going to take action on more often with this co-worker.

*To Be More Supportive*

1. Spend time orienting about the organization's purpose, business or practice areas, functions and general expectations for this individual's role.
2. Provide information that will reinforce the team's purpose (which always is to excel): What is occurring in the organization? What other information of general interest is appropriate and helpful?
3. Spend time thinking about how this person can grow and develop.
4. Identify the person's strengths, roadblocks and challenges, potential, goals and interests.
5. Spend time teaching and coaching the individual to help achieve success.
6. Treat the person according to their unique needs.
7. Hold up the mirror for this person, helping him or her to understand how others see their performance, actions and behavior.
8. Listen carefully and look to be flexible when the person brings up a personal problem.
9. Compliment the person when very good work is observed.
10. Watch for signs of overwork and approach the individual about it.

*To Be More Assertive*

1. Set clear and definitive expectations for evaluating this person's performance.
2. Follow up on projects given to this person to assess if work is on track or in need of redirecting.
3. When an assignment is not completed to satisfaction, ask the person to redo or improve the work until it meets the expected results.
4. If this person is taking advantage of flexible arrangements, address the issue immediately.
5. Directly define and address recurring flaws or difficulties in performance with this person.
6. Stretch the person to take on new responsibilities even if they do not feel comfortably ready.
7. Insist on all aspects of quality: accuracy, timeliness, creativity, clarity of communication and thoroughness.
8. Always establish "Smart" goals: Specific, Measurable, Achievable, Resourceful and Time-based
9. When something is needed or required from this person, ask for it.
10. Watch for signs of underperformance and approach the individual about it.

*Action Plan*

List three actions to manage, teach or coach this person for more productivity each quarter of the year.

That will equal a total of a dozen improvement suggestions per year, obviously. Note: Be sure to have the necessary conversations. That's the icing on the top. Make a copy of the blank four-quarters page and make your list on it to file and reference every 12 to 13 weeks (Quarterly). Make adjustments and GROW:

GROW

First described in legendary executive coach John Whitmore's 1992 book Coaching for Performance, the GROW model is a **4-step system for achieving goals.**

The name is an acronym of the four steps:

1. G… Goal,
2. R… Reality,
3. O… Obstacles (or Options), and
4. W… Way Forward (or Will).

The GROW Model is a good and solid companion for SAMI meetings. Return to it quarterly with each subordinate's meeting to make sure that the subordinate remains goal focused and realistic. GROW is similar to the acronym "DARE,' the sequence of The Six Conversations, and even the OSHAM acronym.

My teacher mind wants you to think of each one as being circular (a spiral) in design and in that is way able to surround and reach inward to The No-nonsense Nine Principles & Disciplines. (See Arriens ref. on page 8).

. First Quarter

1. ______________________________
2. ______________________________
3. ______________________________

Second Quarter

1. ______________________________
2. ______________________________
3. ______________________________

Third Quarter

1. ______________________________
2. ______________________________
3. ______________________________

Fourth Quarter

1. ______________________________
2. ______________________________
3. ______________________________

## A Harry Kraemer Inspired One Sheet: Motivation and Team Engagement

Teams do not come together by themselves. They are developed purposefully and with intention. As the leader, you will need to follow closely the four principles of values-based leadership: self-reflection, balance, true self-confidence and genuine humility.

Healthy Business Management Principles
Principle 4: Resources

| | | |
|---|---|---|
| 9 Reliability | 2 Autonomy | 3 Creativity |
| 8 Community | 1 Purpose | 4 Resources |
| 7 Sincerity | 6 Mastery | 5 Responsibility |

Self-reflection will keep you on track with what your team needs to accomplish and how successfully you are engaging and motivating others. With balance, you are genuinely interested in other people's input and feedback as you make final decisions. In fact, you may discover that their recommendations are better than your initial approach. You want them to challenge you and each other as they explore how best to accomplish the team's objectives. True self-confidence affirms that you do not need to be right; rather, you are committed to doing the right thing as you work with a team of talented individuals. Genuine humility reminds you of who you are and where you've been. You haven't forgotten what it's like to be a junior member of a team. At the same time, you recognize that no matter what someone's title may be, you are neither inferior nor superior to that person. You're all on one team.

To build, motivate, and engage your team members will require that they be as passionate about achieving an objective as you are. Of course, that means you must have a high degree of energy and commitment around what you're trying to accomplish. Your leadership comes not from telling others what to do but from showing them why what they're doing is important to the entire organization. Furthermore, before they agree to follow your lead, they must first place their trust in you.

The thinking among many people, particularly those who start out as single contributors, is often, "It would be so much simpler just to tell them what needs to be done and give them a deadline." These people say to themselves, "As soon as I have some direct reports, I'll be able to assign them specific tasks. Then my life will be easier." This is a fantasy far from reality. Leadership isn't about doling out responsibilities that you can check off your to-do list. Leadership is about forming teams that are motivated and engaged to do the right thing and to make the right decisions for the good of the company.

## Trust: The Foundation of the Team

Even when the right people whose values are aligned with the organization are in place, very often they still act like individual players. However, it is not the individual talent of the star players but their cohesion that matters the most. As we've seen in sports, an assemblage of talented and ambitious individual players often does not make the best team. Players who function well together always put the team first and their own aspirations second.

Your job as the leader is to motivate and engage the group and transform it into a team. For you to succeed, people will need to know that you are true to your word, that you will treat them fairly and with respect. They want to know that if the project goes well, they will all share in the credit for its success. They also want assurance that if things do not go as planned, you will not pin the blame on them. There may be individual issues for each person as well. Some people are motivated by the chance to learn something new. Others look to network outside their departments to advance their careers. For most people, recognition is very important.

As the leader, you need to understand how best to connect with each person you are trying to influence, including those whose backgrounds are completely different from yours. Although many people equate motivation with monetary rewards, other incentives can work just as well if not better than money and cost very little. Staging a good-natured competition with an inexpensive yet coveted prize is one such example. With an understanding of your people and a little creativity, you can motivate people in very simple ways, especially by publicly recognizing them for their work.

As a values-based leader, you must first understand your team members before you can motivate and engage them. When trust and respect are established on both sides, people will devote themselves to the project and to each other. They become committed to a successful outcome because they see how important it is to the entire organization. Knowing that you, as the leader, are genuinely interested in their viewpoints and perspectives is very motivational.

A key component in engaging and motivating others is influence, which is really a two-way street. The more people know that they can influence you because of your open-minded attitude toward feedback and input, the more you will be able to influence them into thinking holistically about the entire organization instead of just focusing on their department or unit. Influencing others doesn't mean being the loudest person in the room, or the most persistent or persuasive. Having influence does not mean being a steamroller, flattening any opposition or contrary opinions in your path. Influence is possible only when others truly understand your values, where you're coming from, and what you consider to be most important.

A Clear, Elevating Goal

Years of research has shown that one factor is far and away the most important in making a team successful: people feeling that they are part of something worthwhile and significant. A team can operate effectively only if it shares an overarching purpose or objective around which the team can be brought together. Without a broader sense of purpose and direction, a team runs the risk of disintegrating into individual players going off in separate directions. (One way to tell if a group is really a team is to ask each member individually what he or she believes the group is trying to accomplish. If eight different people give you eight different responses, you know there is no real team.) Granted, the team will be made up of people who have different tasks and assignments that reflect their expertise or the area of the company in which they work. In the end, however, all these tasks must relate directly to achieving a clear, elevating goal.

Great teams have a leader who explains the purpose to the group—what they are going to do as a team that, if they had not come together, would never happen. The key element is a trusting, caring, and helpful environment. People need to be allowed to be open, direct, challenging, and honest with each other while always being respectful.

Three things to remember:

- Your leadership comes from showing your followers why their work is important.
- Trust is the key to turning a group of individual performers into a true team.
- To be effective, a team must have a clear, elevating goal that is shared by all team members.

The way to tell whether a team is really effective is if there are no sidebar discussions. For a team to be effective, it must be cohesive; everything must be laid out on the table for discussion with everyone in the room. There should be no sensitive topics or taboos that are off-limits. So when ten people are meeting and someone says something that doesn't make sense, one of the team members asks for an explanation. Your team can eliminate sidebar discussions by ensuring that everything that needs to be said is expressed at the meeting. Team members are encouraged to openly, honestly, and respectfully question everyone, including the team leader. People don't see challenging as a threat because they give their fellow team members the benefit of the doubt. They understand that these challenges are being made to present all sides of the issue and arrive at a better answer. How else can the team move forward to determine, in a logical way, the right thing to do?

Sometimes we mistakenly think that teamwork requires some false sense of getting along. But if everyone wants to "play nice" and resists challenging and arguing specific points, you will end up with a mediocre team. Having a great team means holding each other accountable and refusing to accept anything less than doing the right thing for the right reasons. Discussions should be framed as collaborations aimed at achieving the best possible solution for the overall organization. This means shifting from "I win, you lose" to "We win." Decisions should be framed so that everyone shares an interest in achieving and supporting the best solution for the group.

Establish a sense of fairness and equity in the process. People do care about outcomes, but they are also concerned about the process that gets them there. Some team members may not have chosen a particular decision, but as long as these individuals provided input to the process and felt that their opinions were heard by the leader, most likely everyone will be okay with the outcome—even if the leader's final decision is contrary to what some of them recommended. Through open and thorough discussion, the team members understand all sides of the issue and can see that the leader, whom they trust, believes that this decision is in the best interest of the entire organization.

**Adapted from the book "From Values to Action," © 2011 Jossey-Bass with permission from the author, Harry M. Jansen Kraemer Jr.** Note: This brief summary is geared towards providing information in regards to the topic and issue covered. This book is provided with the understanding that this book is commentary, educational summary, comparison, and analysis on some of the original books main ideas and concepts.

Questions for Discussion for Working Better Together (WBT)

1. As a team leader, how does your ability to establish trust relate to key performance indicators (KPIs) and financial performance in your organization? Answer in one or two paragraphs.

2. On a scale of one to ten, rate your organization's leaders on their ability to (a) establish trust, (b) show people why their work is important, (c) create a sense of shared purpose, and (d) maintain team engagement: Rate for different levels of leadership if necessary.

3. On a scale of one to ten, how well do you think you rate on the abilities listed in the previous question?

4. Have you ever worked for someone that you did not trust? Why did you not trust that person? How did the lack of trust affect your work? Describe with concrete examples.

5. Have you ever worked for someone that showed a lack of respect for you or for others? What happened? Describe with concrete examples.

6. Think about your favorite leader under whom you have worked personally. How would you rate that person's ability to lead teams? Do you trust that person? Why? Do you feel respected by that person? Why? Describe with concrete examples.

7. How does a person's dedication to specific personal and organizational values relate to their effectiveness as a team leader?

8. In one sentence, how do trust and respect relate to the effective use of resources within in an organization?

9. What are two or three specific things that you could do to improve your effectiveness as a team leader?

## Addendum to SAMI

One can substitute "Assertive" for "Forceful" and "Supportive" for "Enabling" (See following chart*)

Forceful and Enabling Leadership: You Can Do Both

A report from the Center for Creative Leadership by Kaplan shows business leaders too often believe that being forceful and being enabling are mutually exclusive. While distinctly different behaviors can characterize these two styles, they are both complementary and necessary to effective leadership. Kaplan emphasizes the importance of versatility in response to the demands of the job. The table that follows points out that the controversy over which style is "better" is based on a polarized view of extreme behaviors (the left and right-hand columns, "too forceful" or "too enabling"). The most effective executives are those who have the versatility to use both forceful and enabling leadership behaviors, when appropriate (the two middle columns).

| **Too Forceful** | **Forceful (Support*)** | **Enabling (Assert*)** | **Too Enabling** |
|---|---|---|---|
| Takes over, doesn't give people enough rope. | Leads personally. Is personally involved in solving the unit's problems. | Enables subordinates to lead. Is able to let go and give individuals latitude to do their jobs. | Empowers to a fault. Gives people too much rope. |
| Other people don't speak out, aren't heard. | Lets people know clearly and with feeling where he or she stands on issues. Declares self. | Interested in where other people stand on issues. Is receptive to their ideas. | People don't know where he or she stands. |
| Insensitive, callous. | Makes tough calls -- including those that have an adverse effect on people. | Compassionate, responsive to people's needs and feelings. | Overly accommodating. Is nice to people at the expense of the work. |

| **Too Forceful** | **Forceful (Support*)** | **Enabling (Assert*)** | **Too Enabling** |
|---|---|---|---|
| Harshly judgmental. Dismisses the contributions of others. Is an "unloving critic." | Makes judgments. Zeros in on what is substandard or is not working -- in an individual's or unit's performance. | Shows appreciation. Makes other people feel good about their contributions. Helps people feel valued. | Gives false praise or praises indiscriminately. Is an "uncritical lover." |
| Parochial, a partisan, rivalrous. | Competitive. Is highly motivated to excel and have the unit excel. | A team player. Helps other units or the larger organization perform well. | Sacrifices sharp focus on own unit. |
| Pushes too hard. Demands the impossible. Risks burnout. | Intense can-do attitude. Expects everyone to do whatever it takes to get the job done. | Realistic about limits on people's capacity to perform or produce. | Too understanding. Doesn't expect enough. |
| Arrogant. Fills own space and some of yours, too. | Confident. Gives people the feeling of belief in own self and abilities. | Modest, aware of not knowing everything, can be wrong. | Self-effacing or down on self. Doesn't fill own space. |
| Sticks rigidly to a course of action, despite strong evidence it is not working. | Persistent. Stays the course -- even in the face of adversity. | Flexible, willing to change course if the plan doesn't seem to be working. | Inconsistent, changeable; too quick to change course. |
| Forces issues when finesse would work better. | Raises tough issues. Acts as a "forcing function." | Fosters harmony, contains conflict, and able to defuse tension. | Avoids or smoothes over tense issues that need attention. |

*"PRODUCTIVITY" IMAGE: ANCIENT TEXTILE (JAPAN)*

# #5.
# THE PRINCIPLE OF REPONSIBILITY: POSSESSING PRODUCTIVITY and USING SURRENDER ("Letting Go")

## Leader/Manager-as-Coach in Action

"Sink or swim" management seems more commonplace today. Knowledge workers move from project to project unchecked by a manager, and are often working remotely. And as usual, the dreaded annual performance appraisal does not suffice... often perceived as a waste of time, resources and energy.

Ineffective performance by workers can be attributed to two management failures:

1. Lack of direction
2. Lack of feedback

People won't know what they are supposed to do, how to do it or why they are supposed to do it without direction. People simply lose hope and become stalled and subsequently lose motivation without the second, namely, proper feedback. The remedy is implementing a dependable and consistent commitment to leader/manager-coaching in the workplace.

For satisfaction, growth, and development, employees need to get feedback on what they have done particularly well, what opportunities they have for improvement and what they are doing just right. That does not happen with standard appraisals. Leader/Manager-as-Coach overcomes most of the objections to the traditional performance appraisal process. With the use of ongoing feedback, workers know where they stand and are more open and honest in appraising themselves within the on-the-job coaching relationship.

**The Leader/Manager-as-Coach Process versus Appraisals**

Leader/Manager-as-Coach is a positive process of enhancing strengths to be used productively. While far broader in concept and application than appraisals, Leader/Manager-as-Coach includes feedback and evaluation as a natural imbedded part of the process. Leader/Manager-as-Coach is defined as an ongoing, primarily face-to-face process that influences behavior by which the superior and apprentice collaborate to assist in achieving: increased job knowledge; improved skills in carrying out job responsibilities; higher level of job satisfaction; a stronger, more positive working relationship; and opportunities for personal and professional growth.

Leader/Manager-as-Coach can be contrasted with training and counseling as a process for influencing human behavior. Training emphasizes the development of knowledge and skills.

Counseling focuses on personality and psychological factors of performance. The on-the-job leader/manager-coaching process lies between these two poles and has some characteristics of each.

As a collaborative process that emphasizes the apprentice's strengths, Leader/Manager-as-Coach tends to overcome most of the objections of the performance appraisal process. Because of ongoing feedback, workers know where they stand with their superiors and are generally more receptive to interactions of a developmental nature. Furthermore, since a Leader/Manager-as-Coach is not necessarily linked directly with rewards, workers tend to be more open and honest in self-appraisal and superiors tend to be more comfortable in exploring performance factors.

**Leader/Manager-as-Coach Principles**

The success of the Leader/Manager-as-Coach process depends mostly on the attitude, knowledge, skill, and understanding of the leader/manager-coach. If the process is explored with the genuine spirit of enabling strengths to be used most productively and to contribute to the quality of working life, both the leader/manager-coach and the subordinate (as apprentice) will participate with enthusiasm.

The central principles of being a Leader/Manager-Coach are:

1. Leader/Manager-as-Coach emphasizes the job, not the person. It stresses development of knowledge and skills, not the success or failure of the employee as a person. While managerial awareness of employee personality characteristics and values is helpful, the emphasis is on improving job performance—not changing the employee's personality.

2. Leader/Manager-as-Coach implies respect for the dignity and worth of the individual, for the right to be an individual, and for the right to personal privacy.

3. Leader/Manager-as-Coach starts with the employee's current level of performance as a baseline.

4. Leader/Manager-as-Coach identifies realistic incentives that have personal meaning for the employee and identifies outcomes and competencies valued by the employee. Linking these outcomes with competencies, strengths, staffing and work assignments results in powerful individual motivators to perform at an optimum level.

5. Effective Leader/Manager-Coaching leaves both the leader/manager and follower with greater knowledge and more understanding of the worker's job—in addition to improving the leader/manager-follower relationship.

6. As an ongoing, participative process, Leader/Manager-as-Coach assures that the leader/manager and the follower agree on performance goals, on how performance is to be measured, and on appraising performance against those goals. Thus, Leader/Manager-as-Coach focuses on collaborative measures to attain objectives and results.

7. Leader/Manager-as-Coach effectiveness at the upper and middle management level necessarily starts at the top of the organization, with the president or chief executive officer. Not only does this enable top executives to function effectively, their commitment to the process communicates an important message to the entire workforce.

**When to be a Leader/Manager Coach**

Virtually every contact with the employee provides an opportunity for Leader/Manager-Coaching. The foundation of Leader/Manager-as-Coach, however, is clarity, when the employee is new to the position and as the employee develops or the job changes. Leader/Manager-as-Coach opportunities exist anytime someone wants to (a) discover strengths, (b) align responsibility, (c) renew resources and (d) energize actions. A helpful acronym for this is "DARE," which stands for Discover, Align, Renew and Energize. Leader/Manager-Coaching can be used at every stage in the cycle.

In addition to these many one-to-one leader/manager-coaching opportunities between leader/manager and the individual follower, teamworking sessions also provide excellent time saving Leader/Manager-as-Coach occasions, especially in dealing with team interaction issues such as conflict or change. Group experiences and teamwork perspectives provide valuable opportunity for the Leader/Manager-as-Coach process.

A few Group-oriented Leader/Manager-as-Coach examples include:

- Education: Participatory Learning as part of a small group ("Active Learning") with a group of cohorts or workplace team members.
- Exploring: I recommend NGT* Events. Practical, Philosophical and/or strategic exploration of a subject. *Re-read about NGT versus Brainstorming.
- Establishing expectations, defining and refining outcomes.
- Affirming competencies and standards for achieving excellence.
- Defining goals, tasks and objectives.
- Periodic progress reports on assignments (Use SAMI recommendations from Chapter Four (4).

- Discussing successful and unsuccessful projects
- Oversight of activities within the actual situation

By focusing on the problem as an opportunity for improvement, maintaining a climate of acceptance and dignity, and identifying the issue as a mutual one, the probability of positive outcomes and improved performance are confidently improved.

I might add here, to stay focused on the "solution" versus on the "problem" is a preferred approach (Note: As a reminder, see "Solution Focus Coaching" within the Leadership Spirit pages).

**Leader/Manager-as-Coach Guidelines**

To coach effectively, the manager must be skilled in a number of techniques:

*Observation*

Since most communication is transmitted by tone of voice, inflection, body language, and other non-verbal methods, observation of these methods is a powerful source of information to increase your understanding. Observation of the employee's interactions with co- workers and job performance factors is also an important information source.

*Analysis*

Analysis in Leader/Manager-as-Coach is the process of determining what responsibilities a particular job requires and what degree of authority must go with the job if it is to be done well. In the Leader/Manager-as-Coach process, the analysis is done in collaboration with the employee. An important part of this process is to explore the employee's values, wants, and needs: Integrating these elements into the job and work assignments whenever possible powerfully motivates performance.

*Benefit of the Doubt*

Being tenaciously deliberate with an attitude of humility is that portion of the Leader/Manager-as-Coach process where the manager and follower wrestle with a problem they have discovered. By focusing on this "intake" situation as an opportunity for improvement, maintaining a climate of acceptance and dignity, and identifying the issue as a mutual one, the probability of a positive outcome is enhanced. Remember to use a Solution-Focused Coaching approach.

*Channeling*

Channeling is a means of guiding the Leader/Manager-as-Coach interview to assure that it focuses on a positive, supportive atmosphere, an open exchange of ideas and mutual decision making, and development of action plans that will contribute to individual and organizational development. Active listening skills, such as paraphrasing, summarizing, perception checking, and asking purposeful questions are instrumental. Also essential are assertive "sending" skills such as saying what you want, telling, communicating ideas and intentions, describing behavior, and describing feelings. In an atmosphere of trust and respect, significant progress can be made in developing an individual through an open exchange of thoughts and feelings. This is a first cousin to the art of improvisation: the artful deliberate and consistent use of "Yes and" as an open and always-accepting green light. This is the backbone to the DARE: Discovery, Alignment, Renewal and Energizing processes of Leader/Manager-as-Coach.

*Delegating*

A fundamental aspect of every manager's job is the ability to delegate. Delegation encourages initiative, satisfaction, and personal and professional growth and enables workers to focus on high-priority issues. As such, this tool is an important part of the Leader/Manager-as-Coach process. Effective delegation requires that the manager:

Note: The following can be used a handy checklist:

1. Explain what has to be done and why the job is important
2. Delegate in terms of results. Let the follower determine the means for achieving them where possible
3. Give the worker the entire problem, not just a series of tasks
4. Encourage the worker to think through the entire problem or issue, or come up with possible solutions (using Solutions-Focused Thinking).
5. Assign appropriate authority level: act on own / act and report / consult then act or / wait to be told
6. Agree on a deadline
7. Ask for feedback and check out understanding
8. Provide for follow-up and controls
9. Resist the temptation to get involved in the delegated assignment. And then, Let go! Really let go… I call it "Surrender." Surrender is the main No-nonsense Discipline to the No-nonsense Principle of "Responsibility." This is what saves you as a true Leader/Manager-Coach. Your colleagues and workers must all know that you are a true "hands-off Leader/Manager." So keep your nose out and TRUST. Remember the old saying, "You can teach a man to fish."

*Giving feedback*

One factor that both motivates workers and contributes to their satisfaction is knowledge of results—feedback. For personal and professional developmental reasons, people need to know where they stand, what they are doing well, and what opportunities they have for improvement.

In the Leader/Manager-as-Coach process, a person is encouraged to think through his or her own performance and develop suggested action plans for consideration. Prior to the formal Leader/Manager-as-Coach meeting, the individual completes a self-evaluation and then presents it to the manager for review and feedback. This process reduces or eliminates many of the problems associated with traditional performance evaluations completed by "a manager for the employee" and encourages a more open Leader/Manager-as-Coach dialogue for growth and development purposes. While this process is usually applied to general performance factors, it can certainly be more focused on individual projects as well.

Management expert Peter Drucker encourages managers to ask: "What can I do to enable you to be more effective on the job?" Leader/Manager-as-Coach takes this a step further: A suggested format for the employee self evaluation is as follows. The employee completes the following sentences:

> *To be even more effective, I will do more (or start doing)... action plans.*
>
> *To be even more effective, I will do less of or stop doing... action plans.*
>
> *To be even more effective, I will continue doing... action plans.*

For each of the "do more of" or "do less of", a specific action plan is to be proposed - answering the question, "Who is going to do what by when?"

*Manager feedback*

After the apprentice has been given a best shot at self evaluation, the leader/manager has the opportunity to provide feedback regarding both the points of the evaluation and the action plans. After appropriate modifications are suggested, the leader/manager and follower work through differences and come to an agreement. The final product can then be placed in the worker's file and reviewed at the next formal Leader/Manager-as-Coach session.

*Feedback to manager*

Recognizing that a primary function of managing people is to enable them to be as successful as possible, it is critical that leader/managers be open to feedback from their followers regarding the working relationship, development process, and the job itself.

♦

Encouraging such feedback from the follower will provide ideas to improve leadership/management performance, create a climate for more effective performance, enhance interpersonal trust, and contribute to the quality of working life. The risks are minimal. Some leader/managers may fear getting negative feedback, but this passes shortly and is far, far better in the long run to work through these issues than to permit such feelings to go underground. In an open, caring environment of mutual exchange, both the employee and the manager win.

* * * * *

**Productivity: The Discipline of Surrender in Five Dimensions**

*Identity:*

**Surrender is anchored to the commanding part of our decision-making: Leader/manager-Coaches are productive and exemplars of when to let go of or "surrender" control (and of their own egos)...**

*Understanding:*

**Leader/manager-Coaches who have paid attention to their own development are able to shoulder huge responsibility without having to control everything. Right beneath the surface they are softhearted; when this is tempered with their typical self-confidence, they have loyal supporters and can truly move mountains.**

*Challenging:*

**Unfortunately, Leader/manager-Coaches can also have the reputation of being power mongers and tyrants because it is difficult for them to feel enough trust to acknowledge any vulnerability. Their driving force is excess. Often, they feel it is their responsibility to intervene in and direct situations—they pursue power and control (their behavior set) aggressively. They hold a value for justice—as self-defined! Leader/manager-Coaches can have a "bull-in-the-china-shop" approach because they tend to speak (and often act) in imperatives. The emperor mode of thinking is the curse of Leader/manager-Coaches. This must be managed from within, therefore the need for the Disciplines of Still Point, Steadfastness and Sharing. After all, we are all human.**

***Believing***

- "I've always been very responsible."

- "I have a hard time asking for help—I'll just charge ahead and do it myself."

- "I cannot think of a time when I was afraid."

- "I had to grow up fast as a kid."

***Performing***

Development options include developing their ability to put themselves in others' shoes, collaborative negotiation and active listening skills, and respecting and mentoring others. Their key development need is innocence, approaching life with more of a child-like response to the current situation and to approach a situation without cynical judgments or jaded expectations.

***Leader/manager-Coaches*** need to be decisive and willing to sweat.

About Leader/manager-Coaches and Decision-Making:

Leader/manager-Coaches don't "noodle," they "do." Everybody else has the luxury of "analysis" and Monday-morning quarterbacking. Leader/manager-Coaches can tend to become "Commanders" because they are often faced with a deluge of daily decisions – much of it minutiae: All of it requiring decisions and action.

Being a Commander is about moving the ball forward every day while dealing with a large amount of decisions with some of it being incredibly important.

Commanders accept that the decisions sound so basic to others when they are not the one having to make them.

"Commanding" never ends. That is why making quick decisions becomes critical and the chutzpah to accept that 70% (at best) of the decisions will be right.

Commanders who are "in-tune" acknowledge that some decisions will be bad and that they will have to recover from them.

Especially in business, Commanders do not get timeouts to pause and analyze all of the decisions.... They just do it. Again - Commanders don't "noodle" they "do."

But the goal is to become Leader/manager-Coaches. This often requires someone having to screw in a new brain. It's tough. Hugely tough. But the only way to change of that magnitude is through Practice, Practice, Practice.

About Commanders and Sweating It....

Commanders will get over their failed company, but never get over coming up with a great idea, getting initial traction and then watching someone else get all the glory and financial returns. Commanders are lot like entrepreneurs that way.

It may be unfair, but this is the reality of capitalism: It is the dynamic that drives innovation. In the future commanders won't only be in San Jose but also in Shanghai, Seoul and Bangalore. If you're not prepared to be "all in" then you're not prepared to compete and to cooperate, which are both essentials in today's marketplace

The Discipline of Surrender is big part of maintaining a life while managing your success. They go together, like hand in a glove, like compete and cooperate.

## A Harry Kraemer Inspired One Sheet: "Self-Reflection"

True leadership starts with self-leadership. Self-leadership requires genuine responsibility. Genuine responsibility is based, first and foremost, on taking responsibility for oneself. We cannot truly take responsibility for ourselves without self-awareness, and we only develop self-awareness through self-reflection. Thus, true leadership requires self-reflection.

Healthy Business Management Principles
Principle 5: Responsibility

| | | |
|---|---|---|
| 9 Reliability | 2 Autonomy | 3 Creativity |
| 8 Community | 1 Purpose | 4 Resources |
| 7 Sincerity | 6 Mastery | 5 Responsibility |

Here's a simple way to think about the connection between self-reflection and leadership: If you are not self-reflective, how can you truly know yourself? If you do not know yourself, how can you lead yourself? If you cannot lead yourself, how can you possibly lead others?

Self-reflection is the key to identifying what you stand for, what your values are, and what matters most. Through self-reflection, you are able to step back, filtering out noise and distractions. As your view becomes clearer, you can do a better job of prioritizing how and where to invest your time and energy.

Self-reflection allows you to gain clarity on issues, both personal and professional, because you have taken the time to think about them more deeply. The more self-reflective you are, the easier it is to make choices that are in line with your values, with awareness of the full impact of your decisions.

Self-reflection increases our ability to act with conviction, and it makes us better leaders. When we take time to reflect on what is important to us and why, we become more capable of transforming activity into productivity, through ourselves and others, for all the right reasons.

## Self-Reflection and Productivity

One benefit of self-reflection is overcoming the potential disconnect between mere activity and true productivity. Leading a team or organization effectively requires the ability to continuously evaluate what constitutes true productivity. Without this ability, we can end up finding that a great deal of activity has produced nothing of value.

Self-reflection allows us to:

- Identify what is truly important
- Bring concentration into focus
- Cut out distractions
- Eliminate feeling overwhelmed
- Prioritize effectively
- Have greater impact
- Know what really needs to be done

## Learning to Lead and Developing Your Leadership Style

Self-reflection improves our ability to evaluate the outcomes of our actions, which makes us better able to learn and to build expertise and influence. The more you practice self-reflection, the better you know yourself: your strengths, weaknesses, abilities, and areas to be developed. You know what you stand for and what is most important to you. You are able to connect and communicate with others more effectively. Your leadership becomes more authentic.

Although we can all learn a lot from the examples of others, your leadership must come from your core. You cannot determine the kind of leader you are without first figuring out who you are. Your leadership needs to be rooted in the real world, and it needs to be reflective of your views, your life experiences, and your professional path. Your authentic leadership style is not something that you can choose. You must discover it through self-reflection and develop it by expressing it with self-awareness in your work and your relationships.

Explicit vs. Implicit Decision Making

Self-reflection enhances leadership by helping you become more aware of the decisions you make, as well as the likely outcomes and implications of them. We can refer to this as making decisions explicitly rather than implicitly. With an explicit decision, you understand that you are not making one decision by itself in a vacuum. An explicit decision takes into account all of the factors that are affected by or that have an influence on the decision. There are causes, contributing factors, previous decisions, and direct and indirect outcomes to consider. By being explicit in making decisions, the process becomes transparent. In contrast, implicit decision making takes only a narrow focus without much regard for the big picture—an approach that can lead to surprises, often unpleasant ones.

Making an explicit decision requires you to be self-reflective, ensuring that you stay consistent with who you are, your goals, your values, and your priorities. Therefore, the likelihood of being dealt an unexpected disappointment is far less when you are introspective. Your decision can even be a bit "out of the box" and still have a high probability of producing the expected results, as long as you spend some time in reflection and discernment.

Three things to remember:

- Self-reflection leads to better decisions and higher productivity.
- Self-reflection makes us more dynamic and inspiring leaders.
- To develop self-awareness, we must take time to reflect on important questions on a regular basis.

Self-reflection allows us to be more conscious and more deliberate in our making decisions. It causes us to take in a wider range of perspectives and concerns, while identifying and accounting for any expectations or biases that we might harbor. This helps us to build engagement, because other people sense that we are taking their ideas into account.

Self-reflection helps us to make choices that are aligned with our highest values and goals because we know what is truly important to us. It supports creativity by allowing us to make innovative or unconventional choices that are, at the same time, well thought out. It also helps us to manage risk by identifying and considering potential negative consequences.

The Practice of Self-Reflection

In order to achieve meaningful results, we must practice self-reflection on a regular basis. We cannot wait until a major crisis erupts and then immediately develop self-awareness with sudden, intense reflection. Although a crisis might awaken a hunger for greater self-awareness, we cannot develop deep self-awareness in an emergency as though we are "cramming" for a test.

The key to practicing self-reflection is to find time when you can be silent and really focus on what matters most. Some people are able to do this when they are jogging or walking, others while they are commuting by train or car. For some, it is when they pray or meditate. To practice, focus on the inner voice rather than the outside noise, and reflect on important questions, such as the following.

Questions for Self-Reflection

- What did I say I was going to do today, and what did I actually do?
- If what I did was different than what I planned, what were the reasons?
- What went well, and what did not?
- How did I treat people?
- Am I proud of the way I lived this day?
- If I had the day to live over again, what would I do differently?
- What did I learn today that will have an impact on how I live the next day and going forward?

Ask yourself these and other questions that are most relevant to you. You may want to record your reflections in a journal. Note that all of the above questions relate strongly to you taking responsibility for yourself. Remember: You cannot lead well when your core values are in conflict.

One more thought: Although personal assessment is primary mechanism of self-reflection, you cannot always perform self-reflection without the input of others. In addition to reflecting on your own thoughts, reflect on things that other people say to you and the ways that they respond to you. Even when other people are mistaken, their words and actions can sometimes provide us with important insights about ourselves.

**Adapted from the book "From Values to Action," © 2011 Jossey-Bass with permission from the author, Harry M. Jansen Kraemer Jr.** Note: This brief summary is geared towards providing information in regards to the topic and issue covered. This book is provided with the understanding that this book is commentary, educational summary, comparison, and analysis on some of the original books main ideas and concepts.

Questions for Discussion for Working Better Together (WBT)

1. In your own words, how does self-reflection relate to (a) responsibility and (b) leadership effectiveness?

2. How does your level of self-awareness relate to key performance indicators (KPIs) and financial performance in your organization? Answer in one or two paragraphs.

3. On a scale of one to ten, rate your organization's leaders on (a) the level of integrity they demonstrate, (b) their openness to different perspectives, (c) their ability to inspire enthusiastic followership, and (d) their ability to stay focused on the right things. Rate for different levels of leadership if necessary. Based on your ratings, how much self-awareness do you think the leaders possess?

4. On a scale of one to ten, how would you rate your own level of self-awareness? How does your behavior support your answer?

5. Have you ever been in a situation where you were tempted or urged to violate your core values? What happened, and what did you learn?

6. Have you ever worked for someone that clearly lacked self-awareness? Why do you think so, and how effective were they as a leader?

7. Think about your favorite leader under whom you have worked personally. How would you rate that person's level of self-awareness and why?

8. Ask yourself and answer the Questions for Self-Reflection listed above on this page.

9. In closing these questions for this "one sheet" reading on the No-nonsense Discipline of Productivity and Surrender, ask yourself this: "If I were to establish or improve my own practice of self-reflection, what, specifically, would that involve for me?" I suggest you wait a while and contemplate before answering. Or even better yet, perhaps find someone you trust and have a conversation about this, before answering it in writing.

*"JUDGMENT" IMAGE: CATHEDRAL WINDOW (FRANCE)*

# #6.
# THE PRINCIPLE OF MASTERY: and STEP STONES

Introduction / Overview: "Am I building and demonstrating mastery in my work? Do my colleagues and co-workers value mastery? Does this environment support and encourage the development of mastery?"

## Mastery and The Issue of Change

Ideally we want to gain Mastery over Change. Let me explain. The process of mastering any skill is a long and tedious journey. It involves many hours and a whole lot of trial and error. You may have heard of the 10,000 hour rule, popularized by Malcolm Gladwell, which has more recently been largely debunked. The biggest flaw is that it focuses on the amount of time spent practicing, and not the quality of that practice – and not all practice is equally helpful. The number of hours is arbitrary, and what really matters is what I call "focused practice." It's hard to gain Mastery if you cannot deal with change. You will never escape change. Moreover, what is often neglected in the 10,000 hour rule is the role of psychology. Humans are not machines and do not follow a linear path to mastering a skill, but rather go through various stages of change in understanding, based upon many variables. Therefore to affect or gain Mastery, us humans must first consider having to deal with the issue of change. Change is inevitable. Change is the only constant. Outside forces provoke change, more often than not. Specifically, increased competition increases the rate of innovation, and continually "ups the ante" in the world of work. How can a company, a manager, a worker, or a work group gain Mastery in a sea of change? Consequently, the general rule today is, "If you're standing still, you're falling behind." The changes occur in:

- Personal requirements
- Technologies
- Rationale
- Products & Services
- Organizational structure

**The Problem with Change**

Every human being has a finite tolerance for change. A small fraction of the human race actively seeks change, and is quickly bored with any kind of status quo. An equally small fraction is instantly terrified by even the threat of change. The majority is somewhere in the middle, looking on the one hand for a measure of stability and predictability, and on the other hand looking for a controlled amount of variety.

All of us, however, have a tendency to cling to at least some parts of our status quo. This occurs because all of us have feelings of ownership about things familiar to us. For instance, we tend to get used to:

- Our physical environment, as if it were our "home"
- Familiar equipment, supplies, devices, as if we owned them
- Accustomed physical actions and routines, to the point where they are almost a part of us
- Familiar ideas and opinions, again feeling we "own" them
- The people we work with and our relations with them, as if they too "belong" to us

The central problem with any change is that all change takes away something we are "used to," which is the same as taking away something we "own." That phenomenon is central to understanding the dynamics of change, resistance to change, and the leadership of change.

- A real or perceived loss, which is not accompanied by any apparent gain, will instantly produce *active resistance.* If your salary is cut, but the workload remains the same, you'll fight the change.

- A real or perceived loss, which is simultaneously accompanied by an apparent gain, will produce *conflict.* On the one hand, there is the pain of the loss; on the other, the enjoyment of the gain. *Most organizational change creates this kind of gain-loss conflict.*

**How People React to Change**

First, nearly all people eventually adjust to change. This occurs because the initial loss loses its sting. What was new becomes old, familiar, and thus "owned." However, during the period of change, people are likely to display defensive behavior, such as:

- Denial: pretending the change won't really happen, or denying there is any reason to change
- Withdrawal: various ways of trying to escape the change, such as absenteeism, tardiness, quitting, daydreaming or over-concentration on mundane tasks or sheer busyness to shut out the change
- Selective perception: finding all the good things about the old, only the bad in the new (selective memory is very similar)
- Banding together: resisting the changes collectively to achieve greater strength, often accompanied by pressure on individuals who do not "go along"
- Aggression: displaying anger and hostility toward those persons or agencies who seem to be provoking the change, hoping somehow to "scare them away"
- Surrender: individual or collective "giving up," usually accompanied by loss of self-esteem, passively following orders, doing only enough to "get by"

Remember, these are not the perverse reactions of unqualified people. They are quite normal, human reactions of anyone to a loss – and to repeat, all change involves some degree of loss.

**Tips for Managing Change**

To function with Mastery as effective agents of change, managers need to learn three sets of techniques.

*Preparing People for Change*

Several methods are employed by skilled managers to create a more receptive environment for change, and reduce the built-in psychological (and organizational) tendencies to resist change. These include:

- Get across, constantly, that there will never be a return to the status quo; more, that no status quo is likely to last very long. Everyone needs to learn to "ride loose in the saddle." This message, old as it may be, needs to be repeated over and over again. The most effective approach is to encourage everyone to question every product, process, or technique, searching for new and better ways. When innovation becomes a way of life, rather than an idle slogan, much of the resistance to change melts away. Those who create their own change are much less likely to feel something has been stolen from them.

- Keep everyone in the organization abreast of what is going on in their profession, industry, company, marketplace, and the world if necessary. This kind of "knowledge management" helps employees see for themselves what changes are likely to occur. Consequently, they are less likely to feel blindsided when it does occur. Don't depend on the media to do this for you, and do not assume your employees are keeping up. Force-feed the information if necessary.

- Take advantage of the informal influencers in your organization. This may take a bit of investigation, but all organizations contain individuals who are broadly networked – others who are strong opinion leaders, regardless of their title – others who are privy to lots of information, which has not been shared with higher management. These people usually know one another – and they talk. Furthermore, they have profound organizational influence. They are the "believable ones," and it pays to make sure that they are well informed.

*Replace Victimization with Empowerment*

Any significant change carries with it the risk that some or many people will feel like victims. Those who have been victimized more than once soon become bitter and cynical "prisoners of the system." Whether it is replacement of a product line, a new acquisition, a brand new technology, or a reengineering initiative, the leaders are put to the test.

- The first step is to communicate clearly, firmly, and without reservations what the changes are and why they are occurring. Your people must know, in no uncertain terms, that the changes are going to occur – whether or not they approve. Equivocation at this point only breeds confusion and conflict.

- As much as possible, do this communicating face-to-face, using managers and supervisors. Remember, because of the loss factor, there is no such thing as unadulterated good news. All change carries some bad news – and you do not communicate bad news on video, through a newsletter, or from the mouth of an outside consultant. The best approach, even though it takes some time, is to make change announcements in small groups, so that people can dialogue, not just listen.

- It is at this point that the most critical step needs to occur: now that the people know what is happening and why, immediately involve them in addressing what they can do, need to do, or might do at their own level to implement the change. And do not be too quick to conclude there is nothing employees can do. Let us say the change is a merger with a formerly competitive firm: a large change, indeed, fraught with both opportunities and threats. Could ordinary line employees make such a merger work better? Of course they could, if they're asked. Employees from each firm can familiarize one another with their respective cultures, processes, technologies, and problems. (In fact, they are more likely to do this openly and honestly than the bosses.) Employee teams from both firms can work out new and better processes in manufacturing, customer service, distribution, quality assurance, and other operations. Bear in mind, there is always a body of tacit knowledge resident in any organization. A major change provides rich opportunities to tap into that knowledge.

- All of this is a form of true empowerment. When meaningful responsibility and authority is given in order to implement a change, everyone gains a strong sense of ownership for making the change succeed, and this is the key to avoiding the "victim" syndrome. Management's job, as stated, is to make sure that the "what" and the "why" are clear: as much as possible, it should be employees who work out "the how."

*Avoiding Common Pitfalls*

Change is difficult enough without aggravations such as:

- Springing surprises on your people. Very few situations are so urgent or unexpected that no advance warning can be given. There is no justification whatsoever for deliberately blindsiding your people. Be mindful and actively aware also that changes which do not have direct impact on line employees – such as suddenly reshuffling the ranks of senior management – can nevertheless scare them, create endless rumors, and generally depress morale.

- Confidently announcing one direction, only to follow it with countermarching orders, then changing course still another time. Particularly if each new initiative is accompanied by grandiose claims ("This is not a program; it is a way of life.") you are inviting the Dilbert Syndrome. After awhile, employees learn to ignore every new pronouncement.

- Over-enthusiastic "selling" of changes, exaggerating the benefits and downplaying or simply ignoring the negatives. Salesmanship has its place, but straightforward communication of the why and how from credible sources, including the hard parts, is the only way to convince seasoned employees to accept and work with the changes.

- Ruthlessly jamming change down employees' throats. It is perhaps obvious that most people do not like being forced to acquiesce, or being threatened. However, the mistake here is somewhat subtler. Most leaders are smart enough not to use the "my way or the highway" approach any more. However, when people are taken by surprise – or aren't provided with enough factual information – or aren't asked for their ideas or opinions – they are likely to feel coerced, in spite of your polite tone of voice. At the least, they will start feeling manipulated, become suspicious, and start displaying the defensive behavior described earlier.

There is one more caution. In spite of all we hear about the virtues of rapid-fire change, and ever-more innovation, remember that we are only human.

- Change can involve loss, not just growth and progress.
- Managers need to honor and respect the grief associated with change.
- Managers must listen to their people, acknowledge the difficulties and help them deal with the associated challenges.

Before marching down the next road, give workers a chance to remember the road that got them where they are.

To succeed with a change initiative, it is best to be proactive and enlist "the defenders of status quo" to raise your awareness of the important issues that you may not properly address. As a cautionary summary, know ahead of time that a "sell-it-again" approach to effecting change does not work: Convincing or persuading people will never win over opposition once they have already dug in their heels.

When acceptance to change stumbles, however, two things will work:

- Identify the proposed threat and work to take the threat away.
- Identify what is important to maintain and work to maintain it.

Then enlist the defenders of the status quo… They have the courage and strength to present a challenge, so you want them on your side; and what is NOT necessary is for you to <u>fight</u> for what you believe in order to make "it" happen, whatever "it" happens to be. Do not dig in your own heels.

View the problem from their side. Even argue for their arguments. Only then will you learn their view of the problem. A helpful approach is getting "into their box."

This "reframing" is an approach that enlists these 5 Cs:

**Clarify**... probe for full understanding: "Tell me more. I'm not clear..."

**Confirm**... check out unconfirmed assumptions: "Let us be sure we understand—you are saying that..."

**Credits**... focus on what you like about the ideas: "These make perfect sense..."

**Creative...** Restate your concern as a potential positive outcome: "We can assure that these five requirements (or requests) will be done..."

**Communicate**... First, people resist change when they are worried (have fear) about their credibility, their job security, their sense of autonomy, or their level of competence. Second, people also resist change when they sense a lack of congruence between the proposed change and core organizational values. These are fierce enough foes, but to then not communicate the difference between them is what really drives the opposition's resistance into stalemate. The first and the second are really one in the same – they are both the presence of a threat. When the first and the second are then not differentiated, the details and the differences dangerously blur and must therefore be clearly articulated. People take change personally, even when the change being either proposed or initiated is not really personal at all. Make sure the information is comprehensible, that the change is actually believed and expected to be manageable, and that there is an obvious sense of purpose that can be welcomed.

*Clarify*, *confirm*, *credit*, and *creative* are worthless if not communicated. When 40 percent of managing is about the people you hire and another 40 percent of managing is what you communicate with them, then the other twenty percent has little to do with making change happen with success. Communicate the "story" of change –what you tell is what settles the fears that drive the resistance to change.

* * * * *

**Judgment: The Discipline of Step Stones in Five Dimensions**

***Identity*: Step Stones is anchored to the *reformer* part of our decision-making: Reformers are perfectionists - and the process of change is rarely perfect...**

***Understanding:***

A self-observing Reformer can be wise, tolerant, balanced, and focused on standards of excellence in ways that provide an exemplary vision for others. They are often the purveyors of quality in an organization.

***Challenging*:**

When less well developed, reformers can take their perfectionism too far. Perfection carried too far can become unhealthy business management at its worst.

When a manager carries an internal judging voice that chastises themselves and others for falling short of perfection, they can be viewed (by most people) as "preaching" for higher attainment by others who are more healthy individuals. One critical challenge is that many reformers use a non-discriminating shotgun approach. Another critical challenge is that reformers are also often driven to frustration and then anger, which is typically over-controlled until it erupts as resentment when someone has failed to live up to their expectations. Moral tirades that show a "running amok" side can even occasionally allow them to temporarily escape their own high standards. Gaining Mastery is a tough task master on the emotions, especially when the reformer has to deal with changes happening that are mostly beyond their control.

***Believing:***

"I know I'm right, why should I have to compromise?"

"I'm my own worst critic."

"My whole career, I've been brought in to fix things."

"My message as a kid was always, “You can do better.'"

***Performing:***

Development options include the practice of being curious and unattached, while reducing their internal critical voice; learning emotionally intelligent techniques for channeling anger more effectively; learning to respond to criticism non-defensively, and moving away from black-and white thinking with positive reframing, and moving away from black-and-white thinking with positive reframing, acceptance qnd creative problem-solving. Accepting change is the big one, maybe the biggest. Giving the “benefit of the doubt” is a difficult but an important, healing practice to learn. Their key development need is achieving Still Point’s place of serenity, and thereby gaining the ability to respond where personal intervention is required and to acquiesce when letting go is appropriate.

Having a detail orientation and being hands-on has two cutting edges. At certain points, such as in an early stage business start-up you need to be on top of all your details. You need to know your financial model. You need to be involved in the product design. You need to have a detailed grasp of the sales pipeline and marketing needs. You need to be hands on.

In fact one of the easiest ways to rule out people who are pitching an idea that they say they believe in is when you find they do not know the details of their job, their work group or their business needs. These are easy telltale signs

But this "having to know" also has a downside... the unwillingness to trust others and to let go. Nobody is super human. We are all at our core normal people with strengths and weaknesses, and idiosyncrasies. We all have those too. This reality is why reformers (perfectionists) need to develop a Sense of Humor, what I call "a Sense of Humanity."

The reality is that nobody can be super human on all fronts when it comes to being balanced and wholehearted. As humans in a work community, we all know that change is upon us. We must learn to breathe that in and have it help make us more accepting, even welcoming to the idea of change. That's when Mastery can really take hold. With a new generation of business managers who seem to have an amazing vision for technology and product, who have the willingness and ability to be flexibly adaptive and who know how to take educated risks in a way that is astonishing, the temptation to lose "the sense of humanity" is clear.

Just as not everyone is perfect, not everyone is over-the-top inspirationally either. The healthy view is to understand, feel and act based upon this reality. Perfectionists cannot expect nor be looking for a 10 out of 10 solution on every front. To succeed in business today, people need to be extremely gifted on some fronts – but still remain humane. In tight-tolerance mechanical businesses, engineers, mechanics and no-fail processes, exactness is a must. With safety, exactness is certainly always a must. With numbers that are to be reported to The Board, exactness is a must. Double and even triple checking prior to presentations is a must. Being perfect and really, really tough on tasks, however, is much different than being tolerant and tender on people.

Mastering the Art of Change is the human side. And the Discipline of Step Stones is part of us all.

# A Harry Kraemer Inspired One Sheet: Leadership and Execution

Healthy Business Management Principles
Principle 6: Mastery

| | | |
|---|---|---|
| 9 Reliability | 2 Autonomy | 3 Creativity |
| 8 Community | 1 Purpose | 4 Resources |
| 7 Sincerity | 6 Mastery | 5 Responsibility |

Leaders can easily become disconnected because there is always so much going on. The temptation is to delegate, which in itself is a good thing, but not when it gets to the point that the leader has lost touch with what is happening day to day. As always, the idea of balance comes into play, this time between delegation and involvement. To put it another way, you should develop a great team to whom you can delegate, and you must still involve yourself enough to be aware of what is going on in case there is a necessary change in direction. Good leadership requires both. The better you delegate, the more you guard against micromanaging, which de-motivates your team. The more you stay involved, the more grounded you'll be in what is happening around you. In short, you must become a leader while continuing to be a manager.

**Leading Versus Managing**

Conventional wisdom makes a big distinction between being a leader and being a manager. Managing is all about getting things done, carrying out the orders from "those guys." When you finally get to be one of "those guys," you may think you are supposed to be strategic, visionary, and above all the day-to-day chores of managing. You may believe you are to focus on creating the changes that others have to manage. After all, becoming a leader is a real achievement. Although there are many people who make good managers, very few become strong leaders. The faulty thinking lies in the idea that for you to secure your leadership status, you can't still walk around acting like a manager. This is hardly the case.

The fact is that you will not be a good leader unless you are also a good manager. How can you possibly be effective as a leader if you don't have a track record of executing and implementing? If you are not willing and able to roll up your sleeves and make things happen, you are not going to be around for very long. You can call yourself by whatever title you want, but unless you can produce results, you are going to be an unemployed leader. No one is going to follow you—you are not winning. Your objective is both to elevate your ability to be a manager and to become a leader. The two are not mutually exclusive.

What Kind Of Leader Will You Be?

In the simplest of terms, the job of a leader is twofold. The first responsibility is to think about strategy—deciding where the organization needs to go and what it will take to motivate people to get there. The second is to make sure that the team executes and implements the strategy. Unless the organization "makes it happen," nothing is accomplished, no matter how lofty the goal.

Three things to remember:

- Good leadership involves striking the right balance between delegation and involvement.
- For sustained success, the four processes of strategy, people, operations and measurement must be performed well and in harmony.
- Develop your ability to act effectively with incomplete information.

Knowing the Right Questions to Ask

As you grow, you will shift from knowing the right answers to asking the right questions. A leader must be able to balance all the distractions and still make a decision, such as whether to stay the course or make a midcourse correction. Changing direction when it becomes necessary can only be accomplished if the leader stays close enough to what is going on in the company. Once the direction has been set, the leader cannot decide that now is the time to remove herself; she must remain engaged. Changes can hit the competitive landscape, the economy, or the business environment without much warning.

Determining whether to stay the course or make a change requires the leader to be self-reflective enough to pursue the important questions, balanced enough to see the issue from as many perspectives as possible, self-confident enough to change her or his mind and either alter the direction or accelerate the plan, and then have enough genuine humility to seek the input of every member of the team.

As a leader, you need to remain disciplined and focused enough to make sure that the following management processes are in place in order for implementation and execution to occur. These processes—strategic, people, operations, and measurement—

must work in tandem, instead of occurring in four disconnected phases.

The Strategic Process

The strategic process determines where you are today, where you want to go, and what you want to become. Living and vital, it identifies all the key issues, opportunities, and alternatives that are materializing, from technology to competitive intelligence. Effective strategic process is continuous and ongoing.

The People Process

Have the right people in place who are aligned with the values of the organization. Put together a high-performance team as you manage talent and develop future leaders, who are able to execute on the vision that you establish in the strategic process.

The Operations Process

This deals with what is happening right here, right now. Too often there is little or no connection to what is going to happen in the next twelve months to move the organization in the right direction. Manage both the short term and the long term. The company needs to outline the steps required to achieve the opportunities uncovered through the strategic process. Companies that fail to have an adequate operations process will not succeed.

The Measurement Process

Measurement is too often neglected. What gets measured gets done. Unless there is a measurement process, nothing will happen. Be strategic and discerning about what you measure and why. Strike the right balance between making sure you have the metrics versus being overburdened with reports. Reduce information overload. Focus primarily on exception reports (reports that identify meaningful problems) and eliminate the reports that nobody ever looks at.

Speed is of the essence in business, and you need to be able to make decisions based on accurate yet incomplete information. You also need to inject a sense of urgency into decisionmaking. Most of the time when you lose, it is not so much a result of making the wrong decision as it is waiting too long to make a decision.

Generally, execution and implementation go awry for a number of reasons that have more to do with the individual leader than with the organization or any outside influence. Simply put, execution gets lost because no one really owns the process.

**Adapted from the book From Values to Action © 2011 Jossey-Bass with permission from the author, Harry M. Jansen Kraemer Jr**. Note: This brief summary is geared towards providing information in regards to the topic and issue covered. This book is provided with the understanding that this book is commentary, educational summary, comparison, and analysis on some of the original books main ideas and concepts.

Questions for Discussion for Working Better Together (WBT)

1. Consider the four processes of strategy, people, operations, and measurement. In your organization, how does performance in each process affect key performance indicators (KPIs) and financial performance? Describe in specific terms.

2. On a scale of one to ten, how well does your organization perform each of the four processes? Rate for different levels of the organization as appropriate. For any deficiencies, what do you think is the root of the problem, and what would correcting the problem involve?

3. How quickly do you think your leaders respond strategically to changes in the broader business environment (changes in customer needs, competition, markets, technology, the economy, regulatory issues, etc.)? Provide specific examples.

4. How well does your organization implement its stated strategy? Describe any specific strengths, challenges or problems that you see.

5. In your organization, do problems linger? Do opportunities go unaddressed? If so, provide examples.

6. How well do the leaders of your organization balance leading with managing? Is there a greater tendency toward being disconnected or toward micro-managing? Discuss for different levels of the organization (or for individual leaders/managers) as appropriate.

7. Are there processes or initiatives in your organization that get "lost" because no one owns them enough? Explain.

8. Does your organization measure enough of the right things? Does it produce any unnecessary reports? Provide specific examples.

9. On a scale of one to ten, how well do you contribute to each of the four processes—strategy, people, operations and measurement?

10. How well do you balance leading with managing? Do you have a greater tendency to become disconnected or to micro-manage?

11. Do you prefer planning for the short term or the long term? If you have a bias, what risks does it bring, and how might you adjust?

12. How comfortable are you with acting on incomplete information? (Perhaps use self-reflection to observe yourself over a few days.)

13. Are you more likely to wait too long to act or to act before you have enough information? Provide examples of when you've done both.

14. What, specifically, can you do to improve your business group's performance in each process: strategy, people, operations, and measurement?

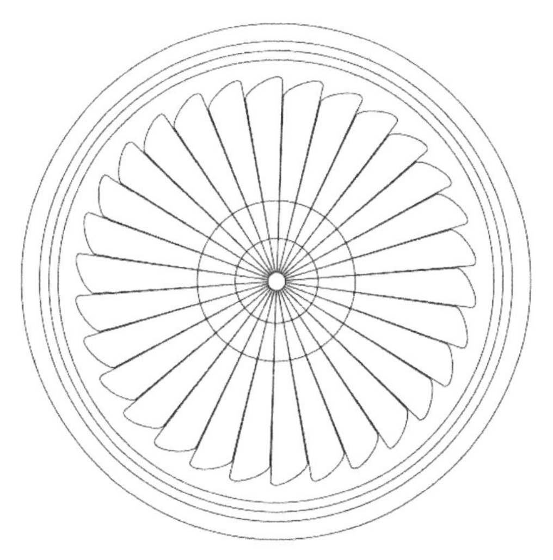

*"HUMILITY" IMAGE: FRIENDSHIP FEATHERS (NATIVE AMERICAN)*

# #7. THE PRINCIPLE OF SINCERITY: STEADFASTNESS DISCIPLINE

Humility is not thinking less of yourself, it's thinking of yourself less. *C.S. Lewis*

The No-nonsense Nine Question: "Do the people around me speak and act with sincerity? Do they really mean what they say and care about the way they affect other people?"

## Effective Group Processes

Within the whole Manager/Leader–as-Coach line up of duties, there is no other more critical than working well in Small Groups. As written elsewhere, small groups are the backbone of doing business. Let's begin with the most critical area: This chapter is a primer on group processes and mainly concerns problem-solving meetings. Many other kinds of meetings happen, but none are as important as those concerning problems and their solutions. Once the basic methods of handling problems as part of a group are well honed, all other forms of meetings will simply fall in place.

**The Need for Explicit Methods**

Mutual humility and sincerity are critical. Inexperienced groups often fail to solve problems, not because of lack of information, sloppy thinking, or conflicting motives, but simply because of conflicting methods. Some individuals are quick to reach for solutions while others are trying to fathom the cause of the problem; some think and speak quickly, others are more deliberate; some want to know the objectives, others want to know the background – and so on.

Unfortunately, the group is frequently unaware that different people are using different agendas, which leads to what is called "unconscious incompetence:" the group gets nowhere, or breaks up, or resorts to fighting.

The most practical solution to this phenomenon is to have and use an agreed upon series of processes.

**The Rule of Consensus**

This is the overarching rule for highly effective groups. It states that the group's mission is to reach enough agreement on courses of action that everyone – including and especially those with reservations – can support and implement those courses of action. This is in sharp contrast to certain other rules, such as –

- Autocracy – those with the most power rule
- Democracy – the rule of the majority
- Anarchy – the agreement to disagree forever

Adhering to the rule of consensus places a number of obligations on all participants. Regardless of personal style, motives, or power, everyone agrees at all times to do the following:

1. Be open – transparent – about what you believe, want, and stand for; i.e., no hidden agendas ever!
2. Speak and write clearly, completely, coherently; i.e., "make your case" effectively and with emphasis.
3. Adapt your communication sufficiently to avoid irritating or confusing those with sharply differing styles of communication.
4. Listen actively, with the intention of understanding others – especially those you do not understand – even more especially, those with whom you disagree, or who seem to have "strange" notions.
5. Draw out the uncommunicative or timid.
6. Do not be uncommunicative or timid.
7. Be grateful for the involvement and insights of others

**The Ground Rules**

Effective groups work out their own particular ground rules, so consider the following as a "starter set."

1. Reach consensus on what issues deserve attention.
2. Share knowledge first.
3. Reach consensus on what the real problem(s) is/are.
4. Share solutions. Create solutions if necessary.
5. If necessary, reach consensus on decision criteria.
6. Reach consensus on what actions to take.
7. Assume ownership for implementation.

Each of these is discussed below.

1. Reach consensus on what issues deserve attention.

This can be done in any of the following ways.

- Have everyone submit his or her preferences to the meeting leader prior to the meeting.
- Have everyone share their ideas with one another prior to the meeting, and then submit their preferences to the leader.
- Proceeding in round robin fashion, list everyone"s preferences at the beginning of the meeting.
- The idea is to make sure everyone has an opportunity to suggest issues and problems. (The exception is a crisis situation, where one or two people call an emergency meeting.)

When there are differences concerning what issues to address, use the familiar "S.U.G." system; i.e., weight each issue in terms of its:

- Seriousness; i.e., actual or potential impact
- Urgency; i.e., the degree to which something needs to be done now
- Growth probability; i.e., the degree to which the problem will become more serious and/or more urgent over time

Note: Over time, most groups get into the habit of creating and distributing meeting agendas well in advance. Whenever possible, this is an excellent idea.

2. Share knowledge first.

This means exactly what it says. Before and/or at the outset of the discussion, everyone is asked to share what he or she knows about the issue at hand. In complex situations, this may and often must take the form of written information. In that case, everyone is obliged to study that information.

Sharing knowledge does not mean sharing ideas, opinions, or analyses! It specifically precludes discussing potential courses of action. Doing so, especially if it is done by those with the most power, guarantees lack of group information.

At this stage, it is permissible and sometimes essential for some people to "pass." This simply means they do not have any information about the issue.

3. Reach consensus on what the real problem(s) is/are.

Sometimes this is obvious. In other cases, it is not obvious, and may be a bone of contention. If one individual thinks the whole problem is money, another thinks it is all about technology, and a third believes the whole issue is human, the group is obliged to decide just what it is about.

This is a more difficult consensus to reach... consequently the ground rules become significant. Specifically, each individual in the group should be given enough time to complete the following sentence:

"The question is what we should do in order to ______________________________."

And then each individual is asked – and required – to state why the person thinks this is the critical action-seeking question. Reminder: no debate during this process. Only courteous active listening to be sure every person is heard and every idea becomes properly aired.

Note: If there is not consensus on what the problem is, and consensus cannot be reached, do not continue the meeting. If necessary, ask everyone to reflect further and submit their ideas in writing, with copies to everyone, before the next meeting. If this is not done, you will conduct meeting after meeting, full of sound and fury, leading to absolutely nothing, except frustration.

4. Share solutions. Create solutions if necessary.

On occasion, you will find that the "real" problem can or should be solved by only one or two people, who possess the specialized know-how needed. When this occurs, of course, the meeting should be terminated so that these people can get to work. They neither need nor in most cases want further input from the other members.

However, a true group problem is one in which everyone's thinking is needed to arrive at the best courses of action. In that case:

- Proceed in round-robin fashion to gain everyone's thinking on possible solutions or courses of action, being sure to record each one.
- Do not debate the relative merit of any idea, but do interrogate one another to be sure each individual's thinking is out on the table. The idea is to understand, not necessarily agree.

If at the end of this process you are dissatisfied that you've found the right solutions, do any of the following:

- Establish an "idea quota" and a time frame, such as "10 more ideas in the next 5 minutes."
- Use inverse brainstorming; i.e., create ideas calculated to keep you from solving the problem, and then reverse them.
- Stop and reconvene after people have had some "think time."

Note: Be sure to capture all ideas in writing. (A flip chart and a laptop computer are handy devices in all problem-solving meetings.)

5. If necessary, reach consensus on decision criteria.

One of two things happens at the point where your group completes the task of creating solutions. Some course of action is obviously the way to go – or not!

At that point, one of two additional things happens. Discussion again yields a clear "winner," or not.

And if that happens, the group probably needs to "decide on how to decide." The method is familiar: stop debating the options, and instead strive to reach consensus on the criteria to be used in evaluating the options, and if necessary weight them.

This admittedly can be a laborious process. Nevertheless, if millions of dollars or human fate is at stake, it is usually worth the effort. Criteria such as time, cost, risk, effort, acceptability to customers, and so forth are well worth debating. Among other things, the debate itself reveals clearly, to everyone, what each individual really values.

The processes, of asking each person to state what s/he believes are the relevant criteria, and their relative weight, then trying for consensus, is identical to those involved in identifying key issues or creating potential solutions.

6. Reach consensus on what actions to take.

This, of course, is the process of deciding what to do. It is best handled by asking each individual – preferably starting with that person who has the least seniority, "clout," rank, or status, and ending with the person who has the most – to state which options s/he prefers, and why.

It is worth remembering that selecting an option is in effect a "bet": a wager that X solution has the highest probability of satisfying Y or Z criteria. Consequently, it is fair and reasonable to challenge people who pick options you do not believe in.

7. Assume ownership for implementation.

No problem-solving meeting should end without specific people who have been given specific responsibilities for implementing the chosen solutions. This is obvious advice, but often violated. The last question that should be answered is:

Who is going to do what, and by when?

## Applying Lubricant

Neither the processes explained above, nor any other, actually work unless there is a conscious and active determination to make them work. This requires sincerity. More than that, there needs to be conscious and active adaptation to the needs and styles of each person in the group, from beginning to end.

- The verbal people need to encourage the less-verbal people
- The less-verbal need to make themselves speak up
- The quick need to slow their pace
- The slow may need to accelerate
- The goal-oriented need to accommodate the people-oriented, and vice-versa
- The idea-oriented need to accommodate the analytics, and vice-versa
- The dominant need to control their dominance
- The receptive need to become more assertive

* * * * *

## Humility: The Discipline of Steadfastness in Five Dimensions

***Identity*:**

Steadfastness is anchored to the *peace seeking* part of our decision-making: Peace Seekers assimilate, influence and guide with self-effacing determination…

***Understanding*:**

Serene and centered, well-developed Peace Seekers bring cooperation to an organization; they are highly capable of dealing with others' problems and building consensus. They have a natural tendency to honor diversity, and can get along with almost anyone.

***Challenging*:**

Even though Peace Seekers tend to merge with the preferences of other people, they may tend to melt into the woodwork and to forget what their own preferences are or might become. Typical to a Peace Seeker is a dogged determination to ruffle no feathers, because their very nature requires of them to empathize with either sides (or even all three sides)… and in so doing end up disappearing. Taking a strong position is particularly difficult for them. Bright and ultimately patient, they see all sides of an issue and because they are essentially non-aggressive they can become indolent. Their tenaciousness has turned sour. Not because they are lazy (they are very hard workers) but because they are out of touch with their own wishes. Determinedly stubborn, their inbred tenacity flips them into a habit of being self-forgetting or even becoming self-effacing: Being tenacious toward consensus-building then flounders into proposing endless solutions to no avail. This is tenacity gone haywire. Though usually quiet, once these guardians of equanimity get started they tend toward epic tales because they hold so many alternative views.

***Believing:***

"I think it is important to always focus on what we need to do to serve others."

"Of all the people in the organization the President could have called, he called me."

"Was that helpful?"

"Both of my parents were alcoholics and I basically took care of them."

***Performing**:*

Development options include learning to focus, to speak up and to confront others and opposing issues. They must be ever alert to recognizing that their own passive-aggressive tendencies are tenacity turned into stalling. Swinging back to behaviors that are more assertive is key; such as putting “a stake in the ground” (anywhere almost), and setting priorities, then sticking to them without distraction. Indolent patience must be replaced by active tenaciousness for initiating change.

The key performance development need is not only taking action, but also learning how to take action. Left alone, a steadfast guardian can become frozen in place, lacking the basic ability to actualize himself or herself by engaging fully with others. The ongoing desire to live with avoidance of conflict is their Achilles’ heel.

Natural tenacity is probably the most important attribute for a manager-coach. This is the quality of the person who never gives up. This is the manager-coach who never accepts “no” for an answer. With a world filled with doubters who say that things cannot be done (and then pronounce after the fact that they “knew it all along”), tenacity is a must.

Digging one’s heels in is admirable… if it’s got a direction. But it is deadly if not aimed at something. If you are not naturally one of these high-end-tenacious people you probably know it already. But if you are one of these people, there is a chance that you do not know it already. So the key for you is listening to and trusting others. When they say that you are "driving them nuts" or to financial ruin by stubbornly refusing to budge; or when you have tenaciously reached the point of someone saying, "Okay you win because you have out-lasted me" - in truth you have lost. Instead, use your tenacity in a true and steadfast way… combined with openness of choice, not "closed-ness" to choice... Be self-managing and self-caring by avoiding "the tenacity fracas" when you see that competitive peer who always pushes things further than you normally would egging you on.

Making choices by "working through" your tenaciousness to the other side is really what separates the wheat from the chaff. Ask yourself this: When am I going to get further out of my comfort zone and be more than just stubbornly tenacious?

Know this about stubborn folks: The advice to "move on" to a person who is steadfastly tenacious will go unheard by that person. That is not only lousy advice but also a lousy way to give advice. Tenacious people need others to say, "let's move through this together." Since unhealthy tenacity itself is excluding, the habitual tenacity over-achievers need an invitation. Being steadfast is having tenacity with companions and a joint purpose attached to it as a guide.

Tenacity is not always pretty. People who have it cannot help it. It is in their DNA. The quality is admirable and a quality that is frankly sought for within top performing leader/manager-coaches. Where resiliency is about taking the punches life gives you every day and not falling down, tenacity is more about delivering the punches. The beauty, however, can be in just pushing hard enough and ever not crossing the line. This takes a certain amount of seasoned knowing and larger amount of willingness to listen attached to it. Mentors and learning groups are ideal for testing the tenaciousness edges. But the "just-right perfect formula" for determining the right amount of tenacity (or chutzpah) does not exist. The right amount of chutzpah is a bit like art – you know it when you see it. Until you do become more artful with your stubbornness, however, a good guideline to follow for tenaciousness is to be sure to combine it with a purpose within a community – this is the steadfast persistence that will pay off. Be stubborn for a reason and with people you trust.

Steadfastness pushes forward with heart every step of the way artistically, never accepting "no'" as a complete answer. Steadfastness awaits "yes" with love.

The Discipline of Steadfastness is part of us all.

## A Harry Kraemer Inspired One Sheet: "Genuine Humility"

Healthy Business Management Principles
Principle 7: Sincerity

| | | |
|---|---|---|
| 9 Reliability | 2 Autonomy | 3 Creativity |
| 8 Community | 1 Purpose | 4 Resources |
| 7 Sincerity | 6 Mastery | 5 Responsibility |

Genuine humility keeps leaders grounded. In fact, the word humility comes from the Latin word humus, meaning "ground, earth or soil." No matter how far you've risen, you should not forget where you started. Genuine humility helps you recognize that you are neither better nor worse than anyone else, that you ought to respect everyone equally and not treat anyone differently just because of a job title. When you embrace genuine humility, your leadership thrives: your team members are willing to work with you to accomplish the mission and will respect your decisions because they know you value their contributions, no matter their roles.

At the heart of genuine humility is never forgetting who you are, appreciating the value of each person in the organization, and treating everyone respectfully whether he or she is a senior manager or a summer intern. Genuine humility enables you to remain authentic, approachable, and open to others. Genuine humility won't hold you down and will enhance every dimension of your life. The more you practice genuine humility, the more your leadership will shine.

## False Humility

Brushing off compliments with an "aw shucks, it was nothing" attitude smacks of false humility because it is often a ploy to get people to heap on the praise even more. Genuine humility is born of self-knowledge. As a leader, you may find that suddenly some people lavishly praise everything you do: That was amazing. Nobody makes decisions like you do. You really know how to get stuff done. If it sounds as though they are buttering you up, they probably are. Even when compliments are well-intentioned, don't let people's praise carry you away. With genuine humility, you get to enjoy the journey as you rise through the ranks, while also making sure that you do not fall victim to an inflated ego that separates you from your team and colleagues or that makes you a target of the criticism of others.

People who have risen through the ranks on the merits of their abilities and what they have contributed to the organization are focused, first and foremost, on doing the best they can do in every job they have. Their emphasis is on doing the right thing and making a positive impact, not on plotting how to climb the proverbial ladder as quickly as possible.

Here are three humble career goals:

1. Make sure that you are always learning and have the opportunity to grow.

2. Add value to your team so that you are making a difference.

3. Make sure that you and everyone around you are having fun.

The natural paradox is that genuine humility can actually do more for your career than tooting your own horn, simply because this allows you to be authentic and become all you are capable of being—which will lead to your getting noticed.

## Raw Ambition

Raw ambition rubs people the wrong way. Plus this type of drive is usually unsustainable. When overly-ambitious people finally claw their way up to the top, they have too few allies to support them, and many more people who would love to see them fail. The downfall for these people often comes when they need help. Their colleagues, peers, and direct reports aren't motivated to help them get ahead.

The value of focusing on those around you, simply put, is that you can be more successful if you help those around you than you can if you focus only on yourself. The better your team functions, the better you are going to perform. Your team will be motivated to do their best because they want you to succeed, and they know you will share the credit with them. If you have a reputation for developing everyone on your team, the best people will want to work for you, which will further enhance your contribution.

## You Are Not Your Job

Most people define themselves by what they do for a living. What is printed on their business cards is synonymous with who they are. This attitude is dangerous for many reasons, not the least of which is that it will keep you from developing genuine humility. If you allow your identity to become wrapped up in your title, your sense of self will be endangered should you ever lose your job for some reason, whether you resign, are laid off, or get fired. If you think that you are too much of a stellar performer ever to be let go by your company, keep in mind that the higher up in the organization you go, the more likely it is that you will be terminated at some point—regardless of your performance. The average tenure of a CEO of a publicly traded company is now four to five years. Often, they are removed for reasons that have more to do with market cycles and other external factors than with their history of performance. Leaders, including many good ones, come and go.

Three things to remember:

- Genuine humility allows you to connect with the people around you in powerful ways.
- Treat every person with respect, and show them that you value their contributions.
- Genuine humility protects your true source of power—your ability to do what you know is right.

Having your sense of self wrapped up in your job title is not only dangerous in the event that you are let go, it is actually a weakness that can threaten your ability to function well and do the right thing on the job. Sometimes, doing the right thing means taking risks that might put a promotion—or even your job—on the line, and if your identity is wrapped up too much in your position, taking that risk might seem too threatening. In this way, over-identifying with your job title steals your autonomy, makes it difficult or impossible to exercise self-confidence, and can make you less effective at doing your job well. Genuine humility can help you avoid the dangers of egotistical inflation, and it protects your true source of power—your ability to do what you believe is right.

### You Can't Fake Genuine Humility

People express genuine humility in many different ways, but at the heart of it, the principle is the same: you recognize the value in everyone; you know you are no better than anyone else; and the higher you move up in the organization, the more you stay grounded. You can't fake this. If you do, people will know you're a phony. You can't decide to spend twenty minutes a day walking the floor to be Mr. or Ms. Open, then close yourself off the rest of the time behind a wall of self-importance. If that's what you're going to do, then it's better not to even try.

If you think that your talent, abilities, accomplishments, educational pedigree, and title on your business card mean you really are better than other people, then you can't even pretend to have humility. No one is that good of an actor. If you do see yourself as superior, however, you will lose out on so much as a leader. Holding yourself above others makes it difficult to build a cohesive team—whether that means five direct reports or thousands of team members. You may not have a team who truly wants you and the organization to succeed.

When you are the leader, people are always watching you. The higher up you go, the more visible you are to more people. From that vantage point, you have an enormous opportunity, one that you can't take lightly: to set an example, influence behavior, and become a positive and uplifting force in the lives of a great many people. They, in turn, will inspire and motivate you.

Genuine humility, along with the other three principles of values-based leadership enhance who you are as a person and allow you to make a greater impact as a leader. The more self-reflective, balanced, truly self-confident, and genuinely humble you are, the more that others will appreciate what they see in you. Because you recognize the value in them, you will lead with the authority that comes from being authentic, and they will follow you. Being grounded in the four principles in your personal leadership, you are now ready to put them into action as you become a leader in a values-based organization.

|| **Adapted from the book From Values to Action © 2011 Jossey-Bass with permission from the author, Harry M. Jansen Kraemer Jr.** Note: This brief summary is geared towards providing information in regards to the topic and issue covered. This

book is provided with the understanding that this book is commentary, educational summary, comparison, and analysis on some of the original books main ideas and concepts.

Questions for Discussion for Working Better Together (WBT)

1. In your own words, how does genuine humility relate to leadership effectiveness?

2. How does the presence or absence of genuine humility relate to KPIs and financial performance in your organization?

3. On a scale of one to ten, rate your organization's leaders on their level of genuine humility. Rate for different leaders and/or different parts of the organization, if applicable. Explain your ratings using specific examples of behavior.

4. On a scale of one to ten, how would you rate your own level of genuine humility? How does your behavior toward other people support your answer? How does the behavior of other people toward you support your answer?

5. Have you ever behaved in a way that demonstrated a lack of humility? What happened? What were the results? Did you learn anything from that experience? If so, what did you learn? Provide details.

6. Have you ever worked for someone who clearly lacked genuine humility? What did that person do that demonstrated their lack of humility? Provide multiple examples of behavior, if possible. How did those behaviors impact the results that the leader produced?

7. Have you worked under a successful leader who demonstrated genuine humility? What did that person do that demonstrated their humility? Provide multiple examples of behavior, if possible. How did those behaviors impact the results that the leader produced?

8. If a person does not possess genuine humility, what types of experiences might make that person aware of their lack of humility?

9. How do you think a person's possession or lack of genuine humility relates to the way they view their purpose in the workplace?

10. In what ways does your organization's culture support and/or discourage the development and expression of genuine humility?

11. What specific things can you do to make sure you are behaving with genuine humility on a consistent basis?

12. What specific things can you do to encourage the development and expression of genuine humility in your workplace?

*"MEDIATION" IMAGE: BISHOP'S EYE WINDOW, ENGLAND*

# #8.
# THE PRINCIPLE OF COMMUNITY: SHARING AS A DISCIPLINE WITHIN COMMUNITY

The No-nonsense Nine Question: "Does this feel like a good community? Do I respect and trust these people? Do we support one another and give each other the benefit of the doubt? Do we share knowledge and resources? Do we inspire each other and coach each other?"

## The No-nonsense Discipline of "Sharing:" Healthy Business Affinity: An Introduction

**Is Social Collaboration the "New Way?"**

The definitions that define the organization do so by defining the communal purpose of the organization. The definitions today are social, based upon people, not machines. At the same time, technology is enabling and requiring a movement away from a classic command and control structure. The World Wide Web flattens and changes the traditional corporate triangular structure of hierarchy: The effect of technological change, according to workplace guru Bill Bridges, is amplified by the very strategies that organizations currently use to cope with change. These strategies include:

- Shortening chains of command
- Flattening hierarchies
- Handing decision-making authority to front-line employees
- Turning over the redesign of processes to cross-trained, self-managed teams
- Shifting to just-in-time systems of materials handling
- Putting suppliers and even customers on product development teams

Companies that have taken leadership positions in their industries in the last two decades typically have done so by narrowing their focus. They have focused on delivering superior customer value in line with one of three value disciplines—operational excellence, customer intimacy, or product/service leadership. They have become champions in one of these disciplines while meeting industry standards in the other two. Implicit to top performance in all three is the healthy balanced necessity for people to have…

1. Comprehensibility: A comprehensive knowledge of performance requirements

2. Manageability: The resources and wherewithal to function properly

3. Meaningfulness: A sense of equability with the values and purpose of the company

These are the three critical elements of being healthy or possessing "wellness"—the necessary implicit ingredients for having an affinity for Healthy Business... and the three essentials that will help make Healthy Business Affinity an on-the-job reality. Comprehensibility feeds the No-nonsense Principle of Autonomy. Manageability feeds the No-nonsense Principle of Mastery, and Meaningfulness feeds the No-nonsense Principle of Purpose. Together these are the essential precursors to building a healthy workplace community of excellence:

**Healthy Business Affinity: The Backbone of Organizational Wellness**

Organizations have proven that if they flatten out their organizations they can improve their productivity. In addition to the flattening out of structure, however, performance improves when knowledge workers become well balanced through behavioral change; which takes place if and when they are enabled by management and circumstance to respond positively in their work to these three simple questions:

1. Do I understand the motivations of my work? Is it comprehensible?
2. Are the resources at my disposal adequate to act upon and manage what is confronting me? Is it manageable?
3. Do I say "welcome" to my work because I know why I am here and I find it meaningful? Does it have meaning or purpose?

According to workplace research in the category of professional services since the 1970s, service professionals who answer any one of the above questions with a strong "yes," will then answer all of them with a strong "yes." And the opposite is also true: if the worker answers "no" to one, then he or she will answer "no" to all three: "If I do not know, I cannot manage… and I do not know why I should."

Let us look more closely at these three important questions:

Questions 1 asks knowledge workers whether the information a worker needs to do his or her job is orderly, consistent, structured, and clear, rather than noise-chaotic, disordered, random, and inexplicable: "Do I comprehend the stimuli about me?"

Questions 2 asks if knowledge workers have the tools and resources they need to manage what bombards them on a regular basis: "Do I have the resources to take appropriate action?"

Questions 3 asks if the problems and demands of their jobs are worth investing energy in, are worthy of commitment and engagement, are challenges that are "welcome" rather than burdensome: "Does my work have true meaning for me?"

In theory, having the ability to "comprehend, manage and find meaning" at work is the "Healthy Business Affinity elixir" to a stressful work environment. With the implicit answer of these three questions, a person instinctively knows how to reduce anxiety. When managers, workers, business executives or entrepreneurs, have these three necessary ingredients in harmony, they will find themselves being more effective and therefore more productive than others, often without even knowing why.

The answers to these are important to every worker, but especially important to high-stress knowledge-working professionals, as within the "STEP" vertical, who are highly identified with their work. In truth, when the person answering these three questions is a high-end professional working in today's high-stress work environment, like a lawyer, doctor, engineer or a senior-level business executive, the positive versus negative answers to these three simple questions can literally be life altering.

The impact of technology, globalization and knowledge are as intertwined as the three tenets of personal performance. While technology seems to be leveling the playing field between the enterprise and the individual in a globalized economy, it is <u>knowledge</u> itself that seems to be the driver of "mission" not what the C-suite or top-management team "declares" as "meaningful." The marketplace and the end-customer now define and thereby "declare" the real purpose, the meaning, and the "mission." And for the knowledge worker, if this market-driven purpose or meaning "just doesn't fit me," they will move on, simply because they cannot make the commitment. Loyalty to the enterprise is no longer the driver. The driver now is personal "motivation," and the end-customer fundamentally drives that motivation and decision.

## In Search of Motivation

According to findings of Victor Frankl, author of "Man's Search for Meaning" and as corroborated by the research of renowned Israeli medical social scientist Dr. Aaron Antonovsky and his colleagues at the Ben Gurion University in Jerusalem and the Institute for Applied Research at Hebrew University in Tel Aviv, the three essential "Healthy Business Affinity" ingredients of 1) comprehensibility, 2) manageability, and 3) meaningfulness are intertwined: all things being equal, high levels in one aspect will result in high levels overall. They are inextricable: Research shows that when there is a high Healthy Business Affinity an individual is able to manage stressful situations more effectively and be consistently more productive.

On one side of the "balance" scale in stereotypical terms, a "culture of concern" would be the result of supportive management. Similarly, a "culture of excellence" would be the result of assertive management. Of course, in the real working world there is no such thing as a stereotypical organization. When working with people, there are always "shades" of "imbalance" - there are and always will be varying pockets of assertiveness and supportiveness active within the same organization. And these shades of imbalance vary from person to person, group-to-group, practice area to practice area, and work team to work team. When the purpose of worker and organization are aligned, the chance of harmony exists and the more likely work effectiveness and productivity will climb.

## The Workplace Opportunity

*Stressors that faced our grandparents and parents face us today: the same fears that are brought on by the uncertainty of change, the fears that influence the daily decisions that make up your life. Whether you realize it or not, these affect you now and will affect all of your tomorrows. Anything that takes up the bulk of a person's life needs to be taken very seriously; namely, the workplace.*

## Our Workplace Now

There are three main forces driving the whirlwind, fast-paced change in the information age today: Technology, Globalization and Knowledge.

Technology: Change is rampant in every aspect of the value chain of manufacturing, distribution, services and retail. We are deep into the world of silicon, networks, cyberspace, social media and "blogosphere."

Globalization: No longer do manufacturers transporters, insurers, financiers, lawyers, engineers, accountants or merchants view themselves as producing, buying or selling within boundaries. They are far beyond the "cottage-industry" walls of yesteryear today, yet often while working online within the cozy confines of their own homes.

Knowledge: This generation of knowledge workers is demonstrated by tight-knit networks of common interest and loyalty to the small group. No longer do young employees quit because they disagree with the "vision" of their company, but quit because they find that their immediate boss and their closest fellow workers are incompatible. How the knowledge worker works and how the "work-pod" functions (or does not) far exceed the importance of any "corporate mission statement."

Headquarters are likely going to become a thing of the past, thereby further distributing workers, no matter what their age or beliefs are. If there is one trend that has demonstrated staying power over the past two decades, it is the movement of strategy formulation away from corporate headquarters and into business units and smaller groups, a move that tends to cluster people of variance in closer proximity to one another. The reason is as obvious as it is sensible: business units are nearer to customers, competitors, and costs. This is where the purpose of the business is most real, and where the meaning to the worker as a result becomes most clear. The tendency today is for workers to find a sense of purpose through relationship building with their co-workers and with their customers.

In theory, every executive, lawyer, doctor, architect, accountant or engineer who has the ability to "comprehend, manage and find meaning" at work already possesses the "Healthy Business Affinity elixir" to a stressful work environment. With the implicit answer of these three, a person instinctively knows how to reduce anxiety. When these knowledge workers, or business managers or entrepreneurs, have these three necessary ingredients in harmony, they will find themselves being more effective and productive than others, often without even knowing why. They answer, "Yes" to the above three questions without even considering otherwise. This "take-it-for-granted" group is often described as a "calming influence." They seem to "have their act together." However, how often do knowledge workers, executives, professionals or entrepreneurs, who work in high-stress environments, when asked, answer all three with an exasperated "no?" The answer: Most likely when they work within an enterprise (or culture) that either (a) lacks a sense of purpose altogether or (b) has a sense of purpose that is inconsistent with that knowledge worker, manager or executive.

The impact of technology, globalization and knowledge are as intertwined as the three tenets of personal performance. More will follow on this later, but while technology seems to be leveling the playing field between the enterprise and the individual in a globalized economy, it is knowledge that seems to be the driver of "mission" not what the C-suite or top-management team "declares" as meaningful. For the enterprise, the marketplace and the end-customer now define their real purpose, their meaning. And for the knowledge worker, if this purpose or meaning "just doesn't fit me," they will move on, simply because they cannot make the commitment. Loyalty to the enterprise is no longer the driver. The driver now is personal "motivation."

**What is your disposition?**

The powerful realization of a "wellness point of view" was originated by studies from the 1950s about concentration camp survivors, made famous by camp survivor and author Victor Frankl, as personal testimony, within his world-renown book entitled "Man's Search for Meaning" (1959).

Whereas pathogenesis deals with the origins of disease, search-for-meaning deals with the origins of health, or wellness. A "wellness theory" of health starts from the assumption that the human and living systems are inherently flawed and subject to unavoidable entropic processes and unavoidable death. In other words, we all die and have varying degrees of wellness along the way. A simple metaphor for health based upon the idea of a river can be helpful to understanding the difference of a "wellness point of view" from being pathogenic or "disease focused": A metaphor... Contemporary western medicine is likened to a well-organized, heroic, technologically sophisticated effort to pull drowning people out of a raging river. Devotedly engaged in this task, and often quite well rewarded, the establishment members never raise their eyes or minds to inquire upstream, around the bend in the river, about who or what is pushing all these people in.

A wellness-point-of-view questions the accuracy of this metaphor and redefines the river as the stream of life. A wellness-point-of-view points out that none walk the shore safely, so the nature of one's river and the things that shape one's ability to swim must all be considered. Therefore, the object is to study the river and to find out what facilitates the capacity to swim well and joyously for some and, for others, makes even staying afloat a constant struggle? The answer is found in one's ability to maintain a wellness-point-of-view. A wellness-point-of-view argues that we are all in the 'dangerous river of life'. A wellness-point-of-view holds that in the end, we will all succumb to its dangers.

The pathogenic view of health sees health as being the absence of disease and sees treatment as an allopathic (remedy-based) system of opposite forces to correct the sickness, e.g. pharmaceutical drugs. This is a reductionist/positivist approach; the answer to illness is to focus in, reducing the problem down to systems and sub systems of pathogens or risk factors; it tends to be mechanistic.

A wellness-point-of-view turns the argument around, suggesting that we need to look at those who stay well despite being high on risk factors. What is different about them? How do they cope? A wellness-point-of-view is a whole life view (integrative, meaning mind-body-spirit), which sees the answers as coming from the big picture. What helps the person to cope? Why do some people cope better than others do? A whole life view sees health as a continuum – that we are all terminal cases, and that we are all, so long as there is a breath of life in us, in some measure healthy.

A wellness-point-of-view sees treatment as enhancing the coping mechanisms not just of this specific illness but in general, giving the person a lift or enhanced coping moving them towards the healthy end of the health/illness continuum. A wellness-point-of-view does not see all stresses as bad: indeed life is full of stresses… the problem is finding the coping resources. Treatments, disciplines and best practices, which support coping, will come more from looking at imagination, love, play, meaning and the social structures that foster them.

A wellness-point-of-view and a pathogenic view of health are often presented as opposites, but the pathogenic view of health is now rarely used in isolation to all other views. There is a growing understanding of support and social policy in whole life views. Researchers do not advocate no longer researching illness, but feel that an "integrative" balance must be struck which is broader and more holistic, but despite a slight merging, these are two radically different views of health that must cooperate and respect one another. A Healthy Business Manager must embrace disease prevention, but must never lose sight of the difference.

## A Wellness Point-of-View

I almost entitled this chapter "A 'Healthy Business' Point of View." The question within a wellness-point-of-view or a "Healthy Business" Point of View is why some of us do so much better in the river of life, or in the river of business life. The whole-life orientation looks at what factors move one towards the healthy end of the continuum, i.e. what predicts a good outcome. Instead of looking for cures, what is sometimes called "whole-life" focuses upon the adaptation of the person - one can look at love, play and meaning as well as physical cures. A wellness-point-of-view is particularly interested in the deviant case, "why did he survive despite being so high on risk factors?" for example. Sometimes the deviant case can be a majority, i.e. smoking causes lung cancer, but a majority of smokers do not die of lung cancer, why not? A wellness-point-of-view argues that:

- We are all, always in the dangerous river of life.
- We need to understand the movement of people towards health.
- This movement to health cannot be explained by simply having low on risk factors.

- The pathogenic focus is on the disease, not on the host or the person as a whole.
- It is impermissible to identify or equate a rich, complex human being with a particular pathology, disability or characteristic, or a particular set of risk factors.
- Pathogenic narrowness is simply poor care.

As a case example, in the early 1960s an American educated medical sociologist (Aaron Antonovsky) was studying a group of women in Israel who were all having similar menstrual problems, but as a sociologist he noticed more than the pathology, he discovered that there was a particular deviant set that was healthier than all the rest. Upon further investigation he sent out his handful of research assistants and subsequently discovered that all of the members of this deviant set were concentration camp survivors. And with this discovery, began the holistic study of wellness - of health, wellbeing and performance… the root of having a wellness-point-of-view.

The ability to overcome the adversities of life is what builds the resistance attributed to those people who possess a strong wellness-point-of-view. These successes are found in their life's story. Life's adversities help build a healthy perspective on life, a "wellness-point-of-view." A life overcoming adversities in time fosters repeated life experiences, which helps a person to see the world as making sense on various levels of thought, emotion and action. This enables a person's ability to consistently move towards a state of health and wellbeing, or in commerce we may describe as "a state of healthy business."

Someone with a *wellness point-of-view* will:

- Believe that a challenge can be understood, that it is comprehensible.

- Believe that they can cope with the situation, that it is manageable.
- And be motivated to cope due to a sense of meaningfulness in life.

*As in life, how do these three apply to business?*

*Comprehensibility*

A person with a high healthy-business-point-of-view sees confronting stimuli as making sense in that they will be expected… or if unexpected, they will be ordered or explicable.

*Manageability*

A person with a high healthy-business-point-of-view has the belief that there is a high probability that things will work out as well as can be reasonably expected. Those people with a low healthy-business-point-of-view see themselves as the ones things always happen to. Manageability is the extent to which someone perceives that the resources at their disposal are adequate (or not adequate) to meet the demands posed by the stimuli that are bombarding them.

*Meaningfulness*

A person with a strong or high healthy-business-point-of-view speaks of areas of their life that are important to them; that they have been very much cared about and that that makes sense to them. People with a low healthy-business-point-of-view give little indication that anything in life seems to matter particularly to them.

♦

Adolescence is an important time for the development of a child's wellness-point-of-view. This is the time that the social structured reality, impedes or facilitates the formation of a weak or strong healthy-business-point-of-view. A strong healthy-business-point-of-view is cultivated by making clear and realistic choices, which are valued and supported by those people close by and important. The person with a strong healthy-business-point-of–view will suck dis-orderliness right out of the environment, which counterbalances the pressures towards disorder, from the internal and external environments. This ability to see order and to view that the best possible outcome will occur leads the person through bad periods of life. Seeing these events more as "challenges" than crushing blows, may challenge the healthy business point-of-view, but will not undermine it completely.

Overall the emphasis in healthy business remains on "keeping people well", this assumption that people are naturally healthy leads to health promotion work being all about mediating pathogens and ensuring social conditions that allow and encourage wise low-risk behavior.

We propose two key questions for health promotion:

1. "How dangerous is our river?" and

2. "How well can we swim?"

We argue that health promotion needs to move people along the continuum to health, not simply encourage people to become low on risk factors: How can this person/community be helped to move towards better health, rather than focusing on risk factors or disease grouping that they may belong to. Measuring someone's healthy business point-of-view is part of the job of a manager-coach as a "Healthy Business Manager."

A healthy business point-of-view is called a "Dispositional Orientation": an indicator of someone's disposition. In life, we are all people of head and heart and gut: thoughtful, emotional and physical. And having a healthy business orientation is a way for a person to know in the truest sense of knowing, of gaining intimate life-witnessing knowledge, and at numerous levels: we can know intellectually, through our head; we can know tangibly by controlling, through our actions; and we can know compassionately, through our hearts. We can know in these three ways - through our curiosity, through our ability to have control and through our heart-felt compassion. And with these three can come a knowing that will heal. This way of knowing is most precious and requires much courage, simply because finding meaning is so difficult: of all three, having compassion is the most difficult. We can all be curious (think much), and we can all seek control (do much), but can we all own and release our compassion (feel much), which is the surest, most enduring way to achieve improved health, wellbeing and performance in our daily work lives. Finding meaning is important to assuring a healthier work environment.

## The Ultimate HR Conundrum

This reconciliation is obviously difficult for one huge and ever-important reason: because when the customer comes first, the organization (and therefore its workers) must come second: Second in terms of job security, wellbeing, stability, and continuity; and more simplistically, there frankly is not anyone on the scene who can provide them. This is the workplace reality. The organization cannot because, economically, the customer will not: they are not a patriarch or a benevolent despot; they are the economical driver who wants top performance. The result: without security, there is no reason to obey, and without obedience, out goes its kissing cousin, loyalty. Therefore, the reconciliation can only come from "employee loyalty to the company" being replaced by "commitment to the business," and this commitment will not come without an employee knowing the "work story" and without having a balanced holistic Sense of Coherence (Comprehensibility, Manageability, and Meaningfulness). This solution is not going to be performance driven, this solution has to be community and culture-driven - by a community and a culture that are motivated to assure top performance.

In Jay Galbraith's business terms, specifically, employee commitment to the customer, their workmates, and their immediate supervisor, and their profession, replaces loyalty to the company. To repeat, in today's high-tech, dispersed, knowledge-age workplace, personal commitment has replaced traditional company loyalty in the workplace, for a variety of reasons, but chiefly because the "benevolent corporate dictator" no longer exists, because **the customer** has become the ultimate boss. That is the real workplace story, personally, socially and structurally: This reality requires the employee to be self-reliant for their overall wellbeing in terms of their learning, their finances and their state of health. In turn, this requires the employer to be culturally-enabling in their HR processes and practices, for the self-starter who has the initiative to grab hold.

As illustrated earlier, the "new organization" is characterized by weaker employee attachment to the company and stronger employee attachments to one's own professional wellbeing, the immediate supervisor, the project team and the end customer. What typically matters most to individuals is not the company, but their own personal and professional health, their peers, and the immediate person to whom they report – that is what and to whom the worker of today is committed to (versus the employer "owning" their loyalty), and is most significant in how a worker finds meaning in their work.

This shift from loyalty to personal commitment motivationally can be very destructive to organizations operationally if not planned for and managed effectively at all of these three levels: the personal level, the social level and the structural level.

Employers historically expected obedience and diligence in exchange for employment security. The foundation of this deal was the premise that to achieve organizational success, a company or firm needed high morale, employee satisfaction, and employee loyalty.

Ignoring this change as a reality has resulted in a loss of people and in a loss of customers. Managed well, to enact change in this can result in improved business results. The shift from loyalty to the company to a more self-reliant worker commitment to the culture and to the customer can clearly benefit all interested parties when understood, planned for and acted upon.

**A Working Community of Engagement**

A new working community of engagement, with learning, competence and justice as its core, becomes possible when managers understand, operate and motivate with a Sense of Coherence. Engagement happens when employee commitment replaces employee loyalty.

With Sense of Coherence comes employee commitment quite naturally. This is the essence of a new work culture of engagement for the modern day organization, within which comes an expected and accepted exchange between worker and organization: initiative for opportunity. When the organization commits to providing order, assuring workload balance and giving a voice to the worker, the organization offers its worker the opportunity to achieve success; in return, the worker promises the organization to self-manage their initiative in creating value for customers and thereby profits for the organization.

As indicated above, a new culture of engagement requires a commitment by the organization to provide an enabling, achievement-focused environment, a culture within which Healthy Business Affinity is supported, an environment where achieving "meaningfulness" at work is supported and communicated, promoted *and possible.*

Offering workers the opportunity to achieve success will require that organizations provide (a) an immediate supervisor who is comfortable and capable of being both supportive and assertive as a "leader/manager-coach," (b) the apprentice (as a lifetime learner) with the chance to engage… to learn new skills and the opportunities to apply them in new arenas, (c) workers with the chance to achieve rewards and enhance personal reputation, and (d) all workers (apprentices and people in charge) with the opportunity to become committed (and have the wherewithal) to self-manage their own professional lives.

This can be accomplished by (a) providing workers with the ability and resources to supply input into the projects that they work on, (b) by emphasizing behaviors and outcomes (results) rather than procedures, (c) by delegating work, the know-how, the tools and the decisions about how to do it and (d) supporting the worker's own personal sense of purpose in their chosen career.

In this way, job advancement and professional growth become based on flexible work assignments and clusters of activity that get organized in sequential and synchronized projects of varying lengths and breadths rather than fixed job responsibilities. The actual work being done when an organization is "flattened out" into migrating "work pods" requires commitment by the workers to the projects and tasks at hand, because they have a Sense of Coherence and are therefore "motivated" – and not because of "command and control."

Organizations must, therefore, culturally support a viable apprenticeship model that connects experts with learners, in order to help people gain the skills and self-reliance to master this new enabling work culture and environment of engagement: to find security and support through "employability" when they can no longer count on their employer to provide job security automatically.

**Needed: A New Human Resource Ethic**

The most complicated hurdle for organizations is meeting the learning needs, the financial security and the health and wellbeing demands of their workers. Yet meeting the basic worker demands for "employability" will help engender the worker commitment that supplants worker loyalty of a bygone era. This worker commitment is very different from loyalties of the past in which the agreements between employee and employer for employee loyalty were more performance based or "contract" based. Now a worker's level of engagement is more "culturally based" than ever.

To successfully achieve this new covenant of engagement, the role of the human resource ethic needs to be revised, must speak a new healthy-culture language of employee health and wellbeing, education and financial enablement versus corporate protection, With this ethic in place, positive change will then begin to take place.

A new human resource ethic that equates with and transcends into today's business world must elicit employee engagement versus demand loyalty. A new human resource ethic must be more explicit about what the organization expects and, more importantly, what employees can expect from the organization. A new human resource ethic must help employees gain the skills and self-reliance to master their new engagement environment. A new human resource ethic must lead the charge in developing organization capabilities, efficient work tools and in turn further enable the new healthier business culture itself. A new human resource ethic must function in ways that help individuals develop their desires and capabilities. The new HR ethic must do so while promoting a "culture of health, wellbeing and performance."

A new human resource ethic of engagement can be accomplished culturally by (a) institutionalizing organizational purpose and values and then (b) integrating them into learning (comprehensibility), resources (manageability) and rewards, incentives and purpose (meaningfulness).

This ethic must be implemented at the individual personal level, the group social level and the organization structural level… both operationally and motivationally. If this is not done the resulting schisms prevalent within un-engaged work cultures will continue to widen.

Ultimately, employers will capture the hearts and minds of employees when the employees can connect their purpose with an honest and well-articulated customer-focused organizational purpose. Reconciling what organizations want with what workers need requires commitment from both worker and employer:

Employers must commit to enabling workers, not through some form of "guarantee" but instead by fostering a culture of enablement in all areas that promote employability.

Workers in exchange must commit to providing value to the customer.

The hinge pin for this to succeed is the role of the immediate boss… as a “leader/manager-coach.” This is the number one cause for employee satisfaction and therefore customer satisfaction. The immediate boss as “leader/manager-coach” is the great connector and the grand enabler of workforce profitability.

A harmonious employer-employee commitment is won or lost at the level of the immediate boss… Companies must focus there if they want to help create a healthier, higher-performing workforce. In response this will cause the organization to “unravel” from an outdated model based upon fear to a healthy model of personal, social and structural wellness affinity… and a Healthier Business Environment.

* * * * *

**Mediation: The Discipline of Sharing in Five Dimensions**

***Identity***:

Sharing is anchored to the *nurturing* part of our decision-making: Helpers are care giving and supportive…

***Understanding***:

Interpersonally oriented, Nurturers are caring leaders who derive satisfaction from seeing and encouraging the development of others; they often play the role of mentor in an organization. When healthy, Helpers are also keenly aware of their own needs. This will bring balance to them and will allow them to participate more freely, without expectation of return.

***Challenging***:

Helpers can become prideful and possessive. They tend to get in the middle of things… giving help and advice (whether others want it or not). They can develop a sense of entitlement and be manipulative in attempting to influence people. If betrayed, they may become vindictive ("after all I've done for you!").

***Believing:***

"I think it is important to always focus on what we need to do to serve others."

"Of all the people in the organization the President could have called, he called me."

"Was that helpful?"

"Both of my parents were alcoholics and I basically took care of them."

***Performing:***

Performance development options include realistically estimating what others need instead of giving to get approval, seeing how they contribute to their own burdens, setting clearer boundaries, and asserting their interpersonal power more directly. Key development need for helpers is humility. They need to be able to acknowledge their own needs, to having the strength say no as well as yes.

Having flexibility is an important development area for helpers. The best manager-coaches get feedback regularly and change their approach based upon the latest information. Excellent manager-coaches are in-tune… they want to be of assistance to their followers and therefore seek advice from everybody that they need on-the-job, learning their lessons and making minor adjustments on a regular basis.

Nurturing manager-coaches can become "the leader others choose to follow." They know from experience that whatever they are working on NOW is likely to be dramatically different than what they will be doing in years 3, 4 or 5. Great manager-coaches know how "to pivot" and to prepare, and then to teach their followers how "to pivot" also. They "pass it on."

Savvy nurturing Leader/Manager-Coaches believe in accountability and in "having the numbers crystal clear." But they also know to not be alarmed or over-reactive. They understand that a financial model is an ongoing compass and strategic. They know that change takes on a regular basis, and especially more so during times of start-up, operational reshuffling or economic turn-around.

Great Leader/Manager-Coaches expect 80% of their decisions to be right… while exceptionally wise Leader/Manager-Coaches know how to spot the other 20% – what they and the others at work are doing wrong. Giving help begets getting honest feedback from followers that is realistic and tough, and critical to future success.

While being a Leader/Manager-Coach may seem terrific, the reality is that the job can be lonely and difficult, filled first with high pressure and then again with many mundane tasks. Being nurturing under such conditions is at times a gritty existence, filled with self-doubt. Leader/Manager-Coaches often struggle with their setbacks. Many even become bitter at bosses, subordinates and/or circumstances.

There are those Leader/Manager-Coaches who seem to "kick it up a gear" and react how Thomas Edison, Abe Lincoln and Winston Churchill reacted... with resiliency. They each understood accountability and knew the stakes - and had been astute enough to make a huge investment in nurturing others… they couldn't have done it all alone.

The Discipline of Sharing is part of us all.

## A Harry Kraemer Inspired One Sheet:<br>Talent Management & Leadership Development

Healthy Business Management Principles
Principle 8: Community

| | | |
|---|---|---|
| 9 Reliability | 2 Autonomy | 3 Creativity |
| 8 Community | 1 Purpose | 4 Resources |
| 7 Sincerity | 6 Mastery | 5 Responsibility |

It's all about the people. This seemingly simple statement cannot be overemphasized. Many companies get things in the wrong order. As soon as the values are clearly defined and put in place, leaders often move immediately into setting the direction for the organization. The thinking goes that once they have the values determined and the strategic direction set, then they can attract the right people to join the team. This approach is backwards. Once the values are in place, before leaders do anything else, they need to focus on the people.

Most of all, the values-based leader is looking for people who exhibit the values that are most important through self-reflection, balance, true self-confidence, and genuine humility. These are the people who can be developed to their full potential for the good of themselves, the team, and the entire organization.

Whether you are leading a small team or you are the CEO of a company with thousands of team members, you are looking for people who are wired in a way that is consistent with the values of the organization. You are looking to identify and develop a phenomenal group of people who are going to help set the direction and move the organization forward. As a values-based leader, you are committed to building a team in which everyone is pulling together to reach the organization's goals.

This can be accomplished only with a focus on talent management and leadership development at every level. Rather than being perfunctory or bureaucratic—with forms to fill out and so-called development goals that no one looks at after the performance review is completed—this process is integral to the values-based organization.

You've Got to Own the People Process

Admittedly, being a leader is often like drinking from a fire hose. It's overwhelming. As a result, you may be tempted to delegate away the people piece as yet another task on an overly long to-do list. Many managers delegate the people process entirely to HR because they don't have the time to deal with it themselves. However, the reason they don't have the time is that they don't have the right people. It's a vicious cycle that can only be broken if leaders emphasize talent management and leadership development. By doing this, they will have the right people in place to whom they can delegate with confidence. The more time you put into the people process, the more productive you and your entire team will be. You will no longer feel the burden of needing to do everything yourself.

The good news is that even though you own the talent management and leadership development process, you don't have to lead everyone by the hand. In fact, you should not micromanage the career development of each individual. It comes down to striking a balance. You must make it a priority to have the right people on your team. At the same time, you empower them to own their development.

Think of it as a partnership. Each person on your team has his or her goals and desires, skill sets, and developmental needs, and should be encouraged to reach his or her full potential. There are tangible ways you can support your team through this process—for example, helping them identify what they want to do, what they are good at, and what they would rather not do.

Ambition and Values

As you advise the people you are developing, you may encounter people who are highly ambitious. They'll tell you they've always known their career goals, one of which is to become the youngest CEO in the history of the company. This kind of ambition is usually all about finding the shortest distance between point A (where they are) and point B (where they want to go). Moving up in the organization is a great goal, but to be authentic, it must be grounded in the person's wanting to contribute more to the organization, instead of merely acquiring a prestigious job title and earning more money.

**So What Are You Looking For?**

There are significant commonalities among the people who are most valued within their organizations. The first is that these individuals are grounded in the four principles of values-based leadership—self-reflection, balance and perspective, true self-confidence, and genuine humility. Second, they have a global perspective on the entire organization, which gives them breadth. Although they have depth in a particular expertise—whether a business unit, geography, or function—they are not limited to that. These are the well-rounded individuals with both breadth and depth who are valued on any team and who can contribute significantly to the overall organization.

Having a global perspective is essential in any organization, large or small, public or private. Rather than staying within their silos, people must operate across multiple businesses, departments, geographies, and functions. They need to have the intellectual curiosity to commit to understanding how their particular role fits into the whole; and the broader the perspective, the better.

Helping your team develop the necessary depth and breadth requires a purposeful approach. It is critical to gain expertise broadly instead of only pursuing opportunities narrowly. Individuals with global perspective can contribute more productively to the team, and the people who most often become senior leaders are those who understand the entire organization.

Admittedly, not everyone is going to want to pursue global perspective. There will always be highly capable individuals who want to specialize in one area and go really deep into it. That's great, because a team should be balanced by a variety of expertise and perspectives that are complementary and helpful. Thank goodness there are people who want to specialize in such things. As a leader, however, you also want to look for individuals who can cut across numerous areas and see how things really fit together. One way to help your team members develop a global perspective is to encourage them to participate in as many projects involving other departments as possible.

The Process

The purpose of talent management and leadership development is to make sure every single person in the organization is being developed to his or her full potential. Development needs to occur on a continuous basis not just when it comes time to fill out the annual performance review forms that get processed by some computer someplace. People should know what they do well and what they don't do well, and a developmental plan should be in place to help them improve over time. As a leader, you need to be highly involved in this process, while making sure that your team members are engaged and empowered to advocate for themselves.

Three things to remember:

- Talent management and leadership development should be continuous and include everyone.
- Take ownership of (but don't micromanage) the people process.
- Develop your skill at providing feedback.

If the key to a values-based organization is really the people, then leaders need to spend a lot more time developing the team than analyzing performance indicators. After all, the numbers aren't going to generate themselves. You need to have the right people in place in order to reach the performance targets.

Talent management and leadership development is not a yearly or even a quarterly process. It happens continuously, with honest feedback that lets people know how they are doing, what needs to improve, and where they stand. Feedback is one of the most important yet difficult parts of the process. Openness and transparency are vital if you want to develop the best team.

Delivering honest feedback is challenging for many managers. Maybe they are afraid of hurting someone's feelings, or perhaps they had bad experiences delivering (or receiving) feedback earlier in their careers. It is important to trust that most people really want meaningful, open, and honest feedback. Concurrent with the feedback process is letting your team know when there are open positions in the company for which they might be well suited.

"So What About Me?"

As a values-based Leader/Manager-Coach, you are highly focused on the development of your team. At the same time, you should also be engaged as part of the organization's overall talent management and leadership development process. Although your boss should play a part in your development, you need to take charge of it as well: asking for feedback, seeking opportunities to make sure you are developing breadth and a global perspective, and looking to see where you can contribute further to the organization.

|| **Adapted from the book From Values to Action © 2011 Jossey-Bass with permission from the author, Harry M. Jansen Kraemer Jr.** Note: This brief summary is geared towards providing information in regards to the topic and issue covered. This book is provided with the understanding that this book is commentary, educational summary, comparison, and analysis on some of the original books main ideas and concepts.

Questions for Discussion for Working Better Together (WBT)

1. On a scale of one to ten, how well does your organization perform talent management and leadership development? Does it treat the people process as fundamental, continuous and all-inclusive? What does it do well and not do well? Provide specific examples.

2. On a scale of one to ten, how well do you think you contribute to the people process? What behaviors of yours support your answer?

3. Do you currently have clear development goals toward which you are working? If so, what are they?

4. When was the last time you discussed your development goals with someone who could provide you with effective guidance?

5. Do you receive regular, constructive feedback that is focused specifically on your progress toward your development goals? Describe.

6. On a scale of one to ten, to what extent do you take responsibility for your own professional development? When you need guidance, do you ask for it? Do you actively seek out development-related feedback?

7. Have you ever worked for someone who was clearly uncomfortable or unskilled at providing feedback? What happened? How did you feel about working for that person? How well did people perform in that environment?

8. Have you ever worked for someone who was especially diligent and skilled at providing feedback? What happened? How did you feel about working for that person? How well did people perform in that environment?

9. For an organization to perform its people process well, why is it important that its leaders practice self-reflection?

10. For an organization to perform its people process well, why is it important that its leaders exhibit balance?

11. For an organization to perform its people process well, why is it important that its leaders possess genuine humility?

12. What specific things can you do to improve the people process in your organization, either as a whole or in your workgroup?

*"TRUST" IMAGE: LOTUS FLOWER (UNIVERSAL)*

# #9.
# THE PRINCIPLE OF RELIABILITY: POSSESSING TRUSTWORTHINESS

Reliability is the precondition for trust

Wolfgang Schaub

The No-nonsense Nine Questions: "Are the people around me reliable? Do they follow through and make good on their word? Do I know that they'll get the job done and come through for each other?"

You will find that the principles are straightforward and universal, and that they provide an all-embracing view of a manager's activities. They also provide an open framework that embraces and supports all other models of good business management.

When it comes to reliability a person has to be concerned with the No-nonsense Nine Discipline of Self Awareness, including self-reflection, as Harry Kraemer so excellently describes within his book, "From Values to Action." I also include Self Care, which is essential when you consider the burden of PTSD (Workplace Burnout). Today's workplace is in need of healing.

Beyond self-reflection and self-awareness and even beyond self-care is what is called Self Differentiation, which is mightily needed in today's workplace.

**Self-Differentiation at the Foundation**

Social Identity comprises the parts of a person's identity that come from belonging to particular groups, including their age, ethnicity, race, religion, gender, sexual orientation, nationality, and socioeconomic status.

Your social identity informs how you manage others and perform as a leader. As well, the social identities of those around you affect how they view you as a manager and leader and how they view and thus work with others.

A variety of questions and activities can help you develop your self-awareness of social identity. Armed with that knowledge, you can decrease the likelihood of misunderstanding, increase your ability to be open to different perspectives, and enhance your skill at accurately interpreting day to day as well as extraordinary situations that call on your ability to manage others and lead initiatives.

Managers by default are given the job of being responsible, trustworthy and value-based. The image is to persevere and to protect.

A healthy business is one wherein practical learning of managers is consistently applied to real-life problems. The learning goal is to place the self in touch with the social self.

On one side of the "balance" scale in stereotypical terms, a "culture of concern" would be the consequence of supportive management. Similarly, a "culture of excellence" would be the consequence of assertive management. Of course, in the real working world there is no such thing as a stereotypical organization. When a manager is working with employees, there are always "shades" of "imbalance" - there are and always will be varying pockets of assertiveness and supportiveness active within the same "social" organization. And these shades of imbalance vary from person to person, group-to-group, practice area to practice area, and work team to work team.

When understanding, purpose and the tools of workers and the organization are in alignment, the chance of workplace harmony exists and the more likely work productivity will climb. A "healthy business culture" is one that recognizes the never-ending journey of trying to achieve a harmonious balance between supportiveness and assertiveness mentally, emotionally and physically. This is the spirit of a healthy business.

**Three Motivational Styles**

David C. McClelland's perspective is similar to Frankl and Antonovsky, but expresses our sense of coherence (comprehensibility, meaningfulness and manageability) through the lenses of three motivational styles. The idea is that each of us draws from all three motives, but one will be predominant and may reinforce the person's habitual way of operating. This also aligns with how people prefer to go about making decisions, such as whether to purchase something, follow someone or adhere to a recommendation.

Therefore, employees will initially respond best to the approach that fits most closely with their dominant motive and how they go about making decisions.

Caution: If you're in a managerial or advising relationship, you could unwittingly strengthen a motive that is not in a person's best interest. For example, if someone constantly looks to you for approval and you give it, that person will be satisfied but continue to rely on you for approval and won't develop independent standards.

*Achievement Motivation*

Standards of excellence are clear, with opportunity to set goals and perform successfully against those standards (includes problem-solving about how to overcome obstacles to performance). People primarily motivated by achievement are usually competitive and work well independently. This motivation is reinforced and maintained by providing challenging work that stretches capabilities, along with concrete standards for success and clear, unambiguous feedback.

Style of support: Specific and descriptive feedback will provide people with a tool to satisfy and/or develop their achievement motive because it allows them to set their own goals and give themselves feedback about the degree to which the goals were accomplished.

These are those people who are dominant in "comprehensibility" in that they prefer to make decisions based on cognitive input: They are more naturally what would be described as energetically curious people.

*Affiliation Motivation*

Primary is being with others, expressing feelings and ideas, and getting others' approval. People motivated by affiliation are often friendly and work best when they feel appreciated and their work environment gives them the opportunity to interact with others. This motivation is reinforced and maintained by providing work where cooperation with co-workers is required, some time for personal interaction is encouraged, and team-building efforts are valued.

Style of support: Positive feedback that is not specific will satisfy and/or develop peoples' affiliation motive because it lets them know they're liked and accepted, but will not develop the achievement or power motive.

These are those people who are dominant in "meaningfulness" in that they prefer to make decisions based upon emotional input: They are more naturally what would be described as empathic or compassionate people.

*Power Motivation*

Impact the working environment. This includes being able to persuade and/or influence others, either through organizational position or through opportunities for group input. People primarily motivated by power usually have an interest in moving up in the organization and are often fluent in their communication style. This motivation is reinforced and maintained by allowing personal control over work pace and methods, as well as opportunities to influence -- especially if they can deal directly with people higher in the organization.

Style of support: Encouraging peoples' involvement in problem-solving and decision-making will satisfy and/or develop their power motive because it gives them influence over their work and other people.

These are those people who are dominant in "manageability" in that they prefer to make decisions based upon experiential input: They are more naturally what would be described as control-oriented people.

## Motivation versus Motive

Motivation is strategic and rooted deeply within a person whereas motive is tactical and therefore more transitory and based upon occurrences or instances. Understanding ones motivation is far different than understanding what a particular motive may be. If a person has a clear view of their longer term grounding in terms of motivation, than they are apt to be more proactive and less hesitant about making choices. When a person is well grounded in terms of motivation, decisions become less reactive-oriented and most often much simpler to make. Knowing the difference between a motive and one's motivation brings clarity to the decision making process and a higher level of performance.

## In Search of Motivation

According to the concentration camp experiences and logo therapy findings of renowned author Victor Frankl ("Man's Search for Meaning") and corroborated by the research of renowned Israel-based medical social scientist Dr. Aaron Antonovsky and his research colleagues at the Ben Gurion University in Jerusalem and the Institute for Applied Research at Hebrew University in Tel Aviv, the three essential "Healthy Business Affinity" ingredients of 1) comprehensibility, 2) meaningfulness, and 3) manageability are intertwined: all things being equal, high levels in one aspect will result in high levels overall. The three are inextricable: Research shows that when a person has a strong wellness point of view, that the individual is more likely to manage stressful situations more effectively and be consistently more productive. In practical experience, the person is not likely to even perceive the same stimuli that intrude upon other people as stressful at all in the first place. And the result: improved motivation, heightened effectiveness and increased productivity. Workers will perform better when they believe that they possess the right balance of understanding (comprehensibility), a welcoming attitude (meaningfulness) and the right work "tools" (manageability).

In these cases of harmonious balance, the majority of these in-tune workers make commitments to enterprise goals and other standards of quality. And at the same time, they feel valued, respected, and honored as individuals and as professionals, and feel a stronger sense of personal identity with the organization, its values, and fellow workers. Higher performance then naturally takes place within organizations that: (a) are deliberate and clear about stating their goals regarding what "excellence" means; (b) are unwaveringly entrenched in what their "real purpose" is, and; (c) are deliberate about balancing supportiveness and assertiveness by being tough on tasks, yet tender on people. Yes, a gentler and kinder workplace. That's essential in today's rushing, crushing and gushing internet-based business world. "It's not Kansas anymore," as the saying from "The Wizard of Oz" so poignantly and practically warns us. Business is not nor will it ever again be "as usual. "

**Self-Differentiation**

Projection is denying a feeling in our self - sensing it as coming from another.

| | |
|---|---|
| **Projection** | We believe what we believe is so. |
| **Doubt denied** | When information doesn't fit but we still insist it is so. |
| **Recognition** | "Small and ugly" self-blame for wrong perceptions. |
| **Empathy** | We can see the other's point of view. |
| **Assimilation** | We shift/include feelings mixed on something/someone. |

The same unconscious, which generates projections, strives to correct them too.

**Meaning Making**

According to John and Joyce Weir (specialists in Self Differentiation), though we typically act as if there is a truth in the world around us, in fact, we create that world based on the meaning we give it. That meaning automatically shows up through the dynamics of our own particular decision-making style. There is a constant stream of neutral input, but we select from that input based upon our unique biases, forming perceptions that constantly reinforce our beliefs; and then we take action, even though they may keep us in ruts of our own making.

This process is mostly unconscious, but can bring it to consciousness if we:

- Assume there is no objective world out there, just a projection of our own,
- Recognize that as adults we keep recreating childhood beliefs
- Take complete responsibility for how we behave

- Accept we cannot change others or choose their behaviors for them

As an experiment, take a look at your language and do the following:

Take responsibility for your projections by internalizing them through language (say these first to yourself as you learn to "try them on"):

- Instead of saying or thinking, "It gave me a headache when my boss made me so mad," say "I gave myself a headache when I made myself so mad over what my boss said."
- Instead of saying or thinking, "Sally cannot be trusted," say "There is a part of me that is like Sally and that I choose not to trust."

Take personal ownership of your language:

- Say "I" or "me" instead of "it", "one", "you", or "we".
- For example, instead of "One should be careful," say, "I should be careful."

Explicitly distinguish feelings from thoughts:

- For example, instead of saying "I think I'm scared," say, "I feel scared." Even if you do not experience the feeling right away, you're giving your unconscious the message to let you feel what you feel.
- On the other hand, be explicit about your thoughts. For example, instead of saying "I feel my boss is unfair," say, "I think my boss is unfair." This gets you in touch with the beliefs that drive your behavior.

## Self-Differentiation in Depth

Extensive work has been done on adult development and behavior that views the business organization as an emotional unit that uses systems, processes and thinking to describe the interactions within it. The workers within are intensely connected. When we feel disconnected or detached from the others around us, it is often more fiction than fact.

People profoundly affect other members of the organization's thoughts, feelings and actions to the extent that it often feels that they are all living under the same "emotional skin." We seek each other's approval support and attention, and we react to each other's expectations, needs and conflicts. This connectedness and reaction to each other makes our functioning in the workplace interdependent. Organizations may differ in degree in their interdependence, but it is always present.

Heightened tensions always intensify the processes that affect unity and teamwork, and this leads to problems. When some members of the firm or company become anxious, the anxiety spreads infectiously. As the anxiety level escalates, the connectedness of members of the organization becomes more stressful than comforting. Eventually, one or more people begin to feel overwhelmed, isolated or out of control.

These are the people who accommodate the most to try and reduce the tension in others. As examples, one person may take too much responsibility for the distress of others in relation to their unrealistic expectations, or a person may give up too much control of the thinking and decision-making in response to others anxiously telling the person what to do. The individual person who accommodates the most literally absorbs the anxiety of the others. This person then becomes the one most vulnerable to such things as alcoholism, depression, affairs or illness. The "helper" in us can make us unhealthy.

**Relationships and the Self**

A three-person relationship can be viewed as a triangle, and is the smallest and most stable relationship system. A two-person relationship is less stable. Very little tension is required before a third person must become involved to stabilize things. The three-person relationship is more stable since the tension can be shifted around. If the tension becomes too high to be contained in this triangle relationship, it will spread to a series of other interlocking three person relationships. Although the spreading of tension can stabilize the organizational system, nothing gets resolved.

People's action in this sort of relationship reflects their efforts to secure attachments to others, their reactions to too much attachment and their taking sides in the conflicts between others. Triangular relationships create an odd man out, a situation not easily tolerated by most people. Anxiety over becoming the odd man out poses problems.

In periods of low tension, two people are the close members in a relationship and one is in the uncomfortable position of being the outsider. As the two insiders work closely together, the outsider works to become closer to one of them. So, someone is always uncomfortable and pushing for a change. When we are put in the position of having someone choose another in preference to us, feelings of rejection naturally occur.

When tension levels become very high, the outsider position suddenly becomes the desirable place to be. When conflict occurs between the insiders, one of the insiders puts himself or herself in the outsider position by getting the other insider fighting with the current outsider. If he or she is successful, he or she gains a much more comfortable position, standing outside and watching the two others fight.

## Organizations and the Self

Organizations substantially affect how people think, feel and act. However, different members of an organization differ in their likelihood to engage in what is called "groupthink." In turn, groups vary in how much pressure they choose to exert to ensure conformity. The differences between individuals and groups are reflections of the person's degree of differentiation of self. The lower the developmental level of self is the more impact others have on his or her functioning and the more he or she tries to control (actively or passively) others.

Once established, the level of self almost never changes without conscious effort on the part of the individual.

People that have a poorly differentiated self, either depend so entirely on the approval of others that they very quickly move to change what they think and say to mirror the others, or they self-righteously proclaim what others should be like and exert pressure on them to conform.

Bullies depend very much on approval and acceptance. They push others to agree with them rather than agreeing with others. A rebel also has a poorly differentiated self that is demonstrated by always opposing the stance of those around him.

A person who has developed a well-differentiated self realistically understands his dependence on others but is calm in the face of conflict, criticism and rejection. This is possible because he or she can differentiate between assessing facts from thinking clouded by emotion.

Carefully acquired principles guide his or her decision about important issues. His or her speech and decisions are reflected in his or her actions. He or she can accept or reject other people's views without becoming polarized.

Much of the No-nonsense Nine communicating and conversing "training and development" is built in response to the above paragraph's bearing.

All organizations have people that are well differentiated, poorly differentiated and people who fall somewhere between these two extremes. The more intense the interdependence is in an organization or group, the less they are capable of reacting to stressful situations or conflicts without escalating the anxiety level throughout the organization.

**Conflict and the Self**

The concept of the organizational emotional system is made up of basic patterns that determine where problems develop in an organization or group. People's attitudes and beliefs play a part in this, but the major driver is the emotional system. Problems typically develop during periods of heightened and prolonged tension within the organization. This tension level is dependent on the stress encountered, and how the organization adapts to the stress. The higher the tension is the higher the chance that the symptoms will become severe and affect more than a few people.

For example, emotional distance is when people distance themselves from each other to reduce the intensity of anxiety, but then become isolated. As tension increases within a two-person conflict, each person externalizes his or her anxiety on to the relationship. Each focuses on what is wrong with the other, each tries to control the other and each continues to resist being controlled by the other party.

One-party dysfunction in a relationship is when one person pressures the other to conform and the other yields to the pressure. Both people may accommodate to some extent to preserve the peace, but one does more of it. If the tension level continues to increase, the subordinate party may relinquish so much control that they become ever more anxious. This anxiety fuels the dysfunction

In general, the more anxiety one person absorbs the less that the others are required to. In an organization, some people can maintain functionality at the expense of others. Whenever anxiety dictates behavior, however, someone is going to be hurt or suffer emotionally.

**With "Other Help,"**

Helping yourself helps the group and helps the business. Here is how:

At the heart of the No-nonsense Nine is my desire to help assuage anxiety and conflict within small work groups. The best way to do that is to do as follows: I recommend you form a little club. Call it "The No-nonsense Nine Club" and get someone you trust to the take the role of teacher/coach and pace and guide you through "The No-nonsense Nine" workplace booklet, chapter by chapter, one week at a time. Get a real raconteur and patient teacher/coach to guide you. Make sure the person is "fun" but not "too funny:" Let's call it "uplifting" and/or "encouraging." Certainly not an "enforcer."

Meet for a half hour to 45 minutes per week (always at the same time) to go through it, a chapter at a time. Make the contemplation and the conversation about real-time business concerns. (I call these "live ammo" Sessions). Run it like an NGT session if you get stuck. Be merciless about staying on track and on task. Do the exercises and the work. You will be a better, different person within one-quarter year. And people will be Working Better Together (WBT) and doing so more productively and profitably. I Promise.

**Group Function and the Self**

Organizational projection describes how managers transmit their emotional problems to those who report to them. This can affect the function of many people in a group and increase their vulnerability. Some possible problems could be (a) a heightened need for attention and approval, (b) difficulty dealing with expectations, (c) blaming oneself or others, (d) feeling responsible for the happiness of others, or (e) that others are responsible for their happiness. (f) Acting impulsively to relieve anxiety rather than tolerating it and acting in a clear thinking manner is another possibility. These are six problems that may require a solutions focus.

Projecting occurs when a manager begins to focus on the fact that they fear or believe something is wrong with the employee and then interprets the employee's behavior in such a way that it confirms the fear. This is a dysfunctional cycle… The boss begins treating the employee as if something is really wrong with them.

The supervisor's fears begin to influence that employee's behavior and the employee will then begin to embody those perceptions and fears. This projection process becomes a self-fulfilling prophecy when the manager tries to fix the problem that has already been decided through a manager's one-way lens that the problem is truly the employee's problem.

## Malfunction and the Self

Emotional cutoff describes people who manage their relationships with other members of the organization by cutting off emotional contact with one, some or all of them. These people may appear to be present, but in reality have cut themselves off by avoiding conflict and sensitive issues. The problems remain unresolved.

On the other side of emotional cutoff, people then attempt to solve their problems by trying to forge new relationships within the group or organization. They often make these new relationships overly important.

## Training and the Self

Recall any training program's promise of "a new way of thinking" or "a new beginning" only to realize later you have no recall of what the new way of thinking or new beginning were. Now ask yourself and try to answer these two questions: "Were the ideas no good in the first place? Or did I just not pay enough attention?"

According to David Rock, corporate coaching guru, a 1997 study of 31 public-sector managers by Baruch College researchers Gerald Olivero, K. Denise Bane, and Richard E. Kopelman found that a training program alone increased productivity 28 percent, but the addition of follow-up and feedback to the training increased productivity 88 percent.

For chronically late people, habits like carrying two timepieces — one fast and the other accurate — or routinely trying to arrive 20 minutes early to meetings may be effective precisely because they focus conscious attention on the improved result. With an attention model, learning becomes possible through many media, not just in a classroom. Also, given the small capacity of working memory, the many small bites of hands-on management specific learning, digested over time, may be more efficient than large blocks of time spent in onsite day-long workshops and remote-based types of "retreat learning events."

## Neuroplasticity and the Self

The term "attention density" is increasingly used to define the amount of attention paid to a particular mental experience over a specific time: The greater the concentration on a specific idea or mental experience, the higher the attention density. With enough attention density, individual thoughts and acts of the mind can become an intrinsic part of an individual's identity: who one is, how one perceives the world, and how one's brain works.

The neuroscientist's term for this is self-directed neuroplasticity.

For insights to be useful, they need to be implicit (generated from within) and not explicit (given to individuals as conclusions). This is true for several reasons. First, people will experience the adrenaline-like rush of insight only if they go through the process of making connections themselves. The moment of insight is well known to be a positive and energizing experience. This rush of energy may be central to facilitating change: It helps fight against the internal (and external) forces trying to keep change from occurring, including the fear response of the brain.

Second, neural networks are influenced moment to moment by genes, experiences, and varying patterns of attention. Although all people have some broad functions in common, in truth everyone has unique brain architecture. Human brains are so complex and individual that there is little point in trying to work out how another person ought to reorganize his or her thinking. It is far more effective and efficient to help others come to their own insights. Accomplishing this feat requires self-observation. Adam Smith, in his 1759 masterpiece "The Theory of Moral Sentiments," referred to this as being "the spectators of our own behavior."

**Ideas on Healthy Business and the Self**

The key is getting employees to learn and pay sufficient attention to ideas… something that the "e-learning" industry has struggled with throughout the professional and corporate arena.

Especially in regard to building a healthy business environment, Martin Seligman, founder of the positive psychology movement and former president of the American Psychological Association, recently studied 47 severely depressed individuals.

As the Gallup Organization published, the study involved two unusual components. First, participants focused their attention on things that were proven to increase happiness — specifically, an exercise called the three blessings, in which people wrote down three things that had gone well that day — instead of on the source or nature of their unhappiness, which is where many mental health interventions focus. Second, communities were allowed to form, which encouraged people to pay attention to the happiness-inducing exercises. Depression in 94 percent of the participants dropped significantly, from clinically severe to clinically mild-to-moderate symptoms. The impact was similar to the effects of medication and cognitive therapy combined.

This sounds in line with Brief Therapy Counseling by Kim Insoo Berg's and her husband, Steve DeShazer's results in Milwaukee, and what today's Solution Focused Coaching has found.

Perhaps any "healthy business" behavior change in the workplace brought about by managers, trainers, teachers, executive-sponsors or executive coaches is primarily a function of their ability to induce others to focus their attention on specific ideas, closely enough, often enough, and for a long enough time.

**The Issue of Change and the Self (A Best Practice)**

How, then, can leaders, and especially managers of small groups, effectively change their own or other people's behavior?

According to Jeffrey Schwartz, author and psychiatrist at the School of Medicine at the University of California at Los Angeles the answer is in being repetitive, to reinforce:

Start by leaving problem behaviors in the past; focus on identifying and creating new behaviors. Over time, these may shape the dominant pathways in the brain. This is achieved through a solution-focused questioning approach that facilitates self-insight, as in using the discipline of "story works," rather than through advice-giving.

At the organizational level, a realistic goal is to "health-fully" help change (a) the ways thousands of managers manage, and (b) the ways tens of thousands of employees think about their lifestyle choices. A common approach would be to identify the current attitudes across the group through some sort of cultural survey. As Google did in "The Oxygen Project," or as David Maister did within WPP years ago as documented within the book, "Practice What You Preach," I recommend concentrating this effort on the manager who works with groups of subordinates. This is the level of management most notorious for being the immediate boss who causes the person directly under them to quit their job.

Teaching Healthy Business Management skills with the No-nonsense Nine Mandala helps managers self-identify the source of the problem. This is what the No-nonsense Nine does: I believe the most effective way to enable the health, wellbeing and performance of employees is to improve the self-management skills of their managers. The teaching and development of Healthy Business Management skills is part of the answer. The real solution is making the manager accountable. I suggest that they become what I call a "Leader/Manager-as-Coach."

Based upon what we now know about the brain, however, a much better alternative would be for hands-on managers operating at the core of the organization to paint a broad picture of being "healthier" without specifically identifying the changes that individuals will need to make. The corporate goal should be for employees to picture the new behaviors in their own minds; and in the process develop energizing new mental maps that have the potential to become hardwired.

The every-day middle manager would then get a team of workers to focus their attention on their own insights, by facilitating discussions and activities that involve being HEALTHIER.

After that, the manager's job would be to regularly provide "gentle reminders" so that the healthy-workplace maps become the dominant pathways along which information, ideas, and energy flow. This of course requires repetition and rewiring to a certain degree, through training and development: Small Group "live ammo" practical skills development.

Catching those who get sidetracked to gently bring them back right when it happens brings focus. The power truly is in the focus, and in the attention that is paid. Talk about health, teach about health, and demonstrate health, and a healthier more productive work environment will grow.

If this all sounds too easy, that the answer to all the challenges of changing to a healthier workplace, is just to focus people on solutions instead of problems, let them come to their own answers, and keep them focused on their insights… well, apparently, that is exactly what research shows that the brain wants. And some of the most successful management change practices have this type of principle ingrained in them.

"Open-book management" at Springfield Remanufacturing and Toyota's production system are proven examples: In both of these approaches, in workplace sessions that occur weekly or even daily, people systematically talk about the means for making things better, training their brains to make new connections. If you took an fMRI brain scan of a Springfield or Toyota employee when that person joined the company and again after 10 years on the job, the two scans might reveal very different patterns.

**Mentoring Groups ("Small Learning Groups") and the Self**

Few managers are comfortable putting these principles into practice. They prefer "company" in the form of other managers as mentors. "Let the group be the expert," is what I recommend and model.

Our management models are based on the premise that knowledge is power. This "transmission" approach to exchanging information (exemplified by lectures and textbooks, where knowledge is "transmitted" to a passive receiver) has always been the prevailing teaching method in academia, including the business schools that many managers attend.

Since many executives assume that the teaching methods they endured "traditionally" are the only teaching methods that work, it is no small matter to have them re-consider trying a different approach in our workplaces. For many executives, leading others in such a new way as *Mentor Group Action Learning* may be a bigger change, and therefore a bigger challenge, than driving on the other side of the road. Even though it is scalable and accountable, companies are change resistant. Therefore this little Workbook as a sort of "Guidebook" is but a sampling of the entire Learning Management Need.

As Peter F. Drucker said, "We now accept the fact that learning is a lifelong process of keeping abreast of change. And the most pressing task is to teach people how to learn." In the knowledge economy, where people are being paid to think, and with constant change, there is more pressure than ever to improve how we learn. Being a STEP manager today, with companies promoting remote workforces, perhaps these findings about the brain can start to pull back the curtain on a new world of workplace learning productivity improvement: in our ability to bring about positive, lasting change in our own health, wellbeing and performance and in that of our colleagues, our employer-operations and within society itself.

Further research is needed to help us better understand how much attention is required to facilitate long-term change and in what kind of format the requisite group mentoring, teaching-facilitating and training can be delivered to foster better performance, but through my coaching, teaching and consulting experience at Workstone, I have managed to serve up this "little" workbook, to try and help. I find reinforced Group Mentoring Action Learning to be a real treasure and a much-needed blast of fresh air into the world of business management training, development and education.

* * * * *

**Reliability: The Discipline of Self Management in Five Dimensions**

***Identity*:**

Self-management is anchored to the *stalwart* part of our decision-making: Stalwarts are skeptical yet courageous self-managers…

***Understanding*:**

Stalwarts at their best are highly team and family-oriented self-reliant people who bring out the best in everyone. These are energetic, practical and friendly managers who attend to interdependent needs, which shows up in their language as expressed thoughts about the group.

***Challenging*:**

The Stalwarts driving force is skepticism and fear, which is manifested through a behavior set of (a) accusation (they will accuse whoever appears to have power), (b) in looking for hidden agendas, and (c) in reaction to their own self-doubt. They may procrastinate and/or blurt out their feelings with a kind of reckless courage (driven by their anxieties), and then worry that they've shot themselves in their own foot—and they very well may have. The good news is that they challenge others in ways that hold them accountable; the bad news is that they too often are looking for the bad news!

***Believing:***

"I've been loyal to this organization for 25 years."

"I don't think we have very competent senior management."

"I wish we could get along better."

"All my life, I've questioned my own ability."

***Performing:***

Performance development of the self is kind of endless. One option includes getting a reality check on what you are afraid of. Another option includes empowering yourself instead of blaming other people. And yet another is to focus more on possibilities rather than what worries you have. Another is taking a positive spin by practicing with regularity the job of centering your verbal communication on a clear message that has a theme and several key points. With these few options well in hand, you can then face your fears, support your cause, lessen your worries and organize your thoughts, plans and actions, respectively. As a definition, those words are the core ingredients of healthy business. (Note: on "fears," see the "Cheat Sheet" on page #236 at the end of Chapter #7).

People who struggle with self-related issues ("fears") have development needs that will fill out what they lack in basic self-care. As listed above, these needs typically fall under the banner of becoming more courageous in what they do. This excludes being audacious and cavalier, which in a true business sense is far from being courageous, or even particularly smart.

Bravery in business begins with people having the ability to take responsibility for their own beliefs, decisions, and actions. In brief, business courage requires having self-confidence. Bravery in business goes beyond tenacity and beyond resiliency, even though each is an admirable manager-coaching quality to have. Bravery in business requires many if not all of the Healthy Business No-nonsense Nine tenets listed in previous chapters, from *Purpose* to *Self Differentiation.*

Circumstances today have brought many middle managers to a point of being way under-resourced with budget (money) problems and STRESS. Organizations have cut into muscle. And as with any other historic times of business anxiety the single "bravest business ingredient" is to maintain a strong sense of integrity.

Unfortunately, integrity is not required to make a lot of money. And integrity is not perfectly correlated to what it takes to be a successful entrepreneur, a rich executive or even a well-paid manager. But integrity is perfectly correlated to being a successful Leader/Manager-Coach, simply because its roots are planted in peer accountability.

Any top-notch Leader/Manager-Coach is all for and into accountability-feedback. Any Leader/Manager-Coach would simply pass on backing somebody that makes his or her money through low integrity. Why? Because it would turn them off to everything that they stand for: Autonomy in what they do for a living: Purpose in why they do the job they do: Mastery in how they work and go about living their life.

Money can buy a lot of things but as the saying goes it cannot in and of itself buy anyone's happiness. True happiness for a Leader/Manager-Coach comes from a sense of fulfillment through learning and giving and then doing what a person's moral compass knows is right. Just look at the No-nonsense Nine Mandala!

Better to be that person; whatever level of business success you achieve in life. So, be brave. Reliability (and Integrity) demand it and depend upon it.

The Discipline of Self Differentiation is available to us all.

## A Harry Kraemer Inspired One Sheet: "True Self-Confidence"

Healthy Business Management Principles
Principle 9: Reliability

| | | |
|---|---|---|
| 9 Reliability | 2 Autonomy | 3 Creativity |
| 8 Community | 1 Purpose | 4 Resources |
| 7 Sincerity | 6 Mastery | 5 Responsibility |

True self-confidence makes us reliable because it produces self-reliance, which is the basis of all reliability. No one else can rely upon us until we can rely upon ourselves. Without true self-confidence, we are dominated—for the most part unconsciously—by fear. Fear makes people hesitant and deceptive—and thus unreliable. Without true self-confidence, we will tend to let ourselves down and fail those who depend on us. True self-confidence allows us to operate without being controlled by fear. Once we know that we can rely upon ourselves—even through moments of "failure"—our integrity shows in all of our actions, and we become reliable for others.

The Nature of True Self-Confidence

With true self-confidence, leaders recognize what they know and what they don't know. When you develop true self-confidence, you don't need to put on a façade that suggests to the world that you have mastered everything. Nor do you wilt at the first signs of a challenge, believing that you are not good enough or strong enough to face it. True self-confidence helps you appreciate your strengths, talents, and accomplishments, while also acknowledging the areas in which you need development. Truly self-confident leaders have a deep awareness of what they bring to the table, and they develop a team with complementary strengths, particularly in areas where they have weaknesses.

True self-confidence enables leaders to accept their own limitations, to operate effectively within uncertainty, and to give up the limiting need to appear all-knowing. In other words, true self-confidence allows us to accept ourselves, to see situations clearly, and to engage challenges with the belief that we can succeed. True self-confidence allows us to learn and develop expertise because it allows us to take risks.

True self-confidence is an inner quality that establishes your leadership and enables you to empower your team. Far more than just competency at your job or mastery of certain skills, true self-confidence is the attribute that allows you to see and accept yourself exactly as you are. With true self-confidence you are comfortable in your own skin, recognizing your strengths as well as your weaknesses. You know what you know, and you know what you don't know. If you have true self-confidence, you are committed to continual self-improvement to become even better in the areas at which you already excel, while developing those in which you are not as strong.

When you are truly self-confident, you know that there will always be people who are smarter, more talented, more articulate, and more successful than you are. With true self-confidence, you recognize your shortcomings, weaknesses, and past failures without the need to hide, overcompensate or beat yourself up. Yours is a lifelong journey. You are never done as long as you are open to learning.

False Self-Confidence

Some people argue that either you are self-confident or you are not, but there are crucial differences between true self-confidence and false self-confidence. There are people who adopt a persona that might make others think that they have self-confidence, but they are not the real deal. Instead, they possess false self-confidence, which is really just an act without any substance. These individuals are full of bravado and are dominating. They believe they have all the answers and are quick to cut off any discussion that veers in a direction that runs contrary to their opinions. They dismiss debate as being a complete waste of time. They always need to be right—which means proving everyone else wrong. Posturing and bragging are not expressions of self-confidence. Instead, they are the signs of a person who has no balance, is disinterested in others' opinions, and will not even attempt to understand alternate perspectives. Incapable of admitting a mistake or changing an opinion, this person cares only about being right and has a limited capacity for growth.

When people with false self-confidence end up in leadership roles, the negative effects are compounded because of the adverse influence their attitudes and behaviors have on everyone else. When these leaders are in charge, team members are not motivated to voice their opinions and challenge the boss. They are too intimidated even to think about it. Communication between the boss and the team is one-way; discussion is stifled, and all learning stops. Sometimes a boss who lacks true self-confidence will resort to being intentionally vague so that he can never be accused of being wrong or making a mistake.

At the other extreme are those individuals who clearly lack self-confidence and who focus, almost fanatically, only on what they are not good at. They cannot recognize or appreciate the strengths they do have because all they can see are their deficits.

Neither of these views results in a strong leader. True self-confidence, in contrast, allows you to appreciate the skills, attributes, and qualities that have gotten you where you are today, while also acknowledging that you can still develop in other areas. True self-confidence is necessary not only for your personal leadership but also for elevating the performance of your team and the entire organization. Leaders with true self-confidence avoid creating ambiguity and want to empower their team to provide feedback, voice their opinions, and challenge others, including the leader.

Truly self-confident leaders have no trouble turning to team members who have greater ability or expertise in certain areas. They do not buy into the myth that bosses shouldn't let their teams know they have weaknesses. They remember when they themselves were in a junior position and knew the areas in which their bosses were less competent. The only thing they didn't know was whether their bosses were aware of their weaknesses. Leaders with true self-confidence are comfortable sharing their strengths and weaknesses openly so that everyone can optimize the combination of abilities and talents across the total team.

The Courage to Speak Your Mind

To develop the courage to speak up—that is, to develop true self-confidence—you first need to master the principles of self-reflection and balance. One strengthens and affirms the other. Suppose you've given your boss a recommendation about a decision that has a direct impact on a project you've been leading, but he chooses to act in a completely opposite direction. In such a situation, it is hard to put your ego aside. By engaging in self-reflection, you can ask yourself why you feel so strongly about your recommendation. Have you looked at every option? What is it your boss sees that you do not? What other factors have influenced the boss's decision? Without any judgment or self-condemnation, reflect further on your motivation: Are you trying to be right, or to do the right thing? It may not be as easy as it seems to discern between the two.

If you are convinced that you have put your ego aside, you can use balance—the ability to look at a situation from every possible angle—to move forward. True self-confidence will empower you to speak up when you know that it is the right thing to do, and to share your opinions when you know they matter. As a leader striving to influence others positively, you must rely on your true self-confidence, along with self-reflection and balance, to guide you. If you do, you will be able to reflect on an issue and ask yourself, "If this were my company, what would I do?" By the way, it is your company. For you to have the greatest possible impact, you should take ownership of everything that goes on in your organization.

Facing Setbacks

One of the many benefits of building true self-confidence is the ability to persevere through the inevitable ups and downs you will face in your life, both personally and professionally. In fact, unless you have true self-confidence, a setback can become devastating and undermine your confidence in the future. With self-reflection, balance, genuine humility and true self-confidence, there is nothing that you cannot face with courage, dignity, integrity, and optimism.

When you face a setback, self-reflection, balance and genuine humility can help you discern what happened. If you really believe that you were trying to do the right thing and that you were doing the best you could, then you will be able to keep your circumstances in perspective. True self-confidence will help you accept that setbacks are part of life, that some disappointments are inevitable.

With true self-confidence, you will always be on the lookout for the lessons these experiences contain. As you learn from these experiences, you will see what you could have done better or differently. Your true self-confidence will be further strengthened as you identify both your strengths and weaknesses. Self-improvement becomes a lifelong journey.

Three things to remember:

- True self-confidence is based on self-acceptance, both of our strengths and of our weaknesses.
- Domineering, posturing and dismissiveness reveal a lack of true self-confidence as much as timidity does.
- True self-confidence enables us to raise the performance of everyone around us, and it enables us to grow.

## Building Confidence and Competence

Developing true self-confidence is not just about learning to speak up. It's also about developing greater competency in areas in which you lack ability or confidence—the places in which you are out of your comfort zone and feel very vulnerable. With true self-confidence, no matter your level or position in the organization, you can minimize your agony over feeling inadequate or unsure and maximize your chance of success as you handle current and future challenges.

Start with self-reflection, which enables you to identify your strengths and weaknesses; then you can devise a plan to overcome the challenges and gain competence in the areas in which you have some weaknesses. However, focusing on weaknesses should not be your top priority. After all, the things you are good at are the areas that played a significant role in helping you reach the level you are at today. It makes sense to continue to improve those areas in order to build mastery and strive for excellence, because those qualities are critical to your future success.

True self-confidence comes down to being comfortable with who you are. Although there will always be people who are smarter or more talented, you know you are okay and committed to getting better. You recognize that your future lies in your existing strengths, not in your weaknesses. You surround yourself with people whose skill sets complement yours.



Questions for Discussion for Working Better Together (WBT)

1. On a scale of one to ten, how much true self-confidence do your leaders demonstrate through their actions and communications? Rate for different levels of the organization, or for specific individuals, as necessary. Support your answer(s) with specific examples.

2. On a scale of one to ten, how much true self-confidence do you think you demonstrate through your actions and communications? Support your answer with specific examples.

3. How might a manager's lack of true self-confidence negatively impact KPIs and financial performance in your organization? Answer by describing one to three different scenarios.

4. Have you ever worked for someone who notably displayed false self-confidence? How did that person's false self-confidence affect the performance of your workgroup? Describe using concrete examples.

5. Have you ever worked for someone who notably lacked self-confidence (was timid)? How did that person's lack of self-confidence affect the performance of your workgroup? Describe using concrete examples.

6. Have you ever been in a situation where you felt it was risky to voice a difference of opinion with a superior about an important matter? What was the situation, what did you do (or not do), and what was the outcome? How did a lack of true self-confidence—either on your part or on the part of your superior—contribute to that situation and/or outcome?

7. Think about your favorite leader under whom you have worked personally. How would you rate that person's level of true self-confidence? Illustrate using concrete examples of that person's actions and communications. How did that person's true self-confidence affect your performance and growth?

8. How can one person's true self-confidence lead other people to build true self-confidence? Illustrate using one or more very short stories.

9. If a person is possessed by false self-confidence, what kinds of experiences will that person have on the way to developing true self-confidence?

10. In one sentence, how would you describe the relationship between true self-confidence and reliability?

11. How does true self-confidence relate to upholding personal and organizational values?

12. In one or two sentences each, how does true self-confidence relate to (a) self-reflection, (b) balance and (c) genuine humility?

13. What specific things can you do on an ongoing basis in order to increase your level of true self-confidence?

14. What specific things can you do to increase the level of true self-confidence of the people around you, both at work and elsewhere?

*IMAGE: CELTIC: PICTISH KNOTWORK*

# #10. Leadership Spirit At Work

Mandalas are often used during prayer, ceremonial blessings, vision quests, and other rituals. Labyrinth mandalas represent birth, death, rebirth, and/or the transition from one world to the next.

The Labyrinth of Chartres, a Cathedral in France, is part of the pilgrim's quest on their journey to the holy land. The Chartres Cathedral labyrinth is the most famous of these, but labyrinths began to appear all over Europe in the 12th century

To find understanding and meaning and to be able to communicate their beliefs, the Oglala Sioux of North America will combine the imagery of the sacred circle with a maze (labyrinth) as a sand painting to create a meandering but purposeful path. As if a part of a Mandala, the maze with its twists and turns they believe is the difficult journey they all will take toward finding deeper meaning in life.

People often find in their life that simply tracing the labyrinth with a finger is an easy way to have the Discipline of a mindful, calming and healing meditation. They often combine the image of a circle with the business meditation practice called "Still Point:" This is achieved when a person imagines in their mind's eye a white floating feather being lightly caressed by a soft wind into a rotating circle as it slowly falls (floats) to rest, around and around, floating down, only to disappear at landing and be replaced by another falling floating white feather again from up above, again and again. As people "reach Still Point," they often achieve a sense of peace, tranquility, or what could be called happiness or a sense of joy. After reaching "Still Point," people report a sense of relaxation or of "coming back mentally," and "not really knowing where they had mentally drifted off to."

This state of mind reminds me to live life as what Harry Kraemer in his writings describes as "a Best Citizen."

Dr. Angeles Arriens writes, "In every culture the circle symbolizes wholeness and the expression of unity. When people are engaged in a search for wholeness they aspire to independence and individuation. What they need most is space, room in which to find their own self and develop their own identity. What they fear most is entrapment, being caught in a situation that will restrict or restrain them." Note: As shown in Addendum #3A through Addendum #3C, The Six Conversations and The TIGERS Series leadership program approach can bring this sort of liberty, and the freedom to grow as a leader/manager-as-coach. This takes patience and practice, a worthwhile journey

9. HJK: "Does the leader have the courage to deal with constant change, controversy, and crisis?"

"As anyone who has been in a leadership position knows, it is not a question of if there will be change, controversy, and crisis, but when. The true leader is prepared for these conditions due to the qualities we laid out earlier, true self-confidence, genuine humility, balance, clear direction setting, people development, effective communications, motivation, execution, and implementation. The values-based leader is well prepared to handle crisis and controversy. He or she realizes that it is much better to proactively manage the issue before the "other side" attempts to monopolize the issue and actually creates change to which competitors must react." (HJK is Harry Jansen Kraemer Jr)

For me, Harry's value qualities bring me "full circle." This Harry Kraemer quotation aligns directly with the No-nonsense Mandala's Principle of Responsibility and the No-nonsense Mandala's Discipline of what I call "Surrender."

"Surrender" is the courage to "let go" and let others learn all on their own: To not be the know-it-all, and let go of your need to be right. Surrendering is not the same as giving up; it's the sign of having the strength to turn over the responsibility and of being hopeful to the other.

10. HJK: "Is the leader a "best citizen," capable of seeing the big picture beyond the organization?"

"The company clearly needs to generate a superior return for its owners. The values-based leader understands this but knows that focusing exclusively on "shareholder interest" is not a winning strategy. He or she knows that "doing the right thing" morally and in a socially-responsible manner as a "best citizen" will help build a great team, build rapport with customers, and lead to shareholder return. Once again, it comes back to balance." (HJK is Harry Jansen Kraemer Jr)

For me, this Harry Kraemer quotation aligns directly with the No-nonsense Mandala's Principles and Disciplines. I honor the role of the "Best Citizen." I also belief that "Best Citizen" can be the result of a practice that is called "Other Help:"

**Other help**

Most of what I have done in my teaching and coaching practice is about career motivation, and improving group connections for others: My teaching, my coaching, and my creating (of the No-nonsense Nine, for example), as well as my follow-up calls, my laid back, joke-telling manner, and my "business ministry" (as I call my "calling,") is mostly about career motivation and improving decision making for other persons.

I call this work I do "other help"- versus "self help," generally because I see a certain "self-help" myopia present in society today that is part of what's gone haywire specifically within this tech savvy world, especially in American high tech, remote-work businesses. By definition, "self-help" is *excluding*, whereas "other help" is *including*. I believe in "other help." It's what raises performance. I wrote about this in reference to the discipline of sharing. Yet, too often, we are subliminally and almost absent-mindedly the defenders of self-help. Just look at all of the self-help bookshelves in the bookstores... it's self-help mania on parade. Plus there have been over a half million books on leadership published in the last 100 years. Most praise the value of self-help. In the first five to ten years of my professional executive coaching and small group coaching/teaching, I saw only one paper published on "followership." I am a firm believer in the importance of Servant Leadership. Self reliance is certainly important, but not more important than knowing how to work well with others, especially when the others are mostly interested in getting help, often times without even knowing it. They are blinded into thinking that mostly anything can be fixed or solved on their own through self-help, which is untrue. Much of the more recent writing and research into Emotional Intelligence has brought more focus on to "followership" and its differences from what would be called power-over Leadership.

**People need help from others**

Yes, people need help from others, but they too often think what they need is self help, when what I believe we really need is NOT "self-help," and NOT more leadership books, but what I call "other help," and not a book at all. People need each other. That's where "other help" comes from, from being in community. I have tried to help with this need with this book.

**The Acronym "LEADERS."**

Consider the Question, "What does it mean to be an emotionally intelligent leader?" I believe the answer is... To learn and possess "Leadership Spirit." According to the Nonprofit Leadership Center's (NLC) website, which promotes the value of Emotional Intelligence, "Leaders" can be defined in most part by the NLC's following seven (7) attributes: "Emotionally intelligent leaders possess seven important qualities that spell out the word LEADERS:"

L = Listening,

E = Equipping,

A = Appreciation,

D = Developing,

E = Enlisting.

R = Relationships

S = Service

**L is for Listening.** Emotionally intelligent leaders place a higher value on listening than they do talking.

**E is for Equipping.** Emotionally intelligent leaders equip their employees with the tools and resources necessary to fulfill their positions' requirements effectively.

**A is for Appreciation.** Emotionally intelligent leaders appreciate the people they work with and invest time, effort and money to show their gratitude.

**D is for Developing.** Emotionally intelligent leaders know that their employees are their most important assets. They consistently create development opportunities to help their people grow and advance.

**E is for Enlisting.** Emotionally intelligent leaders enlist support from others because they know that their employees and team members are critical to implementing change effectively and efficiently.

**R is for Relationships.** Emotionally intelligent leaders understand that their success or failure rests on the quality of their relationships with others. They invest heavily in building and deepening those professional relationships.

**S is for Service.** Emotionally intelligent leaders realize that they must first give the most *to* their employees to get the most *from* their employees. They constantly seek ways to serve their employees instead of waiting on employees to serve them.

Now that you know some of the qualities of emotionally intelligent ("EI") LEADERS, are you in this category? What steps might you take to increase your emotional intelligence?

"WBT" stands for "Working Better Together:"

WBT Exercise 9: In one to two short paragraphs, please write down how you see where the Nonprofit Leadership Center's (NLC's) acronym definition for "Leaders" aligns with the No-nonsense Nine Mandala's Principles:

WBT Exercise 10: In one, two or even three very short paragraphs, please write down how you see where the NLC's acronym definition for "Leaders" aligns with (a) the No-nonsense Nine Mandala's Principles , (b) Maester's "Practice What You Preach" Attributes" and (c) Garvin's "Oxygen Project's Top Ten Manager Behaviors:" (Maister & Garvin References are located within Chapter #2).

## ADDENDUM # 1: KNOWING YOUR OWN STYLE – Social-Dominance Chart Compares to the No-nonsense Nine

Communication and Decision Style Assessment (Public Domain): Having a clear idea about your own "natural" style is useful. This can help prepare you in advance for adapting to the style of others. See Chapter #3 for more about this.. The following exercise will help you know your own style better.

| *Examine each of the pairs of words shown below. Insert a one (1) next to the word that best describes you. If you cannot decide which word best fits, insert one-half (.5) next to each word of that particular pair.* | *Examine each of the pairs of words shown below. Insert a one (1) next to the word that best describes you. If you cannot decide which word best fits, insert one-half (.5) next to each word of that particular pair.* |
|---|---|

| | | | | | | | |
|---|---|---|---|---|---|---|---|
| ___ | challenging | ___ | understanding | ___ | outgoing | ___ | withdrawn |
| ___ | pointed | ___ | indirect | ___ | approachable | ___ | distant |
| ___ | quick | ___ | deliberate | ___ | unstructured | ___ | structured |
| ___ | demanding | ___ | tolerant | ___ | random | ___ | focused |
| ___ | active | ___ | relaxed | ___ | intuitive | ___ | logical |
| ___ | impatient | ___ | patient | ___ | open | ___ | guarded |
| ___ | decisive | ___ | hesitant | ___ | casual | ___ | formal |
| ___ | competitive | ___ | cooperative | ___ | "loose" | ___ | "tight" |
| ___ | confronting | ___ | receptive | ___ | warm | ___ | cool |
| ___ | bold | ___ | cautious | ___ | animated | ___ | poker-faced |
| | **TOTAL** | | **NO TOTAL** | | **TOTAL** | | **NO TOTAL** |
| ___ | | ___ | | ___ | | ___ | |

| TOTAL THE LEFT HAND COLUMN AND PLOT ON THE VERTICAL AXIS OF THE MATRIX ON THE NEXT PAGE. | TOTAL THE LEFT HAND COLUMN AND PLOT ON THE HORIZONTAL AXIS OF THE MATRIX ON THE NEXT PAGE. |
|---|---|

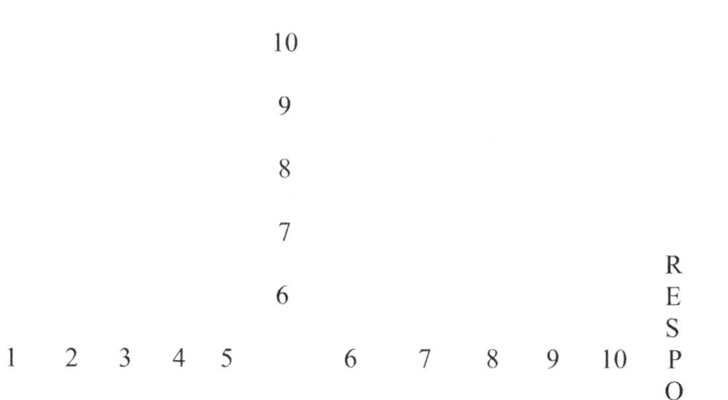


Next, find the vertical and horizontal axis intersection point: In which quadrant do they intersect? The above exercise is an aid to conversation with others. Being aware of your communication and decision-making style will… help reveal your Leader/Manager style, and thereby serve your self-differentiation and your "story-working" processes.. As with all other No-nonsense Nine information, results are held in strictest confidence. For any questions or concerns please contact your cohort-learning group's teacher-facilitator.

Reference: A Public Domain, Social-Dominance Scaling Assessment

"Practice What You Preach"

Causal Model 2001

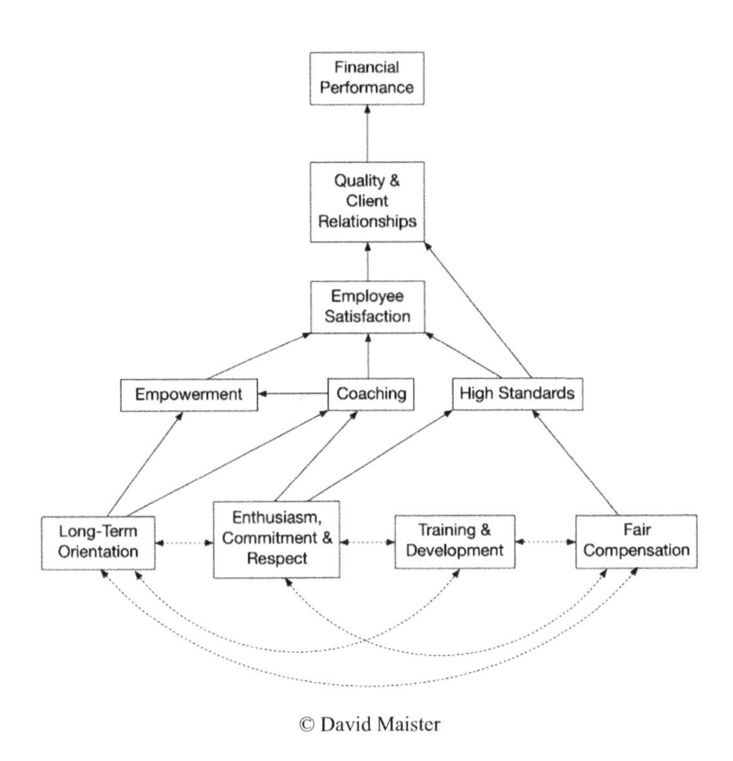


© David Maister

## Causal Thinking Versus Effectual Thinking

Shown above is David Maister's Causal Model derived from his research as described within his 2001 bestselling book entitled "Practice What You Preach." This model stands in stark contrast to Saras Sarasfathy's Effectuation Models as described in Addendum #2 on the following page.

## ADDENDUM # 2: The Effectuation Model

**Principles of Effectuation:** Expert entrepreneurs have learned the hard way that the most interesting ventures are built in a space in which the future is not only unknown, but unknowable. Still yet, they do shape this unpredictable future. They use techniques that minimize the use of prediction to shape the future. The five principles, listed below, make up effectual logic. ©Saras Sarasfathy U of Va. Darden School of Business.
Note: See the Previous page regarding Causal Modeling by David Maister

**1. "Bird in Hand" {START WITH YOUR MEANS}:** When expert entrepreneurs set out to build a new venture, they start with their means: who I am, what I know, and whom I know. Then, the entrepreneurs imagine possibilities that originate from their means.

**2. "Affordable Loss" {FOCUS ON THE DOWNSIDE RISK}:** Expert entrepreneurs limit risk by understanding what they can afford to lose at each step, instead of seeking large all-or- nothing opportunities. They choose goals and actions where there is upside even if the downside ends up happening.

**3. "Lemonade" {LEVERAGE CONTINGENCIES}:** Expert entrepreneurs invite the surprise factor. Instead of making "what-if" scenarios to deal with worst-case scenarios, experts interpret "bad" news and surprises as potential clues to create new markets.

**4. "Patchwork Quilt" {FORM PARTNERSHIPS}:** Expert entrepreneurs build partnerships with self-selecting stakeholders. By obtaining pre-commitments from these key partners early on in the venture, experts reduce uncertainty and co-create the new market with its interested participants.

**5. "Pilot-in-the-plane" {CONTROL V. PREDICT}:** By focusing on activities within their control, expert entrepreneurs know their actions will result in the desired outcomes. An effectual worldview is rooted in the belief that the future is neither found nor predicted, but rather made.

**Effectuation matters:** Expert entrepreneurs prefer an effectual logic vs. a causal one because of the details it offers of a comprehensive alternate frame for tackling problems. Which frame entrepreneurs use influences how they formulate problems; what alternatives they perceive and generate; which constraints they accept, reject, and/or manipulate and how; and why they heed certain criteria rather than others in fabricating and implementing new solutions. Logical framing matters because it makes a real difference in the world and makes a world of difference in the reality entrepreneurs perceive and make possible or impossible.

Effectual framing, as opposed to causal framing, is about redrawing the problem space and reconstituting existing realities into new opportunities. This is often paralleled to having a "Solutions Focus" versus a "Problem focus" as a way of approaching problems, difficulties or opportunities.

# Addendum #3A & 3B:

## Twelve "Getting More" Invisible Strategies Mapped into The Nine Square Grid

## Addendum #3A: The No-nonsense Nine Principles (Nine Square Grid)

| | | |
|---|---|---|
| 9. RELIABILITY | 2. AUTONOMY | 3. CREATIVITY |
| 8. COMMUNITY | 1. PURPOSE | 4. RESOURCES |
| 7. SINCERITY | 6. MASTERY | 5. RESPONSIBILITY |

# Addendum #3B: 12 Invisible "Getting More" Strategies

## by Stuart Diamond of The Wharton School
## Mapped to The No-nonsense Nine Square Grid
## Note: See Diamond's list on the next page as a handy, quick reference

| | | |
|---|---|---|
| **RELIABILITY**<br>Be Transparent and Constructive and Not Manipulative (#8) | **AUTONOMY**<br>It's About Them (#2) and Every Situation is Different (#4) | **CREATIVITY**<br>Embrace Differences : Different is good (#11) |
| **COMMUNITY**<br>Always Communicate, State the Obvious and Frame the Vision (#9) | **PURPOSE**<br>Goals Are Paramount (#1) | **RESOURCES**<br>Trade Things You Value Unequally (#6) and Find the Standards (#7) |
| **SINCERITY**<br>Make Emotional Payments (#3) And | **MASTERY**<br>Incremental is Best (#5) | **RESPONSIBILITY**<br>Prep and Practice With a list |

| | | |
|---|---|---|
| Find & Make Real Problems into Opportunities (A "Solutions Focus") (#10) | | (#12) |

## Addendum #3C:

**List: These are the Twelve (12) "Getting More" Invisible Strategies**

**Special Note: These exact same "12 negotiating" strategies and the Parabola image below apply as well to the No-nonsense Nine disciplines of superior Conversational Communication as well.**

1. Goals are paramount
2. It's about them: You can't persuade people unless you know what's in their heads.
3. Make emotional payments: When people are irrational, they're emotional and they can't listen or be persuaded. You must use empathy
4. Every situation is different: There is no one-size fits all.
5. Incremental is best: People often fail by asking too much at once.
6. Trade things you value unequally: Find out what each party cares about and trade things one person cares about but the other doesn't.
7. Find their standards: What are their policies, precedents, etc.
8. Be transparent and constructive, not manipulative: Don't deceive people. Be yourself.
9. Always communicate, state the obvious, frame the vision: most bad negotiations come from bad communication.
10. Find the real problem and make it an opportunity: Few find the real underlying problem in negotiations. Find out why the other is acting the way they are.
11. Embrace differences: Different is good, it's profitable, creative.
12. Prepare — make a list and practice with it: list the collection of negotiation strategies, tools, models.

Note: The above twelve strategies apply "invisibly" to conversations as well as to Negotiations

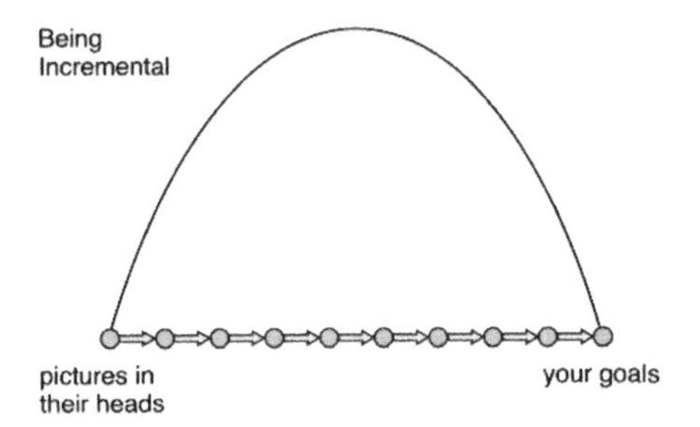


Professor Stuart Diamond's picture here summarizes his world famous negotiation course at Wharton. He wants to make sure people have "the picture in their head." He writes "…the summary of my course: what are my goals, who are they, what will it take to persuade them… Here is the model in a nutshell." © Stuart Diamond in his best selling book, "Getting More: How to Negotiate to Achieve Your Goals in the Real World."

**Addendum #4**

# STEADFAST GROUP

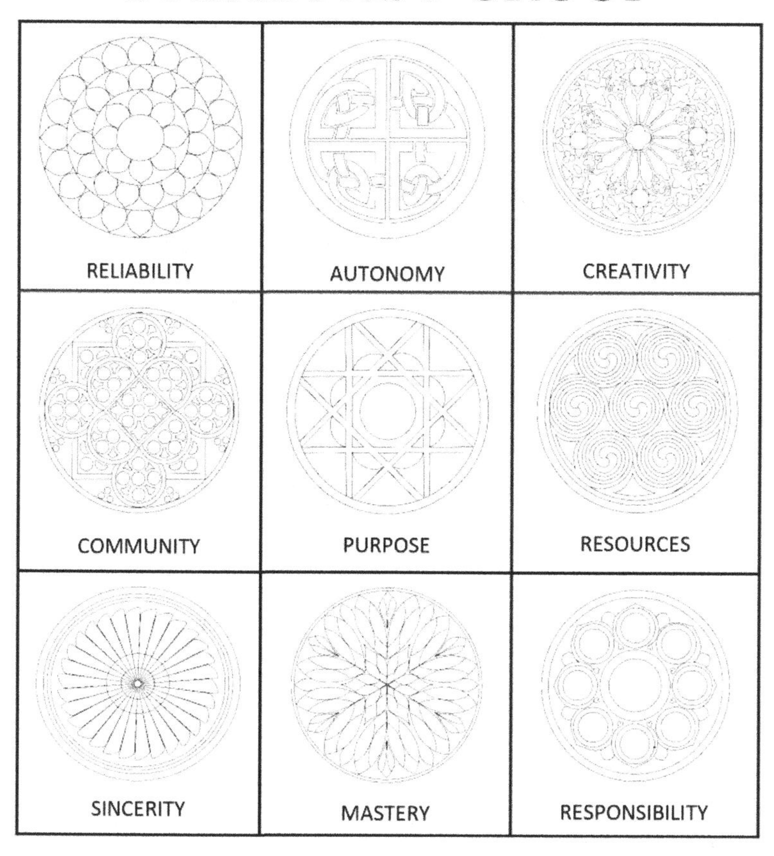


# NINE SQUARE

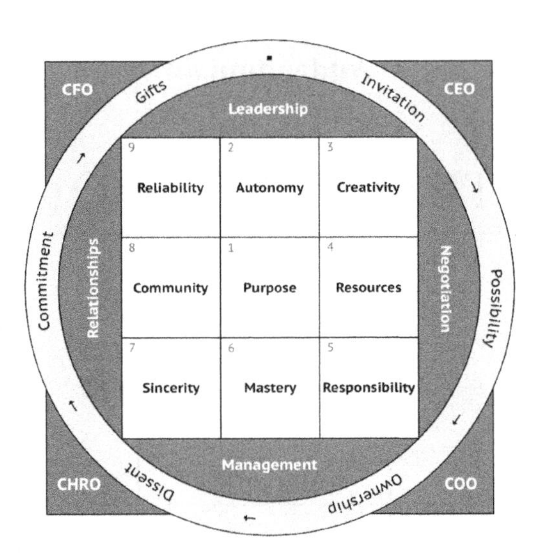


The No-nonsense Nine Mandala with Six Conversations "Driving Wheel" overlay.

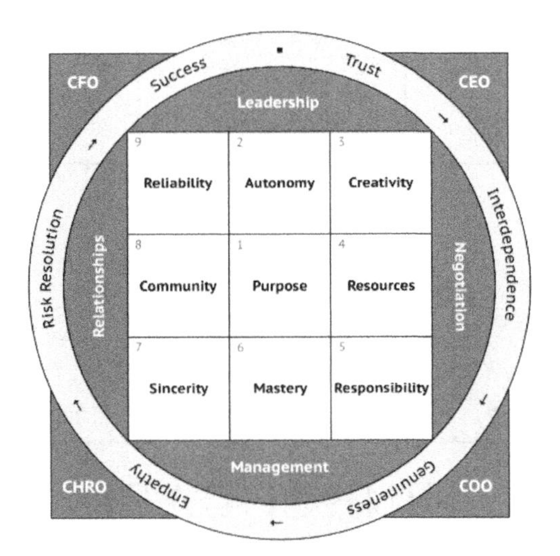


The No-nonsense Nine Mandala with TIGERS©Series "Driving Wheel" overlay.

The two pictures here help summarize the No-nonsense Nine book and coursework:

I want to make sure that people have these No-nonsense Nine Mandala pictures in their head.

Primary Sources:
"Threshold Leadership Development" Workshops for Baker & McKenzie Chicago
© 1998 by Clark Anderson Riley
"Threshold Leadership Development" Workshops for Owners & Account Managers at Hewitt Associates, Lincolnshire, IL © 1997 by Clark Anderson Riley
"Finding Meaning Within Your Work" © 2006 by Clark Anderson Riley
A "Garrett Post-Graduate Thesis, written and published with the advisement of Rev. Dr. Professor Kenneth Vaux (Director of The Center for Ethics & Values, located within Garrett Seminary) and Professor Dr. Lawrence Eugene Lavengood, eminent professor of Business History of The Kellogg Graduate Business School at Northwestern University in Evanston, Illinois.
Secondary Sources:
"Getting More: How to Negotiate to Achieve Your Goals in the Real World"
© 2010 by Stuart Diamond / Crown Business, Crown Publishing - Random House
"Effectuation: Elements of Entrepreneurial Expertise" © 2008 by Saras Sarasfathy / New Horizons / The Darden School of Business
"From Values to Action" © 2011 by Harry M. Jansen Kraemer Jr. / Jossey-Bass, a Wiley Publishing Imprint
"Managing the Professional Service Firm" © 1993 by David Maister / Simon & Schuster, NY
"Practice What You Preach" © 2001 by David Maister, Free Press, A Division of Simon & Schuster, NY
"How Google Sold Its Engineers on Management- Hint: It's all about the data." © 2013 by David A. Garvin, Harvard Business Review
"Managing" © 2009, 2011 by Henry Mintzberg / Berrett-Koehler, San Francisco

"The Balanced Scorecard" © 1996 Kaplan and Norton / Harvard Business Press

© 2020 by Dianne Crampton, "Becoming TIGERS: Leading Your Team Success" Paperback/Three Creeks Publishing. Special Note: Dianne Crampton's "T.I.G.E.R.S." acronym aligns respectively with Peter Block's progression of "The Six Conversations" as described on pages 67, 68, 69 and 350 (Illustrated): Contact The Six Tigers Series (c/o Dianne Crampton) for more information about Tigers Series Program Leadership training for your organization or individually.

<u>© 1996 by Clark Anderson Riley / Garrett-Evangelical Theological Seminary</u>

"Supportive-Assertive Management Initiative" (See Note and Chapter #4)

(Developed for Hewitt Associates in Workshops from 1995-1997 )

Made in United States
North Haven, CT
29 June 2023

38374096R00183